D1348885

THE HEALTH GAP

THE HEALTH GAP

The Challenge of an Unequal World

MICHAEL MARMOT

BLOOMSBURY

LONDON · OXFORD · NEW YORK · NEW DELHI · SYDNEY

Bloomsbury Publishing
An imprint of Bloomsbury Publishing Plc

50 Bedford Square
London
WC1B 3DP
UK

1385 Broadway
New York
NY 10018
USA

www.bloomsbury.com

First published in Great Britain 2015

British Library Cataloguing-in-Publication Data
A catalogue record for this book is available from the British Library.

ISBN: HB: 978-1-4088-5799-1
TPB: 978-1-4088-5800-4
ePub: 978-1-4088-5798-4

2 4 6 8 10 9 7 5 3 1

Typeset by Newgen Knowledge Works (P) Ltd., Chennai, India
Printed and bound in Great Britain by CPI Group (UK) Ltd, Croydon CR0 4YY

To find out more about our authors and books visit www.bloomsbury.com.
Here you will find extracts, author interviews, details of forthcoming events
and the option to sign up for our newsletters.

For Alexi, Andre, Daniel and Deborah

CONTENTS

Introduction

Why treat people and send them back to the conditions that made them sick?

The woman looked the very picture of misery. Her gait almost apologetic, she approached the doctor and sat down, huddling into the chair. The dreariness of the outpatients clinic, unloved and uncared for, could not have helped. It certainly did nothing for my mood.

'When were you last time completely well?' asked the psychiatrist in a thick middle-European accent. Psychiatrists are supposed to have middle-European accents. Even in Australia, this one did.

'Oh doctor,' said the patient, 'my husband is drinking again and beating me, my son is back in prison, my teenage daughter is pregnant, and I cry most days, have no energy, difficulty sleeping. I feel life is not worth living.'

It was hardly surprising that she was depressed. My mood dipped further. As a medical student in the 1960s I was sitting in Psychiatry Outpatients at Royal Prince Alfred Hospital, a teaching hospital of the University of Sydney.

The psychiatrist told the woman to stop taking the blue pills and try these red pills. He wrote out an appointment for a month's time and, still a picture of misery, she was gone. That's it? No more? To incredulous medical students he explained that there was very little else he could do.

The idea that she was suffering from red-pill deficiency was not compelling. It seemed startlingly obvious that her depression was related to her life circumstances. The psychiatrist might have been correct that there was little that he personally could do. Although, as I will show you, I have come to question that. To me, that should not imply that there was nothing that could be done. 'We' should be paying attention to the causes of her depression. The question of who 'we' should be, and what we could do, explains why I discarded my flirtation with psychiatry and pursued a career researching the social causes of ill-health and, latterly, advocating action. This book is the result of the journey that began in that dreary outpatients clinic all those years ago.

And it was not just a question of mental illness. The conditions of people's lives could lead to physical illness as well. The inner-city teaching hospital where I trained in Sydney served a large immigrant population, at that time from Greece, Yugoslavia and southern Italy. Members of this population, with very little English to explain their symptoms, would come into the Accident and Emergency Department with a pain in the belly. As young doctors we were told to give them some antacids and send them home. I found this absurd. People would come in with problems in their lives and we would treat them with a bottle of white mixture. We needed the tools, I thought, to deal with the problems in their lives.

A respected senior colleague put it to me that there is continuity in the life of the mind. Perhaps it is not surprising that stressful circumstances should cause mental illness, he said, but it is inherently unlikely that stress in life could cause physical ill-health. He was wrong, of course. I did not have the evidence to contradict him at the time, but I do now. The evidence linking the life of the mind with avoidable ill-health will run right through this book. Death, for example, is rather physical, it is not just in the mind. We know that people with mental ill-health have life expectancy between ten and twenty years shorter than people with no mental illness.[1] Whatever is going on in the mind is having a profound effect on people's risk of physical illness and their risk of death, as well as on mental illness. And what goes on in the mind is profoundly influenced by the conditions in which people are born, grow, live, work and age, and by the inequities in power, money and resources that influence these conditions of daily life. A major part of this book is examining how that works and what we can do about it.

The more I thought about it at the time, the more I thought that medicine was failed prevention. By that I mean most of medicine, not just pain in the belly in marginal groups or depression in women suffering domestic violence. Surgery seems a rather crude approach to cancer. Lung cancer is almost entirely preventable – by eliminating smoking. I didn't know it at the time, but about a third of cancers can be prevented by diet. Heart disease – surely we would want to prevent that, rather than simply wait for the heart attack and treat. Stroke ought to be preventable by diet and treating high blood pressure. We need surgery for trauma, of course, but could we not take steps to reduce the risk of trauma? That said, having had a bad bicycle accident, I am very grateful for high-quality surgical care, free at the point of use (thank you, National Health Service).

As for prevention, it seemed to me then, and I have evidence now, that taking control of your life and exercising, eating and drinking sensibly, having time off on happy holidays, was all very well if you were comfortably off financially and socially (and going to the private clinics, not the public hospital where I was then working). Were we going to tell the woman in Psychiatry Outpatients that she should stop smoking and, as soon as her husband stopped beating her, she should make sure that he and she had five fruit and vegetables a day (we did know about healthy eating then, even if we didn't have the 'five a day' slogan)? Were we going to tell the immigrant with a marginal, lonely existence to stop eating fish and chips and take out membership in a gym? And for those who assert that health is a matter of personal responsibility, should we tell the depressed woman to pull her socks up and sort herself out?

The thought then occurred that a preponderance of the patients I was seeing were disadvantaged socially. Not in desperate poverty: the husband of the depressed woman was working; the migrants, like probably most migrants, were working hard to get a toehold in society. But they were at the lower end of the social scale. In fact, all the things that happened to the depressed woman – domestic violence, son in prison, teenage daughter pregnant – are more common in people at that end of the scale. I was seeing social disadvantage in action; not poverty so much as low social status leading to life problems that were leading to ill-health.

She had an illness. The fire was raging. Treating her with pills might help put out the fire. Should we not be in the business of fire prevention as well? Why treat people and send them back to the conditions that made them sick? And that, I told myself, entails dealing with the conditions that make people sick, not simply prescribing pills or, if interested in prevention, telling people to behave better. At that time, and since, I have never met a patient who lost weight because the doctor told her to.

As doctors we are trained to treat the sick. Of course; but if behaviour, and health, are linked to people's social conditions, I asked myself whose job it should be to improve social conditions. Shouldn't the doctor, or at least this doctor, be involved? I became a doctor because I wanted to help people be healthier. If simply treating them when they got sick was, at best, a temporary remedy, then the doctor should be involved in improving the conditions that made them sick.

I had a cause. I still do.

It was not a cause, though, that many of my seniors in medicine were prepared to endorse. They were too busy putting out fires to expend effort improving the conditions that promoted these fires.

While thinking these thoughts and working as a junior doctor in the respiratory medicine ward, I had a Russian patient with tuberculosis. When I 'presented' the patient to my seniors, I didn't start with his medical history but, I now blush to recall, said that Mr X, a Russian, was like a character out of Dostoevsky. He had stubbed his toe on the highway of life (cringe). He had been a gambler down on his luck, an alcoholic, unlucky in love, and now, as if in a Russian novel, had developed TB.

A few days later the consultant chest physician drew me aside and said: I have just the career for you, it's called epidemiology. (Anything to get me out of his hair.) He said that doctors, anthropologists and statisticians all work together to figure out why people have different rates of illness depending on where and how they live. I was dispatched with a fellowship to the University of California Berkeley to do a PhD in epidemiology with Leonard Syme.

The idea that one could actually study how social conditions affected health and disease was a revelation. Walking round the hospital wards, I had been saying to myself that if social conditions caused physical and mental illness, then perhaps the rate of illness of a society could tell us something about that society. I know, it sounds obvious, but I was trained in medicine, not in thinking. It meant that the term 'healthy society' could do double duty. A healthy society surely would be one that worked well to meet the needs of its citizens, and hence would be one where health was better.

In Spanish they say *Salud* (health); in German *prosit* (may it be good for you); in Russian *Vashe zdorov'ye* (for your health); in Hebrew *L'Chayyim* (to life); in Maori *Mauri ora* (to life). In English when we are not saying Cheers, Bottoms up or Here's lookin' at you kid, commonly we say: Good health. People value health. Even when they get together for something not favourable to health, alcohol, people remember to wish each other good health. Health is important to all of us.

But other things take priority.

I asked some people in a poor part of London, forty or so years after the experiences in Sydney, what was on their mind. They talked about the importance of family and friendships; concern for their children – safe places to play, good schools, not getting into trouble with unsuitable friends; having enough money to feed the family and to heat the home, and perhaps for the occasional indulgence; having adequate housing; living in a neighbourhood with green space, good public transport, shops and amenities, and freedom from crime; having reliable and interesting work, without fear of losing their job; older people not being thrown on the scrapheap. Actually, had I asked people in a well-heeled part of London, the answers would have been little different.

Then I asked what they thought about health. I was told that in poor countries, ill-health is the result of unsanitary living conditions and lack of health care. In rich countries, now that we all have clean water and safe toilets, they told me that ill-health is the result of difficulty getting to see the doctor and our own indulgent behaviour, we dreadful feckless drinkers, smokers and overweight sloths (I am translating slightly), or just plain bad luck in the genetic lottery.

My point in writing this book is that my informants were not wrong about what is important for health, just too limited. The depressed woman in outpatients, the migrants with pain in the belly, the Russian with TB – they are the rule, not the exception. We now know that the things that really matter to us in our lives, minute to minute, day to day and year to year, have a profound impact on our health. The conditions in which people lead their lives, all the things my London informants told me were on their minds, are the main influences on their health.

The central issue is that good conditions of daily life, the things that really count, are unequally distributed, much more so than is good for anything, whether for our children's future, for a just society, for the economy and, crucially, for health. The result of unequal distribution of life chances is that health is unequally distributed. If you are born in the most fortunate circumstances you can expect to have your healthy life extended by nineteen years or more, compared with being born into disadvantage. Being at the wrong end of inequality is disempowering, it deprives people of control over their lives. Their health is damaged as a result. And the effect is graded – the greater the disadvantage the worse the health.

Finding this out has been not only wonderfully interesting, thrilling even, but it turns out that the evidence provides us with answers. How to improve the conditions of our lives and improve health is the substance of the chapters that follow. The knowledge that we *can* make a difference is inspiring. The argument that we *should* make a difference I find utterly convincing.

My Damascus moment may have been in Sydney, but the journey of compiling the evidence began in Berkeley. As Len Syme, still in Berkeley, puts it, they sent me off from Sydney because I was asking too many awkward questions and thought that Berkeley, soon after its experiences of the student rebellions of the 1960s, was a better place to ask awkward questions. A great place, actually!

Syme, in Berkeley, shocked me by saying: just because you have a medical degree it doesn't mean that you can understand health. If you want to understand why health is distributed the way it is, you have to understand society. I have been trying ever since.

An American colleague enjoys scrambled eggs for breakfast. He studies the impact of stress on health but he doesn't rule out the importance of fatty diet, so limits his egg indulgence to Sunday mornings. One day he opened his carton of eggs and found a printed insert, a bit like a box of pills. Poor desperate souls, we addictive readers, we'll even read package inserts in egg cartons. On the insert he was intrigued to discover that Marmot's study of Japanese migrants in California, reported in the 1970s, proved that cholesterol was *not* bad for the heart. Stress was important, not diet.

Not quite.

I am, of course, delighted that academics in Massachusetts can learn about my research over breakfast simply by reading what's in the egg carton. I would be even more pleased if the advertising copywriter had got it right. Admittedly, it is just a tad complicated; it entails the ability to hold two ideas in your head at the same time – but writers of egg-carton inserts should be able to manage that.

As Japanese migrate across the Pacific, their rate of heart disease goes up and their rate of stroke goes down.[2] Would I like to work on this for my Berkeley PhD? Would I! It was a brilliant natural experiment. If you were trying to sort out genetic and environmental contributions to disease, here were people with, presumably, the same genetic endowment living in different environments. Japanese in Hawaii had higher rates of heart disease than those in Japan, Japanese in California higher rates than those in Hawaii, and white Americans higher rates still.

This was terrific. You couldn't have designed a better experiment to test the impact on health of 'environment', broadly conceived. Most likely, the changing rates of disease are telling us something about culture and way of life, linked to the environment. Simple hypothesis: Americanisation leads to heart disease, or Japanese culture protects from heart disease. But what does that mean in practice?

Conventional wisdom at the time was, and still is, that fatty diets are the culprit. Indeed, I have chaired committees saying just that.[3] Japanese-Americans had diets that were somewhat Americanised, with higher levels of fat than a traditional Japanese diet, and as a result had higher levels of plasma cholesterol than did Japanese in Japan.[4] Diet and high levels of cholesterol were likely to be playing a part in the higher rate of heart disease. What's more, the higher the level of plasma cholesterol, the higher is the risk of heart disease. So much for the egg-package insert. It missed idea one. It grieves me to say it, but conventional wisdom is not *always* wrong.

Now for idea two. Japanese-Americans may be taller, fatter and more partial to hamburgers than Japanese in the old country, but their approach to family and friends resembles the more close-knit culture of Japan more than it does the more socially and geographically mobile culture of the US. That's interesting, but is it important for health? A Japanese-American social scientist with the very Japanese-American name of Scott Matsumoto had speculated that the cohesive nature of Japanese culture was a powerful mechanism for reducing stress.[5] Such a diminution could protect from heart disease. I particularly liked the idea of turning the study of stress on its head. Not looking at how being under pressure messes up the heart and blood vessels, but how people's social relationships were positive and supportive. We humans gossip and schmooze; apes groom. If, whether human or non-human primate, we support each other it changes hormonal profiles and may lower risk of heart attacks.

If this were true, I thought, then perhaps the Japanese in Hawaii had more opportunity to maintain their culture than the Japanese in California – hence the lower rate of heart disease in Hawaii. It seemed a reasonable speculation, but I had no test for it.

I had the data to test the hypothesis much more directly among the California Japanese. Men who were more involved with Japanese culture and had cohesive social relations should have lower rates of heart disease than those who were more acculturated – had adopted more of the American way of life. That is what I found. And this research result, perhaps, is where the egg cartons got their 'news'. The apparent protection from heart disease among the California men who were more 'Japanese' culturally and socially could *not* be explained by dietary patterns, nor by smoking, nor by blood pressure levels, nor by obesity. The culture effect was not a proxy for the usual suspects of diet and smoking.[6]

Two ideas then: conventional wisdom is correct, smoking and diet are important causes of heart disease; and, while correct, conventional wisdom is also limited – other things are going on. In the case of Japanese-Americans, it was the protective effect of being culturally Japanese.

Everything I will show you in this book conforms to that simple proposition – conventional wisdom is correct, but limited, when it comes to causes of disease. In rich countries, for example, we understand a good deal about why one individual gets sick and another does not: their habits of smoking, diet, drinking alcohol, physical inactivity, in addition to genetic makeup – we could call that conventional wisdom. But being emotionally abused by your spouse, having family troubles, being unlucky in love, being marginal in society, can all increase risk of disease; just as living in supportive, cohesive social groups can be protective. If we want to understand why health and disease are distributed the way they are, we have to understand these social causes; all the more so if we want to do something about it.

The British Civil Service changed my life. Not very romantic, a bit like being inspired by a chartered accountant. The measured pace and careful rhythms of Her Majesty's loyal servants had a profound effect on everything I did subsequently. Well, not quite the conservatism of the actual practices of the civil service, but the drama of the patterns of health that we found there. Inequality is central.

The civil service seems the very antithesis of dramatic. Please bear with me. You have been, let's say, invited to a meeting with a top-grade civil servant. It is a trial by hierarchy. You arrive at the building and someone is watching the door – he is part of the office support grades, as is the person who checks your bag and lets you through the security gate. A clerical assistant checks your name and calls up to the office on the fifth floor. A higher-grade clerical person comes to escort you upstairs, where a low-grade executive officer greets you. Two technical people, a doctor and a statistician, who will be joining the meeting, are already waiting. Then the great man's, or woman's, high-flying junior administrator says that Richard, or Fiona, will be ready shortly. Finally you are ushered in to the real deal where studied informality is now the rule. In the last ten minutes you have completed a journey up the civil service ranking ladder – takes some people a lifetime: office support grades, through clerical assistants, clerical officers, executive grades, professionals, junior administrators to, at the pinnacle, senior administrators. So far so boring: little different from a private insurance company.

The striking thing about this procession up the bureaucratic ladder is that health maps on to it, remarkably closely. Those at the bottom, the men at the door, have the worst health, on average. And so it goes. Each person we meet has worse health, and shorter life expectancy, than the next one a little higher up the ladder, but better health than the one lower down. Health is correlated with seniority. In our first study, 1978–1984, of mortality of civil servants (the Whitehall Study), who were all men unfortunately, men at the bottom had a mortality rate four times higher than the men at the top – they were four times more likely to die in a specific period of time. In between top and bottom, health improved steadily with rank.[7] This linking of social position with health – higher rank, better health – I call the social gradient in health. Investigating the causes of the gradient, teasing out the policy implications of such health inequalities, and advocating for change, have been at the centre of my activities since.

I arrived at Whitehall through a slightly circuitous route, intellectual as well as geographic.

You couldn't be interested in public health, or even just interested, and not be aware that people in poor countries have high rates of illness and die younger compared with those in rich countries. Poverty damages health. What about poverty in rich countries? It was a niche interest in the US of the 1970s. After all, the USA thought of itself as a classless society, so there could not be differences between social classes in rates of health and disease, right? Wrong – a piece of conventional wisdom that was completely wrong. The actual truth was handed around almost like Samizdat literature in the former Soviet Union in the form of a small number of papers, one of which was written by Len Syme and my colleague Lisa Berkman, now at Harvard.[8] People with social disadvantage did suffer worse health in the USA. It was, though, far from a mainstream preoccupation. Race and ethnicity were dominant concerns. Class and health was not a serious subject for study. Inequality and health was completely off the agenda, bar a few trailblazers, writing about the evils of capitalism.[9]

If there was a country on the planet that was aware of social class distinctions and had a tradition of studying social class differences in health, it was the United Kingdom. And if there was a place in Britain that excelled at social stratification it was the British Civil Service, familiarly known as Whitehall.

From Berkeley, then, I came home. It had taken a while. Born in North London, I went to Australia with my family when I was four years old and, after a few years playing cricket in the street and declaiming in the school debating team, studied medicine in Sydney, then went off to Berkeley. Donald Reid, Professor of Epidemiology at the London School of Hygiene and Tropical Medicine, offered me a job with the encouragement that if I wanted a position of low pay, limited opportunities for research in different places (such as Hawaii, for example), low research funding, but high intellectual activity, London was the place for me. How could I turn down such an attractive offer? Donald Reid said he was worried about me in 'Lotus Land', i.e. Berkeley. It was too much fun. He was a Scottish Presbyterian and thought a bit of hard living would be good for me. London provided it. The British economy in 1976 had just been bailed out by the IMF. A sense of doom prevailed, and the Labour government, staggering its way to a dismal end, was cutting public expenditure like there was no tomorrow. We wondered if that might well be the case. But, after being in London for about six months (I had arrived at end October 1976), I saw the sun come out, people shed their woolly sweaters, the roads dried out, the flowers bloomed, I stopped writing daily letters to friends back in California, and started to enjoy what Donald Reid promised. It was privilege, not hard living.

At first experience, London's Whitehall was as much of a culture shock as San Francisco's Japantown. Whitehall is home to the British Civil Service, and it looks it. To the east, in 'the City', financial giants now flaunt their hubris in soaring glass constructions, reaching for the skies, like their occupants. Whitehall's buildings, heavy and stolid, proclaim stability. Even in the newer buildings, the corridors of power feel as though unchanged from the days of Empire. It is certainly a place to study class distinctions, but not poverty. There are no poor in Whitehall.

The Whitehall Study, a screening study of 17,000 men, had been set up by Professors Donald Reid and, another great teacher of mine, Geoffrey Rose. Why civil servants? A little more culture shock. Donald Reid had lunch at the Athenaeum Club with one of his friends who was the chief doctor for the Civil Service, and the study was born. Athenaeum Club? Think Gentlemen's Club, with a classical façade and an Athenian-style frieze at the front, in a lovely setting not far from the Royal Parks in London, a stuffy dining room and overpadded armchairs.

Twice is a coincidence, three times a trend. In the 1970s I had done only two big studies, Japanese migrants and now Whitehall civil servants, and both had flown in the face of conventional wisdom. At the time, everyone 'knew' that people in top jobs had a high risk of heart attacks because of the stress they were under. Sir William Osler, great medical teacher from Johns Hopkins University and the University of Oxford, had, around 1920, described heart disease as being more common in men in high-status occupations. Osler fuelled the speculation that it was the stress of these jobs that was killing people.

We found the opposite. High-grade men had lower risk of dying from heart attacks, and most other causes of death, than everyone below them, and as I described earlier, it was a social gradient, progressively higher mortality going hand in hand with progressively lower grade of employment.

Further, conventional explanations did not work. True, smoking was more common as one descended the social ladder, but plasma cholesterol was marginally higher in the high grades, and the social gradient in obesity and high blood pressure was modest. Together, these conventional risk factors accounted for about a third of the social gradient in mortality.[10] Something else had to be going on. In that sense, it was similar to my studies of Japanese-Americans. The conventional risk factors mattered, but something else accounted for the different risks of disease between social groups. In the Japanese case we thought it was the stress-reducing effects of traditional Japanese culture.

You may think: stress in the civil service? Surely not! My colleagues Tores Theorell in Stockholm and Robert Karasek, the man who was eating eggs in Massachusetts, had elaborated a theory of work stress. It was not high demand that was stressful, but a combination of high demand and low control.[11] To describe it as a Eureka moment goes too far, but it did provide a potential explanation of the Whitehall findings. Whoever spread the rumour that it is more stressful at the top? People up there have more psychological demands, but they also have more control.

Control over your life loomed large as a hypothesis for why, in rich countries, people in higher social positions should have better health.

I have written about the Whitehall Studies at length in a previous book, *Status Syndrome*, and will not rehearse all the evidence here.[12] More recent evidence will make its way into chapters of this book. Suffice it to say that the social gradient that we found in the Whitehall studies has been found in British national data, and now all over the world. There is much effort going into understanding it. In this respect, if no other, British civil servants do still lead the world!

More than that, some social scientists from Oxford beat a path to my door. They said that they had a view of how work, not just in the civil service but more generally, should be classified into hierarchies. They thought that the span of control was central: higher status, more control.[13] The second Whitehall Study showed that span of control was important for health.[14] They loved it: evidence that their theorising was important for people's lives.

At the start of this section, I went a bit over the top and said Whitehall changed my life. The social gradient and 'control' certainly changed my approach to health and inequalities in health. It says we should focus not only on poverty but on the whole of society. Poverty is bad for health. There are good reasons for wanting to do something to reduce poverty, and among them is the harm it does to health. The gradient, though, is different. All the way, from top to bottom of society, the lower you are the worse your health. The gradient includes all of us below the topmost 1 per cent. You are thinking, perhaps, that we will always need people to watch the doors and staff the front desk, to serve the great man. Hierarchies are inevitable. Does that not mean that health inequalities, the social gradient in health, are inevitable?

Read on. The evidence shows that there is a great deal that we can do to reduce the social gradient in health, but it will take committed social action, and political will. But before we get to that, we will need to consider the huge amount of work that has been done in connecting our understanding of these social determinants of health in rich countries to the global picture of health and health inequalities.

A remarkable thing happened in 2012. According to the World Health Organization (WHO), life expectancy in the world was seventy, a biblical three score years and ten. Regrettably, that statistic is nearly totally useless. It tells us that China and other countries with life expectancy greater than seventy are balanced by India and other countries, mainly in Africa, with life expectancy less than seventy. The more relevant figure is the spread of thirty-eight years: from life expectancy of forty-six in Sierra Leone to eighty-four in Japan – in Japanese women it is eighty-six.

My first experiences of life expectancy at the wrong end of the scale were in New Guinea and Nepal. To be sure, there was little medical care available in remote villages, but one could hardly start there in looking for causes of ill-health. Dirty water and inadequate nutrition seemed a much better place to start. In the lowlands of New Guinea, particularly, malaria was also a problem, but prevention with impregnated bed nets and mosquito control, even then, seemed better options than waiting for people to get sick and then treating them. In the highlands, everyone had a cough, mostly because of open fires inside their huts to keep warm in the chilly highland nights. Safe cooking stoves would make a difference.

In the early 1970s it seemed a bit hopeless to think that health could improve in such unpromising circumstances. Not so. In Nepal, life expectancy improved by about twenty years, to sixty-nine, between 1980 and 2012. This is astonishing. Let us assume that the figures are more or less correct. Twenty years of improvement in thirty years means two-thirds of a year of improvement for every calendar year. That is sixteen hours of improvement every twenty-four hours. In rich countries, now, the rate of improvement is only(!) about six to seven hours every twenty-four hours.

My point is twofold. First, there are huge differences in health and life expectancy across the world, not just Sierra Leone and Japan but every shade of light and dark in between. Second, health can improve really quickly. Such rapid improvement fuels what I call my evidence-based optimism.

Some time around 2008, I gave a lecture in San Francisco. After it, a friend said to me: 'I have heard you lecture many times, but that is the first time I've seen you wagging your finger. There is something else going on. Not just scientific evidence but an urgency, a demand for action.'

He was right. I had been studying social causes of ill-health, having a fascinating time doing research and writing papers, but underneath there was a low, insistent rumble: it is not right that social conditions should be so unequally distributed across the world, and between social groups within countries. It means that much of the inequality in health that we see is unfair. The rumble grew louder. Research is immensely rewarding, but shouldn't we, and that includes me, be trying to do something about it?

At the end of every scientific paper there is a familiar coda: *more research is needed, more research is needed*. What, I wondered, if we added a new coda: *more action is needed*. It need not be discordant with the first.

Around this time, the turn of the millennium, Professor Jeffrey Sachs, now at Columbia University, and a great advocate for development aimed at the world's poor, had led a Commission on Macroeconomics and Health (CMH) set up by the World Health Organization. The CMH concluded that there should be major investment, globally, aimed at reducing killing diseases. The resultant improvement in health would lead to economic growth.

My thought was that investment in reducing the global burden of tuberculosis, HIV/AIDS and malaria had to be applauded. Much better than global expenditure on armaments, for example. If arguing that disease control would lead to economic growth helped get action, well done. There is a 'however', however. From my standpoint, they got it upside down. Health should not be a means to the end of a stronger economy. Surely the higher goal should be health and well-being. We want better economic and social conditions in order to achieve greater health and well-being for the population.

As an idealistic young student, I did not decide to study medicine out of a wish to further economic growth. I studied it because

I wanted to help individuals get healthier. I went into public health, and social determinants of health, because I wanted to help societies become healthier. I discussed this with the economist and philosopher Amartya Sen, then of Cambridge, England, now of Cambridge, Mass., and suggested we get a group together to say that it was important to improve social conditions to improve health. Not to criticise the CMH, but to say that we needed action, globally, on the social determinants of health. Amartya Sen agreed.

One thing led to another, and in 2005 the Director-General of WHO, J. W. Lee, set up the Commission on Social Determinants of Health (CSDH), with me as chair and Amartya Sen as a distinguished member. We had consultations before the Commission started properly. One prestigious academic said that he had served on commissions where the report was essentially written before the commission met. He said that would not be true here, because: 'Michael doesn't know enough.'

Absolutely right. I ran the CSDH as a mutual learning exercise. I learned from the former heads of government, government ministers, academics and representatives of civil society who made up the global commission, and we all learned from global knowledge networks that we set up. The learning that came from the CSDH, and two subsequent exercises that I will mention below, informs this book.

You produce a commission report. Is anyone listening, or will its fate be that of most such reports – worthy dustiness on shelves? The CSDH was a global report. We were concerned with health inequalities within and between countries from the poorest to the richest. A recommendation is going to look somewhat different in Gujarat and in Glasgow, in Nigeria and New York. We made a virtue of necessity and recommended that countries set up mechanisms to 'translate' our recommendations in a form suitable for that country. Brazil set up its own Commission on Social Determinants of Health. The CSDH met the Brazilian commission and shared emerging findings. Chile got active, as did the Nordic countries.

In the UK, the Labour government, under Prime Minister Gordon Brown, invited me to conduct a review of health inequalities in the light of the CSDH report. The aim was to translate the CSDH's recommendations into a form suitable for Britain. To inform the review we set up nine task groups involving scores of experts who contributed their knowledge in each of our key domains. The Marmot Review, as it was known, was published as *Fair Society, Healthy Lives* in 2010.[15]

More international task groups, more knowledge synthesis, more deliberation informed the production of the *European Review of Social Determinants and the Health Divide*, which we published in 2014. The *European Review* was commissioned by Dr Zsuzsana Jakab, the Director of the European Office of WHO. The so-called European Region contains, in addition to Europe, all the countries of the former Soviet Union. It stretches all the way to the Bering Strait, practically to Alaska. It means that we are getting social determinants of health on the agenda in many countries. The CSDH report was not forgotten.

Society and health, by its nature, is a highly political issue. When we published the CSDH report, one country labelled it 'ideology with evidence'. It was meant as criticism. I took it as praise. We do have an ideology, I responded: health inequalities that can be avoided are unjust – a case I will make later in the book. Putting them right is a matter of social justice, but the evidence really matters.

The *Economist* weekly newspaper said what it thought of our commitment. It gave a full two pages to covering the Commission's report, thank you, and ended with: 'it would be a pity if the new report's saner ideas were obscured by the authors' quixotic determination to achieve perfect political, economic and social equity.'[16] I particularly liked 'quixotic'. In Cervantes's masterpiece, Don Quixote woke up one morning and, imagining himself to be a medieval knight, rushed round doing chivalrous deeds – tilting at windmills, slaying wine gourds – while everyone chuckled at him. I told the Spanish Minister of Health – Don Quixote being part of the Spanish psyche – that the cap, or rather the tin helmet, fitted me rather well: a knight idealistic in a faintly ridiculous way, wanting to make the world a better place, and no one quite taking him seriously. Ah, said the Minister, we need the idealism of Don Quixote the dreamer, but we also need the pragmatism of Sancho Panza. I call that ideology with evidence.

In presenting the CSDH we made clear that we were driven not by the economic case for action, but by the moral case. We even put on the back cover: 'Social injustice is killing on a grand scale.' That sounds rather political. Yet we were criticised for being insufficiently political in our analysis.[17]

Health is political, yes. I have tried, though, to steer clear of party politics. As far as is possible I want the evidence to speak for itself. As societies indulge in the very real debates between the role of the state and freedom of the individual, I want to foreground the implications for health and health inequity. Since wandering around hospital wards in Sydney, I have maintained the view that the scale of health inequalities in society and the world tells us a good deal about the quality of our society and the way we organise our affairs.

I left clinical medicine because I did not think that the causes of ill-health and of social inequalities in health had much to do with what doctors did. We had to improve society. I was therefore surprised, to say the least, to be invited to be President of the British Medical Association for the year 2010–11. I thought they had the wrong person.

I had to make a speech when I was installed. I thought that since there were a lot of doctors in the audience, I could pick up some useful advice. I told the doctors that while doing the work described in this book, I had developed three medical conditions. Perhaps they could help.

The first is optimism. I feel unreasonably optimistic all the time. Despite all the doomsayers, the people who argue that all has been ruined, I judge that the evidence shows that things can improve. There must be some pills I can take for this condition.

The second, related to the first, is that I have developed selective deafness. I don't hear cynicism. If people say that no one will ever do things differently, it won't happen, people don't change, and the like, it bounces off. I no longer hear it. Realistic yes, but not cynical.

Third, I have developed a watery condition of my eyes. We were having a CSDH meeting in Vancouver. At the end of it, Pascoual Macoumbi, former PM of Mozambique, who was a member of the CSDH, said: 'I haven't felt so energised since my country got independence.' The watery condition of my eyes developed. When we were in Gujarat, and saw how the Self Employed Women's Association was working with its members, the poorest, most marginalised women in India, to triumph over adversity, I found my eyes watering. As they did when seeing young people developing self-esteem in the slums of Rio, or Maoris finding dignity in New Zealand. This watery condition seems to come on not when seeing people in distress, so much as when seeing them triumph over difficult conditions.

My purpose in writing this book is to let you know about the evidence of what we can do to improve people's lives – be they the poorest in the world or the relatively comfortably off. When we launched the CSDH in Santiago de Chile, I quoted the Chilean poet Pablo Neruda. Let me do so now, and invite you to join me and: 'Rise up . . . against the organisation of misery.'

I

The Organisation of Misery

It was the best of times, it was the worst of times, it was the age of wisdom, it was the age of foolishness . . . it was the season of Light, it was the season of Darkness, it was the spring of hope, it was the winter of despair . . .

Charles Dickens, *A Tale of Two Cities*

I have a one-track mind. I see everything through the prism of health. It is indeed the best of times. Health is improving globally. In many countries of the world we are much healthier and living much longer than we would have been when Dickens was writing. It is the worst of times. This enjoyment of good health is most unequally spread. For some countries their health is nearly as bad as if they were still languishing in Dickensian squalor. Currently in the world the unhealthiest country has a life expectancy nearly forty years shorter than the healthiest. That is the same as the gap between Dickensian and modern-day London. Within many countries, too, inequalities in health are increasing – the health of the best off is increasing more rapidly than that of the worst off. The best and worst of times coexist.

It is the age of wisdom. Advances in medical science and knowledge of public health give us the tools to make dramatic health advances.[1] It is the age of foolishness – I would have preferred it if Dickens had written hubris. Knowledge of medicine and public health is not so much wrong, as too limited. Health is too important to be left solely to doctors. Health is related not only to access to technical solutions but to the nature of society. We are being foolish in ignoring a broader array of evidence, which shows that the conditions in which people are born, grow, live, work and age have profound influence on health and inequalities in health in childhood, working age and older age.

It is the spring of hope. We may be foolish to ignore such knowledge, but we do now understand how society influences health – my purpose in writing this book – and there are inspiring examples from around the world of how such understanding is transforming lives and improving health. It is the winter of despair. When the 1 per cent and the 99 per cent have diverging interests and the head of the US Federal Reserve Bank says that inequalities of income and wealth have gone too far,[2] when banks in Europe and the US have, since 2008, been fined a total of £100 billion for banking crimes and misdemeanours which damage their customers' interests,[3] when rich countries compete to make the most of Africa's resources, when people of ill will misuse race and religion to spread chaos, when in functioning democracies people's faith in their governments is at a low ebb, and in other countries governments seem to have little interest in the well-being of their populations, then despair may set in.

In this first chapter, I want to show why, in terms of health, it is the best *and* worst of times. Wisdom and foolishness, hope and despair, will make their appearance to introduce the topics for the rest of the book. I am an evidence-based optimist. Armed with knowledge, we can transform a season of darkness into one of light. It will take commitment and political will, but the knowledge and experience is there that can make a huge difference.

A TALE OF TWO CITIES . . . AND THEY
ARE BOTH IN GLASGOW

'I know you have been contrasting shockingly poor health in Calton with the estimable health of Lenzie [areas of Glasgow]. We talk about it in Glasgow. Even in the pub. Especially in Calton, as people raise their glasses to the memory of drinkers past, so many of them gone. I live in Lenzie and drink regularly in the pub with a friend who lives in Calton. We were chatting the other night and it turned out that my friend had no plans for pension or other retirement arrangements. When I asked him why not, he said: "Because I'm fifty-four."' So said a Scottish professor to me at a meeting.

My response: oh dear! That's not what I wanted at all. It is great to have one's research discussed, in Scottish pubs, and elsewhere I hope. I did publish data on life expectancy in Calton and Lenzie.[4] The point was for discussion to lead to change, not to fatalism.

If a man dies in his prime in Calton, a down-at-heel part of Glasgow, it may be a tragedy, but it's not a surprise. Actually, the question of what constitutes his 'prime' in Calton is moot. Life expectancy for men, when I first looked at figures from 1998–2002, was fifty-four. In Lenzie, a much more upmarket place a few kilometres away, 'in his prime' has an altogether different meaning: life expectancy for men was eighty-two.[5] That converts to a twenty-eight-year gap in life expectancy in one Scottish city.

Calton is an unlovely place. Its residents say: 'Nowhere to walk, really bad', 'Can't let granddaughter out', 'Side streets, terrible prostitution'. There might be a park with some green space but it has 'prostitutes, alcoholics and druggies at night', there is 'usually a man parked on a bench with a bottle'.

Calton is the environment in which Jimmy, a typical resident, lives. In truth, Jimmy has always been something of a rascal. He was born in Calton in an unstable home, was in trouble in school, and delinquency problems led to trouble with the police as a teenager. Jimmy was enrolled in an apprenticeship but dropped out; he has never had a 'proper' job, but had short-term temporary manual work. As with his subculture, any money Jimmy gets goes into drink and drugs; his diet, if you could call it that, consists of pub food, fast food and alcohol. Jimmy has had a series of short-term girlfriends, but there is a question of alcohol-fuelled violent behaviour. He is known to the police for his various gang-related violent activities.

It is men like Jimmy who can expect to live shorter lives than men in India. Average life expectancy for men in India was sixty-two at the time that it was fifty-four for men in Calton. Jimmy's poor health prospects will not be improved by telling the adult Jimmy to pull his socks up and behave better. We should have started a bit earlier in his life.

The twenty-eight-year gap in life expectancy in Glasgow was as big as I could find anywhere within one city that gathers good data.[6] The current figure is probably closer to twenty years.[7] Twenty years is ridiculously large. Twenty years is the gap in life expectancy between women in India and women in the USA. We can see differences in life expectancy as big as twenty years within London, too – even within the London borough of Westminster, one of the richest spots on the planet.[8] In the US, if I said that a poor part of the city, in Baltimore or Washington DC for example, had life expectancy twenty years shorter than a rich part, many Americans would think 'race'. Perhaps they would be less quick to think 'race', whatever that means, if they knew that London and Glasgow have a twenty-year gap in life expectancy that cannot be attributed to ethnic differences. We need to go beyond simple categories such as race and social class to find out what is going on.

Perhaps you are thinking: I am not the richest, and I am not the poorest. If I were in Glasgow I would be living neither in an elegant Georgian town house nor in a tenement. Similarly, in the London borough of Westminster where the gap is nearly twenty years I would be neither in the fanciest parts of Mayfair and Knightsbridge nor in the run-down area of Church Street. If living in a rich area corresponds with good health, and in a poor area with poor health, where do I fit in to all of this, you might ask.

You and I, dear reader, fit right at the heart of all this. If we live in a neighbourhood that is somewhere between the humblest and the most exalted, our life expectancy is somewhere in between the low level in the poor areas and the higher prospects in the richer. The richer the area, the better is our health, *on average*, as illustrated in Figure 1.1.[9]

Here every neighbourhood in England is ranked according to level of deprivation. In the top line, each dot represents life expectancy for one neighbourhood. Suppose you live in a neighbourhood with middling levels of deprivation (or affluence), your life expectancy, on average, is middling. If you live in a neighbourhood

FIGURE 1.1: ALL THE WAY FROM TOP TO BOTTOM

Life Expectancy and disability-free life expectancy (DFLE) at birth:
England 1999–2003

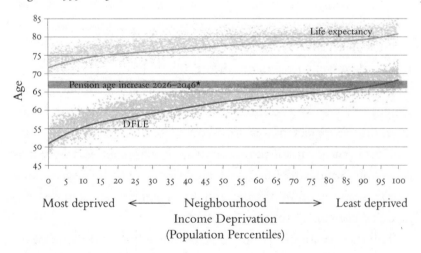

*Policy has been to increase pension age to 68 by 2046.
Source: Office for National Statistics.

that is right up there, but not quite at the most affluent level, your life expectancy is near the highest. The link between deprivation and life expectancy is remarkably graded: the greater the deprivation, the shorter your life expectancy.

The social gradient in life expectancy runs all the way from top to bottom. It doesn't just feel better at the top. It *is* better. At the top, not only do you live longer but the quality of life is better – you spend more years free from disability, as the bottom line in the graph shows. The social gradient in disability-free life expectancy is even steeper than it is for life expectancy. 'Disability' here is quite broadly defined: any limiting long-standing illness. Talk about adding insult to injury: the more deprived people spend more of their shorter lives with 'disability'. On average people at the top live twelve years of their lives with disability, people at the bottom twenty years.

A similar graph could be reproduced in any number of countries round the world. The social gradient in health is a widespread phenomenon.

A decade or so ago, I wrote that if you caught the Washington Metro from the southeast of downtown Washington to Montgomery County, Maryland, life expectancy rises about a year and a half for each mile travelled – a twenty-year gap between ends of the journey.[10] Since then, colleagues in London have said that if you catch the Jubilee tube line, for each stop east from Westminster in central London, life expectancy drops a year.[11]

The point of these exercises is to make vivid the social gradient in health. Subtle differences in neighbourhood, or more importantly in other conditions affecting the people who live there, have grave import for health and length of life.

The first reaction of most of us to the social gradient in health is: hey, this is about me. 'Health inequalities' is not only about poor health for poor people, it covers gradations in health, wherever we are on the social ladder. It is not about 'them', the poor, and 'us', the non-poor; it is about all of us below the very top who have worse health than we could have. The gradient involves everyone, rich, poor, and in-between.

A sampling of the popular press demonstrates a huge variability in attitudes to the fact that the poor have worse health than everyone else. For some, the poor are poor and sick because they are feckless. This fecklessness extends to not looking after themselves and their children. Elsewhere, a more sympathetic view might be that you do care about the poor health of the 'poor' in your own country or 'over there' in another country. It is a concern, it says something about your sense of what you think a society should be for, but it does not touch you more than that. The social gradient in health, though, affects all of us. We are not just interested, we are engaged. This is my life and yours. You and I are neither feckless (I am making an assumption) nor deserving of sympathy because of our poverty, yet all of us below the very top have worse health than those at the top.

The gradient changes the discussion fundamentally. The gradient implies that the central issue is inequality, not simply poverty. As we will see, poverty still remains hugely important for health, but relief of poverty is conceptually simple, even if politically and practically difficult. Inequality, on the other hand, implies that not only is having enough to make ends meet important, but so too is what we have relative to others.

Inequality puts us into entirely different terrain. In many countries, economic inequality has been seen as a good thing. Lowering taxes on the rich, for example, a policy that has the clear and predictable effect of increasing economic inequality, is justified as being good for the economy. Set the wealth producers free and we will all benefit, runs the argument. But what if such a policy made health inequality worse? In Britain, a senior Labour politician said that he was 'intensely relaxed' about how much the rich earned.[12] Governments of the centre-right and centre-left have both contrived to do very little to reduce economic inequality. The centre-left wants to reduce poverty; the centre-right appears to believe that if they get the incentives right, and the economy grows, poverty will look after itself. But neither has seen economic inequality as a problem, although that is now changing.

We should change our focus. We should focus on the rich, not only on the poor. I do not mean social workers calling on the rich to see if they are managing their money all right. Of course, we still want to solve the problem of poverty and health, but if all of us below the top have worse health than those at the top, surely we should aim to improve *everybody's* health towards the high level of those at the top.

The potential gains are enormous. I once calculated that if everyone in England over the age of thirty had the same low mortality as people with university education there would be 202,000 fewer deaths before the age of seventy-five each year – almost half of the total. This equates to 2.6 million extra years of life saved each year.[13] Health inequalities are not a footnote to the health problems we face, they *are* the major health problem.

Common sense tells us that if we want to solve a problem we should focus on it. I am arguing that the problem of health inequalities within countries is the social gradient – from top to bottom, the lower our social position the worse our health. Focusing on the problem of the health gradient implies improving society. But what about the poor at the bottom who have the worst health? My answer is that improving society, improving everyone's health up to that of the best off, does not preclude extra effort on improving health for the poor. Rather than 'them' and 'us', we need to expend extra effort where it is needed: improve society *and* effort proportional to need. The point is made even more clearly if we look at a broader range of countries.

Social gradients? Focus on the richest?
Don't poor countries have
to worry about poverty?

Some health workers in sub-Saharan Africa believe that the social
gradient in health is an effete concern of rich countries. In the
most deprived parts of the world, they argue, we should focus on
the poorest of the poor. That is not what the evidence shows. It is
difficult to obtain figures for inequalities in adult mortality from
most countries – they are simply not available. Many countries do
have figures for mortality rates of children under age five, and those
for a few selected countries are shown in Figure 1.2.[14]

These figures reinforce the importance of concentrating not on
the poorest, but on the richest. We should be asking not only how
can we improve things for the poor, but how can we get everyone's
health up to the standard of the richest? Were we to focus only on
the 'poor' of Uganda, we would miss the fact that the most affluent

FIGURE 1.2: ALL RIGHT FOR THE FEW

Under-five mortality rate (per 1,000 live births) by wealth quintile

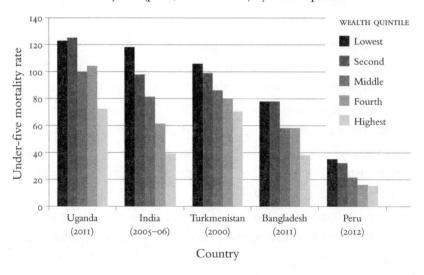

Source: Demographic and Health Surveys.

20 per cent have a higher child mortality than the poorest of Peru.
If you are in India, would you be happy if only the child mortality
rate of the poorest fifth were reduced? Wouldn't you want everyone to have child mortality as low as the top fifth? For that matter,
surely if you are in the best-off fifth in India you would want to get
the child mortality of people like you down to the low level of the
top fifth in Peru, who would want to get theirs as low as the average for high-income countries – 7 deaths per 1,000 live births.

In other words, the implications of the gradient in Uganda, India
or Peru are the same as in Glasgow, London or Baltimore. Yes, it
is important to improve the lot of the worst off, but the gradient
demands that we improve conditions, and hence health, for everyone below the top. Not only do we need to reduce poverty, we
need to improve society and have effort proportional to need.

You may be thinking that a social gradient in health in Glasgow
and in India are quite different. Thinking about Jimmy in Calton,
described above, destitution does not come to mind. He has clean
water and shelter and does not suffer from malaria, or dysentery.
Surely in India it is different, where the basics are lacking. The
basics *are* wanting, but in other respects it is not so different. Here
is Gita.

Gita sells vegetables on the street in Ahmedabad in the state of
Gujarat in India. She has no formal education, lives in an 'informal settlement' (a slum made of makeshift housing) and has two
children who sit with her by the roadside as she sells her vegetables, and an older girl who helps with the vegetable trade. To
keep her business going Gita takes out short-term loans, at 20 per
cent a month interest, to buy vegetables from the middle man in
the wholesale market. Her husband is a migrant worker who is
living in another state and sends a few rupees back each month.
Gita was just about making her tight budget work, but it was time
for her daughter, aged fourteen, to marry, and instead of paying off
her debts she put money into a dowry and a wedding party for her

daughter. Some aid workers are tearing their hair out at what they see as this 'irresponsible' waste of money, as her interest payments have gone up.

What links Jimmy and Gita is disempowerment. They simply have little control over their lives. This disempowerment is linked to ranking low in the social hierarchy. Until they are in a position to take control of their lives it is going to be very difficult to improve their health. Yet the evidence shows that this is far from hopeless. It is to capture the season of light that I have written this book.

In saying at the start that it was the worst of times, I pointed to two types of inequality in health. We have just been looking at inequalities within countries – the social gradient in health. There is a second type of inequality. Figure 1.2 shows big differences between countries as well as within them. It implies that poorer countries have worse health. They do, in general. To see that that is not the whole story, however, I want to turn to the US.

RICH COUNTRIES, GOOD HEALTH?

You are a fifteen-year-old boy in the USA. I'll call you Andy. You are secure in the notion that you live in nearly the richest nation on the planet. Life will be good. Like all fifteen-year-olds you have many preoccupations, some linked to your quick mind and wild enthusiasms, others to your growing body and raging hormones. Apart from being a bit overweight and prone to the occasional bout of hypochondria – it's acne not cancer – health is not a concern. You live in a rich country and everyone says that rich countries have good health because of good medical care and public health. Poor countries have poor health because they lack those things. Anyway, you think, when a country's health suffers it is babies and young children and older people who die. Fifteen-year-old boys are practically indestructible. Given what you get up to, that is a welcome notion. If you reach the vigorous age of fifteen you can almost guarantee you will reach sixty. Reassuring, but not quite right.

Go into a typical American school and count one hundred boys aged fifteen. Thirteen of you will fail to reach your sixtieth birthday. Is thirteen out of a hundred a lot? The US risk is *double* the Swedish risk, which is less than seven. The UK looks more like Sweden, but not quite as low. Yes, thirteen out of a hundred is a lot. It may also be the tip of the iceberg. If so many young people are dying, there may be a good deal more that are suffering non-fatal illnesses and injuries.

You and your family might be shocked to find out that the survival chances of a fifteen-year-old boy in the US are about the same as in Turkey and Tunisia, Jordan and the Dominican Republic. The US figure is worse than Costa Rica, Cuba, Chile, Peru and Slovenia. In fact, in the US the likelihood that a fifteen-year-old boy will survive to celebrate his sixtieth birthday is lower than in forty-nine other countries. The US ranks around fifty on what is called male 'adult mortality'. There are 194 member states of the United Nations. Fifty out of 194.[15] Not looking good. The US is a very rich country. Rich countries are supposed to have good health. What happened?

I have lost count of the number of Americans who have told me that they have the best health care in the world. Let us, for the moment, assume it is true. Why, then, would young adults in the US have less chance of surviving to sixty than young adults in Costa Rica, Cuba or Slovenia, let alone Sweden, the UK and most other European countries?

The answer is because medical care, and even public health, has little to do with it. The high mortality of young men comes from homicide, suicide, car crashes, other accidents, drugs, alcohol and some other disorders. To blame homicide or other violent deaths on lack of medical care is a bit like blaming broken windows on a lack of suppliers of new window panes. If someone heaves a rock through your window, it is quite helpful to have someone to call who can come and fix it. It wasn't difficulty in finding someone to call that led to the rock being thrown . . . or not directly. (There is a broken windows hypothesis which suggests that if you don't fix the windows it encourages rock throwers.) Could the relatively poor survival chances of young men be linked to the nature of society?

For American readers here is a little consolation, albeit not much for Russian readers. Russia does dramatically worse. If you are one of a hundred fifteen-year-old boys in Russia, look around and take note: a third of your group will be gone by the age of sixty. In Russia you simply cannot assume, as you can in Sweden, that if you are alive and kicking at fifteen you will still be breathing at sixty. On this particular health measure, Russia would not look out of place in sub-Saharan Africa. Its figure is the same as in Guinea-Bissau, and only marginally better than Sierra Leone.

This second type of health inequality – the first is the social gradient within countries – is the dramatic variation in health between countries, even among relatively rich countries: Sweden, the US and Russia.

Perhaps you are thinking that Sweden and the US is not a fair comparison. Perhaps, Sweden being a more homogeneous country, the Swedes are genetically programmed to be healthier young adults than the ethnically and racially diverse US. Or is it misleading to compare a country with a population smaller than New York with the whole of the US?

What if I told you that twenty years ago, the survival chances of fifteen-year-old Swedes were worse than now and looked a lot like that of Americans today? Sweden was *more* homogeneous twenty years ago than it is today – there has been a great deal of immigration – so the homogeneity explanation does not hold much water. Put simply, if Sweden could improve its health from a US level of health to a Swedish level, so today could the US improve its health to the new Swedish level. After all the US, too, has improved over the last twenty years. It just hasn't caught up. There is no good biological reason why you, fifteen-year-old Andy in the US, should not have the same health prospects as fifteen-year-old Johan in Sweden. Why don't you, then? Read on.

Obviously, it is not simply about rich and poor countries. National income per head is a third higher in the US than in Sweden, but health is poorer in the US.[16] The US is richer than almost all of the forty-nine countries that rank ahead of it in the survival stakes. Russia's national income per head (adjusting for purchasing power) is twenty times Guinea-Bissau's, yet boys in the two countries have the same poor survival chances.

OK, not simply rich and poor, but we know, don't we, why people get sick and die. Isn't it lack of health care? And if not that, in poor countries it is destitution that leads to death from communicable diseases. In rich countries it is smoking, drinking, obesity and general failure to look after ourselves that cause diabetes, heart disease and cancer. We will look at these explanations and see that they are not so much wrong, as too limited, and they scarcely apply to the life prospects of fifteen-year-old boys.

I rather ruled out of hand the idea that differences in medical care could explain the differences in survival among fifteen-year-old boys – broken windows are not caused by lack of window fixers. Perhaps such quick dismissal is inappropriate when it comes to the more robust gender. Differences in medical care might provide a readier explanation for international differences in fifteen-year-old girls. Women have to face something special before they reach sixty: pregnancy and childbirth. We visited a boys' school. Let's visit a girls' school.

Go into a school in Sierra Leone, and count twenty-one fifteen-year-old girls. One of those twenty-one will die during her childbearing years of a cause related to maternity. In Italy, one school would not be enough. You would have to count 17,100 fifteen-year-old girls to be fairly sure than one would die of a maternal-related cause. I was shocked by the differences among boys. I am horrified by the differences among girls.[17]

My horror comes not just because of the magnitude of the difference between Sierra Leone and Italy, but because it is all so unnecessary. This loss of young lives should not happen. Medical science knows how to make pregnancy and childbirth completely safe for the mother. One maternal death in all the reproductive years of 17,100 women is as close as we can get to completely safe. Conventional explanations suggest that we know what to do to prevent this tragedy.

Skilled birth attendants present before, during and after labour can make a dramatic difference to survival. Lack of access to health care, then, is the beginning of an answer to the differences in risk of maternal deaths. It is only the beginning because the obvious question is, why is there lack of access? Do countries not know what is needed? Do international donors not know what is needed? When I say that conventional explanations are not wrong, they are just too limited; this is part of what I mean.

If it were simply a 'medical care' issue then the US would have the lowest maternal mortality in the world, wouldn't it? The US spends more than any other country on health care. Arguably, it has the best obstetric care in the world, but it does not do very well. In the US, you would have to count 1,800 fifteen-year-old girls to get one maternal death in their childbearing years. One in 1,800 is enormously better than one in twenty-one in Sierra Leone, but significantly worse than Italy, at one in 17,100. In fact, sixty-two countries have lower lifetime risks of maternal deaths than the US. Let that one sink in a bit. No woman should die during pregnancy and childbirth, yet in one of the richest countries in the world, which spends the most on medical care, the risk is higher than in sixty-two other countries.

It is possible that some countries don't count maternal deaths properly and there may be some error in the calculations. For this purpose I will adopt a 'northern' bias, cut out the global south, and limit the comparison to Europe, by which I mean the fifty-three countries that make up the European Region of the World Health Organization, including all of the former Soviet Union, Turkey and Israel. Were the US a European country then it would have only forty-six countries ranking ahead of it in lifetime risk of maternal death. The US would rank forty-seventh among these 'European' countries, and be on a par with Armenia, just ahead of the republic of Georgia.

Invited to address a meeting of the American Gynecological and Obstetric Society, I told them this home truth about US maternal risks equalling Armenia, congratulated them on being ahead of Georgia, and said that I was willing to accept that the US has the best obstetric care in the world. I was also willing to guess that if I asked them to jot down on a piece of paper which US women died of a maternal-related cause, all their notes would say much the same thing: the socially excluded, the very poor, illegal immigrants, people with chaotic lives in one form or another. Some of the good doctors might have mentioned 'race'. I take race as a proxy for other forms of social exclusion, but I'll come back to that.

When people get sick they need access to high-quality medical care. Medical care saves lives. But it is not the lack of medical care that causes illness in the first place. Inequalities in health arise from inequalities in society. Social conditions have a determining impact on access to medical care, as they do on access to the other aspects of society that lead to good health.

I don't have it in for the US: some of my best friends . . . If you are a young person in the US, though, it is reasonable to ask why your prospects for a healthy life are no better than in Armenia and worse than in Costa Rica, Chile or Cuba, quite apart from most high-income countries.

I assumed that you, Andy, are a typical American fifteen-year-old. But there isn't, is there, a typical fifteen-year-old. There are rich and poor, urban and rural, inner-city and suburban, immigrants and descendants of immigrants, indigenous and others, different ethnic groups, red states and blue states. Often, inequalities in health within countries are as big as the differences among countries. We need to get behind the averages, to unpick them. In other words, we need to keep both types of inequalities in focus: those between countries, and those within countries – the social gradient.

Before we go on, there is something that may be nagging at you, as you read this. How can I make such generalisations? You and I are unique. There has never been in the history of the planet another you or another me. Even if you have an identical twin, who is the same as you genetically, the two of you have somewhat different life experiences that mark each of you out as unique. However, if you thought that your uniqueness meant that we could not make any generalisations about you, I would advise against going to the doctor when you get sick. All she could say in that case would be that she had never seen another person quite like you; research data didn't apply; treatment was out of the question. Your doctor doesn't say that. She says people with your symptoms and signs have disease of the heart, or lungs, or toenails. We have good experience of treating people like you; we will therefore recommend the following. It turns out that the treatment has more or less the same effect on you as it has, *on average*, on other unique individuals with the same medical condition that you have. You may be unique but you share characteristics in common with others of our species . . . and other species. Those common characteristics allow us to learn from experience.

The same reasoning applies to all the social facts in this book. Each American is unique; so is each Swede, and each Russian. Yet consistently Russians have higher adult mortality than Americans, who have higher mortality than Swedes. They did last year; they did the year before; and in all probability they will again next year. Unique as you are, your shared experience with your fellow countrymen and women changes your risk of health and disease, and of life and death; and marks you out as different, *on average*, from people in other countries. Similarly, if you are rich and in professional employment, you share characteristics with others in those groups that mark you out as different, on average, from people who are poor and not employed professionally. Health and disease vary with these characteristics of groups, as they do with characteristics of countries.

MONEY – DOES IT MATTER OR NOT?

In the previous section, when discussing American Andy's poorer health prospects than Swedish Johan's, I said that it was not about rich and poor. The US is richer than almost all of the forty-nine countries that have lower chance of death of fifteen-year-old boys. Similarly, I pointed to Russia's 'African' level of mortality despite having much higher national income than Guinea-Bissau. What I did not say is that the 144 countries with higher adult mortality than the US are poorer countries.

It is not as contradictory as it sounds. Among poor countries, higher national income is associated with better health. Among rich countries, getting richer does very little for health. Other things are more important. Figure 1.3 illustrates these two phenomena, by plotting the span of countries' life expectancy against their national income in dollars. A dollar in a poor country can buy much more than a dollar in a rich country, so national incomes are adjusted for purchasing power. This adjustment brings up the figures for national incomes in poor countries.

If you have little of it, money is crucial to your life and your health. For poor countries, small increments in income are associated with

FIGURE 1.3: RICHER AND HEALTHIER — UP TO A POINT

The relationship between wealth and health, 2012

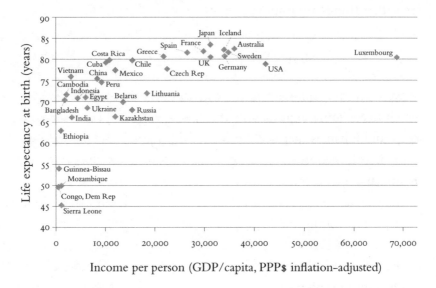

Income per person (GDP/capita, PPP$ inflation-adjusted)

Note: PPP = purchasing power parities, i.e. adjusted for purchasing power.
Source: Data from Gapminder.

big increases in life expectancy. It makes sense. A country with a per capita national income of less than $1,000 can afford little in the way of food, shelter, clean water, sanitation, medical and other services — relief of what I have called destitution. With a small increment in income, more things are possible.

Even more money, though, does not guarantee good health. Above a national income of about $10,000 there is very little relation between national income and life expectancy. When describing the fate of fifteen-year-old American Andy, I pointed out that he does worse than Swedish Johan. Here, taking a slightly different measure of health, life expectancy at birth, we see that Cuba is doing as well as the USA, and Costa Rica and Chile are doing somewhat better, though they all have lower national incomes. Russia does remarkably poorly: much lower life expectancy than would have been expected from their national income.

The conclusion is that money does matter if you are in a poor country and have little of it, less so if your country is relatively well off. Other things are important.

NOT JUST INCOME, SOCIETY!

I have three simple ideas that animate this book – only the third of which needs some explanation. The first, as I said when comparing Andy and Johan, is that there is no good biological reason for most of the health inequalities that we see within and between countries. Health and inequalities in health can change rapidly. Second, we know what to do to make a difference. Arguing for what can be done is the purpose of this book. The third relates to the relatively flat part of the curve in Figure 1.3 – the fact that above a national income of $10,000 there is little relation between income and life expectancy.

This third proposition is simply that health is related to how we organise our affairs in society. Currently, we measure a society's success by an economic metric – the growth of Gross Domestic Product. There is recognition that GDP captures only one aspect of what the good society means.[18] A measure that gets closer to people's lives is happiness or life satisfaction.[19] Health is another. We all value health, probably more than we value money. The argument for health as a measure of social success goes further. Many of the other things we value are related to health of individuals and society: good early child development, education, good working conditions, a cohesive society – all are linked to better health, as subsequent chapters will show.

I will make the case that our social arrangements are crucial to the level of health of our society. The US is doing better than Russia, but not as well as Sweden, or forty-eight other countries. My case does not rest on whether I personally would rather live in the US or Sweden, UK or Russia; it rests on the data. If I say that the US ranks fiftieth, and is therefore doing badly by its citizens, it is not because I start out liking, or not, the way the US does things.

My case rests on the data on health. I know Russia is doing badly, not because of prior views that I hold, whether about communism, post-communism, Putin-ism or some other -ism. I say Russia is doing badly by its citizens because its health is disastrously poor. I knew that communism in Russia was a disaster in the post-war years because health suffered. Post-communism was worse. But we'll come to that.

So close is the link between the nature of society and health that you can use it both ways. By which I mean the level of health, and magnitude of the social gradient in health, tell us about how well the society is doing. And if you are concerned about improving health, then the conditions of society that influence health – its social determinants – loom large.

POVERTY: ABSOLUTE OR RELATIVE?

Two of the ways that societies can affect health are the level of poverty and the magnitude of inequalities. They are linked. Absolute poverty is of clear importance in explaining the close link between national income and life expectancy in the steep part of the curve in Figure 1.3, for countries with national income less than $10,000 per head, adjusting for purchasing power. Degrees of absolute poverty are also likely to be important in explaining the gradient in child mortality in India or Uganda, for example. The higher up the wealth scale, the more likely that people have the basic necessities of life.

Think, though, about the gradient in health in rich countries, the subway rides, and Figure 1.1. It is odd to think of people in the middle of the distribution as being somewhat in poverty, yet they have worse health than those at the top. We need to look for something other than absolute poverty to explain their worse health – perhaps relative deprivation, or being the wrong side of inequality.

What about poverty in Glasgow? Most people visiting Calton would have no hesitation in calling it poor, and yet it is fantastically wealthy by, for example, Indian standards. A third of Indians live on $1.25 a day. No one in Glasgow lives on so little. Average income per person in India, adjusting for purchasing power, is $3,300. That is way below the poverty line in Scotland. There are a few rough sleepers in Glasgow, but almost everyone has shelter, a toilet, clean water and food. Yet life expectancy for men in Calton was eight years shorter than the Indian average.

A clear implication of this contrast is that the meaning of poverty differs with the context. While $3,300 a year is not considered poor in India, it would count as remarkably poor in a high-income country. It is not simply the money in your pocket that defines poverty, or determines health risks.

In the 1980s Amartya Sen and Peter Townsend, two distinguished social scientists concerned with poverty, had a vigorous debate as to which was more important: absolute or relative poverty. It makes for amusing reading as they aimed respectful, elegant, courtly even, academic blows at each other. But rereading it now, I am struck by how little difference there seems to have been between them.[20]

Which is more important for health, absolute or relative poverty? Surely the answer is both. The people of Calton are deprived relative to the standards of the UK, but the absolute amount of money they have matters too. It is reasonable to suppose that if they had more money their lives would change, and if the community had more cash, conditions in Calton would also change.

Amartya Sen resolved the debate by saying that relative inequality with respect to income translates into absolute inequality in capabilities: your freedom to be and to do. It is not only how much money you have that matters for your health, but what you can do with what you have; which, in turn, will be influenced by where you are.[21] If the community provides clean water, and sanitation, you don't need your own money to ensure these solutions. If the community provides subsidised public transport, health care free at the point of use, and public education, you don't need your own money to access these necessities.

Poverty, then, takes different forms depending on the context. There is, though, something that links poverty in countries at all levels of income and development, that links Jimmy and Gita. For its 2000–01 World Development Report, the World Bank interviewed 60,000 people in forty-seven countries about what relief of poverty meant to them.[22] The answers were: opportunity, empowerment and security. Dignity was frequently mentioned. Indeed, dignity has strong claims for consideration by those of us concerned with society and health.[23] A similar exercise in Europe showed that people felt themselves to be poor if they could not do the things that were reasonable to expect in society: for example, entertaining children's friends, having a holiday away from home, buying presents for people.[24] In other words, in Europe the ways of doing without have changed – no longer lack of clean water and sanitation, but not having the means to participate in society with dignity.

Poverty? Inequality? Empowerment? Don't
we know the causes of ill health?

A massive and truly impressive study, the Global Burden of Disease, looked at the causes of everything, everywhere.[25] I am exaggerating only slightly. The study really did look at all diseases in every region of the world in 2010 and, heroically, came up with estimates of the major causes of ill-health globally. The list was, starting at the most important and working down in order: high blood pressure, smoking, household air pollution, low fruit intake, alcohol use, high body mass index, high fasting plasma glucose level, childhood underweight, ambient particulate matter pollution, physical inactivity, high sodium intake, low nuts and seeds, iron deficiency, suboptimal breastfeeding, high total cholesterol, low whole grains, low vegetables, low omega-3, drug use, occupational injury, occupational low back pain, high processed meat, intimate partner violence, low fibre, lead, sanitation, vitamin A deficiency, zinc deficiency and unimproved water.

Three things strike me about this list. First, where are the causes of infectious disease? Sanitation, vitamin A and zinc deficiency and unimproved water bring up the rear of the list. Childhood underweight, which makes children more vulnerable to infection, comes in at rank 8, *after* high body mass index, i.e. overweight. Today, considering all countries, high-, middle- and low-income, the major diseases affecting people are similar – so-called non-communicable diseases: heart disease, lung disease – note the importance of indoor air pollution, a cause of chronic lung disease in low-income countries – cancers, diabetes. AIDS, Ebola, TB and malaria remind us that there is still a long distance to go in eradicating major infectious disease epidemics. That said, already in middle-income countries, and increasingly in low-income countries, the causes of suffering and death are similar to those in high-income countries.

Second, the list contains a mix of physiological risk factors: high blood pressure, high blood glucose, high total cholesterol; behaviours: smoking, diet and alcohol consumption; and environmental exposures: air pollution, lead. There is no causal analysis in the sense that diet can cause high blood pressure and high plasma cholesterol. Think about two ways to control high blood pressure: pharmacologically, or through changing diet and environmental factors. The pharmaceutical industry may not like me for saying it, but my preference is for seeing how we could deal with the causes of high blood pressure, high cholesterol and high blood sugar, rather than simply wait for them to get raised and then treat.

Third, and related to the last point, there is no social analysis. Overwhelmingly, most of these risk factors are related to people's social circumstances. We might call these the 'causes of the causes'.

Diet, indoor air pollution and high blood pressure are potent causes of disease globally. We need to ask why, increasingly, these risk factors are linked to social disadvantage. Remember the discussion of maternal mortality? We may call lack of access to medical care a cause of a mother dying in childbirth. We need to look at the causes of lack of access – the causes of the causes.

My argument is that tackling disempowerment is crucial for improving health and improving health equity. I think of disempowerment in three ways: material, psychosocial and political. If you have too little money to feed your children you cannot be empowered. The material conditions for well-being are vital. The psychosocial dimension can be described as having control over your life. We will look at evidence that people have difficulty making the decisions that will improve their health if they do not have control over their lives. Further, disempowering people in this way, depriving them of control over their lives, is stressful and leads to greater risk of mental and physical illness. The political dimension of empowerment relates to having a voice – for you, your community and indeed your country.

My approach to empowerment and the causes of the causes has a history. Over a century ago, Robert Tressell, describing the foul living conditions in which poor labourers in Britain slept, wrote in *The Ragged Trousered Philanthropists*:

> The majority of those who profess to be desirous of preventing and curing the disease called consumption (tuberculosis) must be either hypocrites or fools, for they ridicule the suggestion that it is necessary first to cure and prevent the poverty that compels badly clothed and half-starved human beings to sleep in such dens as this.[26]

Tressell was a novelist and polemicist and not a scientist, but he is still bang up to date. Should we, as much of modern medicine tries to do, at great expense, look for technical solutions and educate people and patients about healthy behaviour? Or should we, in the tradition of Tressell, seek to create the conditions for people to lead fulfilling lives, free from poverty and drudgery? In my view we should do both.

For an illustration of the potent health effects of disempowerment we can return to Glasgow. Sir Harry Burns is a remarkable man. He was a practising surgeon in Glasgow. He concluded that treating people surgically was too late in the course of their illness. His own clinical observations led him to the clear insight that the illnesses he was seeing resulted from people's social conditions. He wanted, then, to treat those conditions to prevent illness rather than wait for the illness to occur. We met in the early 1990s when he made the shift from surgery to public health. His clinical insights led him to the view that the way social conditions got into the body was through the mind. As I was doing research on how psychosocial factors affected heart disease we had a great deal to talk about. When Harry Burns was appointed Chief Medical Officer of Scotland he brought these insights with him – a force for good.

Harry Burns and his colleagues from Glasgow compared mortality rates in Glasgow with rates in Manchester and Liverpool in England.[27] All three cities are post-industrial, in the sense of having lost their heavy industry, and have similar levels of poverty and of income inequality. The causes of death with the biggest relative excess in Glasgow were: drug-related poisonings, deaths associated with alcohol, suicide and 'external' causes, i.e. accidents and violence apart from suicide.

The causes that show the biggest relative excess in Glasgow are all psychosocial. Harry Burns says that to understand Scottish, and in particular Glaswegian, health disadvantage, you have to understand that people feel they have little control over their lives – they are disempowered. This will be most evident for the poorest people in Glasgow, but it will not be an all-or-nothing phenomenon. It gives us a way to link poverty and the gradient. The lower they are in the socio-economic hierarchy the less control people have over their lives.

All over the world, babies that would have died had they been born a generation ago are now surviving. Middle-aged people can expect to live longer. Older people are healthier. In terms of health, it is the best of times. Unfortunately, there are dramatic inequalities in health, life chances and length of life. There are steep social gradients in health within countries and stark inequalities in health between countries. It is the worst of times. The knowledge we have of the causes of the global burden of disease, and of advances in medical care, qualifies us for an age of wisdom. Age of foolishness is putting it a bit strongly, but it is ignoring the social determinants, the causes of the causes, that accounts for our lack of success in reducing health inequalities within countries and, in some signal cases, between countries.

Money is important for health if you have little of it, but it is not only absolute income that matters. The amount of money you have relative to others influences your degree of empowerment, your freedom to be and to do. Empowerment, or freedoms, in their turn are related to better health. As we shall see, there are ways of contributing to empowerment, or freedoms, other than money.

I want to finish this chapter on what sounds like pedantry, but is actually fundamental. I have used two terms, health inequalities and health inequities. From now on, I am going to use the term health inequities to refer to those systematic inequalities in health between social groups that are judged to be avoidable by reasonable means. Such an approach does not cut off debate. There is ample disagreement as to what are 'reasonable means'. But it focuses the argument. Why is this fundamental? Because if people are suffering from ill-health in ways that could be remedied but are not, that is quite simply unjust.

2

Whose Responsibility?

Dost thou think, because thou art virtuous, there shall be no more cakes and ale?
> William Shakespeare, *Twelfth Night* (Act II, Scene iii)

Here are ten top tips for health. This list was published in 1999 by England's Chief Medical Officer, but it differs little from the kind of advice you would receive from any public health source in a high-income country.

1. *Don't smoke. If you can, stop. If you can't, cut down.*
2. *Follow a balanced diet with plenty of fruit and vegetables.*
3. *Keep physically active.*
4. *Manage stress by, for example, talking things through and making time to relax.*
5. *If you drink alcohol, do so in moderation.*
6. *Cover up in the sun, and protect children from sunburn.*
7. *Practise safer sex.*
8. *Take up cancer-screening opportunities.*
9. *Be safe on the roads: follow the Highway Code.*
10. *Learn the First Aid ABC: airways, breathing, circulation.*

Two questions: do you find the list helpful? Is it likely to change your behaviour, or that of others?

With that in mind, here is an alternative ten top tips for health compiled by David Gordon and colleagues at University of Bristol.

1. *Don't be poor. If you can, stop. If you can't, try not to be poor for long.*
2. *Don't live in a deprived area. If you do, move.*
3. *Don't be disabled or have a disabled child.*
4. *Don't work in a stressful, low-paid manual job.*
5. *Don't live in damp, low-quality housing or be homeless.*
6. *Be able to afford to pay for social activities and annual holidays.*
7. *Don't be a lone parent.*
8. *Claim all benefits to which you are entitled.*
9. *Be able to afford to own a car.*
10. *Use education to improve your socio-economic position.*

Hard to argue with any of the first, public health, list; it is all very worthy, well-meaning, based on sound science . . . and unlikely to make much difference. 'I was about to drink and drive and have unsafe sex and then, just in time, I remembered the Chief Medical Officer's advice.' 'I was about to feed the children takeaway chips, but remembered the one about fruit and vegetables, so gave them a salad and fresh fruit instead.' 'I'm worried about losing my job, which probably means losing my flat, pretty stressful, but I made time to relax, so it's all right now.'

The problem with the public health list is not that it's wrong – it is not – but that simply conveying advice is unlikely to lead to change in those who have most to gain. Here are three possible reactions to that list:

'I know all that. I take the trouble to get informed and look after myself and am already doing what the advice says.'

'Smoking and too much alcohol are bad for me? Fancy that. Who knew? That makes everything different.'

'I knew that, but so what? It won't change what I do. I have other things to worry about.'

In relation to these possibilities, there is good evidence that most people in countries such as the US and UK do know that smoking harms health,[1] and, in England, a majority of people who are obese claim to be on a diet.[2] The reasons that people continue to smoke and that obesity continues to spread do not stem from ignorance. In other words, advice is useful, but it is not how much people know that determines whether they behave as the advice suggests.

And the second, David Gordon's, list of tips? It too is based on sound science. There is good evidence to support the proposition that each of the ten items in the list is related to health, although that is less widely known. The issue that the Gordon list highlights so effectively is that even if people did know that these things were bad for health, there is very little that they could do about them.

The question that I wish to explore in this chapter is: whose responsibility is health? When we published the report of the Commission on Social Determinants of Health, *Closing the Gap in a Generation*, one senior politician asked: where is personal responsibility in all this? A leading economist and public policy expert based his critique on the fact that *Closing the Gap* mentioned 'social' many more times than it did 'individual'. It was the report on *social determinants*, why was he surprised? My response was, and is, that personal responsibility should be right at the heart of what we are seeking to achieve. But people's ability to take personal responsibility is shaped by their circumstances. People cannot take responsibility if they cannot control what happens to them.

The second list of ten top tips, quite obviously, contains advice that is outside the control of the individual to follow, although some commentators think that unemployment is a lifestyle choice and suspect that poverty results from laziness. Less readily appreciated is that the first top ten list is also, to some extent, outside individuals' control. At the very least, individual behavioural choices are influenced by where people find themselves. Smoking, diet and alcohol are causes of disease and contribute to the social gradient in ill-health. We may think of the determinants of these causes as the 'causes of the causes'.[3]

Trying to influence behaviour by addressing the causes of the causes evokes strong reactions. On one side of the argument, public health activists demonstrate that big business has too much influence on health policy – in relation to tobacco, alcohol and food, for example. The other side alleges that any government interference is an intolerable erosion of liberty, that letting business have a say is not lobbying against government policy, it is simply democracy. Citizens and public health people can have a say, too. The fact that a multi-billion-dollar corporation may have a louder megaphone than individual citizens is beside the point, they claim.

An exchange between two commentators on alcohol policy is revealing and typical. A journalist, Jonathan Gornall, wrote a piece in the *British Medical Journal* saying that big business had been instrumental in changing government policy on alcohol and health. Gornall pointed out that it had been the stated policy of the Conservative-led coalition government in Britain to introduce a minimum unit price for alcohol. After all, the data show what economists would predict: raise the price of alcohol and consumption declines. At the time the policy was announced, I publicly praised the Conservative Prime Minister, David Cameron, for taking this step that would benefit the public health. The government then reversed itself. Jonathan Gornall claimed that it was pressure on government from the alcohol industry, the dreaded big business, that led to the policy reversal.[4]

A rejoinder from the Institute of Economic Affairs (IEA), a free-market think tank, was strongly critical of Gornall and others who pressed for government action on public health. The author, Christopher Snowdon, found it hard to doubt that raising the price would reduce consumption but said that the policy was misguided and based on sloppy science, because a minimum price for alcohol might have other bad effects – people might pay more for alcohol and stop feeding their children.[5] He accused Gornall of 'personal attacks and grubby insinuations'.

Gornall's riposte was robust. His scientific objectivity was being criticised by an Institute whose stated policy was summed up in these words from its director-general: 'Through detailed research, we will be seeking to show that free market mechanisms produce better outcomes than heavy-handed and restrictive state regulation.'[6] If you already know that the outcome of your research will favour free markets before you do it, claims of objectivity are ludicrous. Further, the claim that the IEA is an independent voice is undermined by its refusal to disclose its funding sources. When the same Institute opposed steps for tobacco control, including plain packaging, detailed research in tobacco industry documents revealed that the industry had given funding to the Institute of Economic Affairs.

I could report scores of such exchanges. They make clear that discussions of how to address the 'causes of the causes' of behaviours relevant to health involve both political views of the role of the state and vested interests. The overlap makes for a distorted debate.

The fact is that the conditions to which we are exposed influence behaviour. Most of us cherish the notion of free choice, but our choices are constrained by the conditions in which we are born, grow, live, work and age. How far we accept constraints on behaviour varies.

With smoking, for example, most people nowadays do not find steps society may take to limit tobacco consumption particularly troubling. Most people accept restriction of smoking in public places, bans on advertising and warnings on labels. As a result of these measures, smoking rates have declined in many countries, with consequent benefits to health. Even with smoking, though, a proven toxic practice that kills up to a half of regular smokers, there is a hardy bunch that claims that steps towards tobacco control are an erosion of their freedom.[7] One would be more inclined to listen to the viewpoint of those not funded by the tobacco industry.

For smoking, the healthiest amount is zero. Diet is different. We all eat. More than half the world's population live in cities and do not grow their own food. The food industry plays a crucial role, as do governments and others, in getting food to people. If you are critical of markets, as I am when it comes to health care and education, spend a moment imagining how a Soviet minister of food in Moscow might have ensured that 10 million people and their food were matched up every day, without the help of markets. The market works amazingly to match people to food. That said, there are market failures. Some people have too little food to eat, and some too much. The type of food we eat influences obesity, heart disease and cancer. As a result there have been 'food wars' – the *Economist* labelled one in which I was an unwitting combatant as the 'Battle of the Bulge' – over healthy eating. These food wars illustrate the issue of whose responsibility is healthy eating. In addition, the food wars are highly relevant to health inequities because diet can influence and determine levels of non-communicable disease, which in turn contribute to health inequities.

FOOD AND FASCISM

It is diverting to find yourself described in the *Daily Mail*, a national newspaper, as a health Nazi. When it happened to me, in 2007, I commented to a journalist friend that I thought Joseph Mengele was a health Nazi. Why me? My friend told me not to take it so seriously; the writer did not mean I did ghastly experiments on humans in concentration camps. Just that I was a health fascist. That was not terribly reassuring, especially as the newspaper in question described my pronouncements as 'grotesque and increasingly irresponsible'. Another national newspaper, the *Telegraph*, fulminated that I was leading 'an unholy alliance of puritans, health fascists and nanny-state control freaks'. For good measure, another national daily chimed in with 'Fat lies of the food fascists'. One or two of the tabloid headlines were clever. The *Sun* had: 'Save our bacon' and 'Careless pork costs lives'.

What might have led to so much frothing at the mouth? Who were my gang of fascistic liars that a perceptive press uncovered?

Our camouflage was good. I had chaired a panel convened by the World Cancer Research Fund, to review the evidence on *Diet, Nutrition, Physical Activity and Cancer*.[8] The panel consisted of more than twenty internationally acclaimed scientists. Ingenious fascists, covering our tracks by having day jobs as professors from the UK, US, Japan, China, India, Chile, Mexico, Africa, New Zealand and Australia. The strength of our report was that the recommendations were based not on one study but on 7,000 scientific papers. More than 200 scientists were involved in the five-year process of assembling the 400-page report, and UNICEF and the World Health Organization were among the observers – hardly *Mein Kampf*.

Our conclusion, based on *all* the quality scientific evidence, was that people who were overweight had higher risk of cancer, so it was important to be as lean as possible within the normal body-weight range. We reported that processed meat increased risk of cancer and should be avoided if people wished to reduce their risk; and red meat consumption above 500 g a week increased risk of cancer.

As a way of framing our conclusions we made recommendations. It was these scientific conclusions, reached after a painstaking process, that were labelled as 'fat lies of the food fascists'.

I had been here before a dozen years previously: that time about dietary prevention of heart disease.[9] Then the sober reflections of my committee of scientists and professors were described as 'the food Leninists' latest onslaught . . . The nanny state is going to tell you what to eat for breakfast, lunch and dinner.'[10] Leninist or Nazi?

The point is that anyone who seeks to influence individual behaviour in the interest of the health of the public is a totalitarian.

What is the argument – science or something else?

What is going on? How can sober scientific conclusions generate such hostility? Drawing conclusions on the basis of careful review and debate of 7,000 scientific papers was lying? Spending five years culminating in careful formulation of meticulously worded recommendations that were subject to seemingly endless debate was irresponsible? Reporting that people could, if they followed our advice, reduce their risk of cancer was fascist?

The clue is in the fact that it was only the populist press with a libertarian streak who thought we were lying fascists. Acceptance of our scientific conclusions – that there were steps that could be taken that might reduce the risk of cancer – should lead to a serious debate: whose responsibility is it to prevent disease and promote health? Somewhere beneath the hyperbole and, indeed, lies of the journalists was an argument that ran along the lines of: if people want to make themselves sick by their freely chosen behaviours, that is nobody's business but their own.

There is an intellectual smokescreen working here. If he can claim that our scientific conclusions are incorrect the commentator does not have to face the difficult question of what to do about them. It's easier to label us liars than to grapple with the matter of whose responsibility it is to prevent disease, or where the balance of responsibilities should lie between the individual and the community. Or again, and relevant to my core concern, to consider whether social disadvantage renders some people less able to make healthy choices.

It is reasonable to disagree about evidence. Scientists disagree frequently, and vigorously, because the evidence is never as firm as we would like. It does not mean that because there is disagreement no conclusions can be drawn. Some 'scientists' think the earth is flat, and some don't, so can we draw no conclusions? Some think creation science is a more valid theory than evolution, so should we present both theories equally? Of course not. We must distinguish between situations where most scientists, with only a few exceptions, conclude that evidence points a certain way – manmade climate change, for example – and those where it is genuinely more uncertain.

When I first started doing research on determinants of the health of the public I noted a division even among scientists in their view of the evidence on diet and disease. Rather than views of the evidence determining scientists' willingness to take action to improve the public health, the reverse was true: willingness to take public health action was determining views of the evidence. Scientists who were inclined to want to take public health action found the evidence more convincing than those who were philosophically averse to action.

Let us assume, as the evidence shows overwhelmingly, that increased body weight does increase risk of cancer. What should we do? The answer from the political right is that 'we' should do nothing. It is up to the fully informed individual actor, in possession of all the information, to make his individual choice. If he chooses to be fat it should be of no concern to anyone else.

RATIONAL OBESITY?

Gary Becker, Nobel Prize-winning economist from the University of Chicago (sadly, he died in 2014), applied rational choice theory to everyday life. We weigh up the costs and benefits of different actions and make rational choices to maximise our utility, roughly our satisfaction. In general, people value the present more than the future, so future consequences of our actions will weigh less heavily than present benefits, argue rational choice theorists. Becker and his

University of Chicago colleague Kevin Murphy write on rational addiction.[11] In their view, addiction, not just to alcohol, tobacco and cocaine, but to television, work and food, can be explained by rational choice theory. The more people discount the future the more can rational choice account for addiction. Simplifying (following Lord Byron): wine and women, mirth and laughter, now, count for more than sermons and soda water the day after. Eat, drink and be merry because the future, well, is in the future. They argue that it is precisely because some people do value the future that we are not all addicts.

The theory is brilliant and creative and has influenced large numbers of economists, but I wonder if a rational totting up of benefits and harms, discounted at the market rate of interest or some other suitable rate, is what really determines our behaviour. It assumes perfect information which will of course be lacking much of the time.

I have asked rational choice theorists why someone overweight and worried about it might eat a huge slice of chocolate gateau. The conversation goes like this.

RATIONAL CHOICE THEORIST: It is because the utility of doing so is greater than the utility of abstaining.

ME: How do you know that?

RCT: Well, they wouldn't have done it otherwise.

ME: Even if they enjoyed it for five minutes and spent the rest of the waking day in an agony of self-loathing? Is that maximising utility?

RCT: Steep discounting; they value the present ecstasy of chocolate gateau more highly than avoiding the future agony of self-loathing.

ME: Would you ever conclude that someone is not rationally maximising utility?

RCT: No, why else would they do the behaviour?

Having read Dostoevsky, let alone Freud, as a medical student, I thought behaviour was a little more complicated than that. But if you never have to measure utility, simply infer it from the behaviour, it is always perfectly consistent: whatever people do maximises utility, by assumption. Danny Kahneman, psychologist and winner of the Nobel Prize in Economic Sciences, showed that all kinds of things influence our choices, other than simple rational calculation of utility – what we remember, how the evidence is presented, and a whole slew of biases to which we are all subject.[12]

At a meeting, an economist lecturing on rational choice theory as applied to obesity was asked by someone, rather unkindly I thought, why he was obese. His response: because I choose to be. I have to say: I doubt it. It is most unlikely that he gets up in the morning and says: I think I shall spend the day making myself fatter. I presume his answer was shorthand for: the utility I get from my present pattern of eating outweighs the disutility in the future from the effect of obesity on my health. I value health but that's in the future and, right now, I value a quarter-pounder, fries and a large Coke more.

Even if it were the case that, in his model, obese people chose to be so rationally, how then does he account for the prevalence of obesity rising in the USA and elsewhere? And why are more Americans obese than Frenchmen? Telling me that it is because more and more Americans choose to be obese has no explanatory power at all. It simply shifts the question: why are more Americans choosing to be obese?

Rational choice theory is probably implicit in the oft-stated notion that people are responsible for their own health. Growing obesity is a result of people increasingly valuing present consumption more highly than future disbenefits; or, in more everyday language, growing more irresponsible. But if increasing fecklessness accounts for increasing obesity, why have rates of smoking declined dramatically? Why are we responsible when it comes to smoking and feckless when it comes to eating? Even were it true that people value present consumption more highly than the future effects on health, why has the balance changed? Or, if the balance hasn't changed, and people always valued the present more highly than the future, why is that balance more likely to cause obesity now than it did in the past?

With the rise in obesity in mind let's return to the question of whose responsibility is health. A dispassionate view of the evidence would surely acknowledge that the rise in obesity was the result of more than individual choice – it was due to changed circumstances. Why then assume that any attempt to change circumstances is fascism and that it must be left to the individual actor to change things for himself? Yet, if social actions caused the problem, surely it must be legitimate to discuss what social actions we are willing to take to solve it.

INEQUITIES IN HEALTH AND 'LIFESTYLE' – THE CAUSES OF THE CAUSES

The smaller the dress size the larger the apartment. This received wisdom in New York sums it up: there is a social gradient in obesity. Particularly among women in middle-income and high-income countries, the lower the status, the greater the obesity. But why?

My concern is with inequities in health within and between countries, and the role of social determinants. 'Social determinants' is a language unfamiliar to many epidemiologists and others who are more concerned with individual risks. Relative deprivation, social relationships, conditions enabling a life of dignity, empowerment and the items in David Gordon's top tips are not the bread and butter, or even the five a day, of traditional health concerns. Where, I am challenged, are smoking, alcohol, obesity? Social determinants do not exclude these health behaviours. When considering inequities in non-communicable disease, smoking, alcohol and obesity are right at the centre. One way the social environment is causally linked to health inequity is through these behaviours – hence this chapter. Another way is through stress pathways which will feature in later chapters.

I argue that central to improving people's health and well-being is empowerment of individuals and communities. At first blush, the language of personal responsibility would seem to be consistent with empowerment, with people taking control over their lives and freely making health choices. Certainly individuals must make the choice to smoke or not, how to drink and to eat. But when we see regular social patterns of behaviours it suggests that there are broader, social, causes.

I can illustrate with data on the development of these unhealthy behaviours. With colleagues at UCL and the National Centre for Social Research, I was at one time involved with the Scottish Health Survey. I was catching the flight from London to Edinburgh to present the findings and reviewing my PowerPoint presentation on the plane. The data showed that as girls went through the age of puberty, smoking rates rose dramatically. It was almost as if smoking, along with the bodily changes, was another sign of puberty. Participation in exercise went down as girls passed through the puberty years, and girls also started to experiment with alcohol. A woman flight attendant looking over my shoulder said: I did all that, and more besides. I showed her the social gradient in these behaviours, which starts early: the lower the status the more unhealthy the behaviour patterns. 'Yup. That was me, too,' she said, 'modest background like my friends.'

All young people experiment. But we see social gradients in obesity, and smoking already appearing in childhood and adolescence. It is too narrow a view to see this as simply each single one of these young people making an individual choice and ignoring the social pressures on them to behave in certain ways.

I have been asked by a concerned public health doctor: unemployed young people are hanging around in downtown areas, smoking, drinking too much, doing drugs and getting into trouble. What would I suggest? My response, not helpful, is that I would not start from here. I would start with early child development and education. Empower young people, help them develop the attributes that will give them control over their lives and a stake in the future, and they will have more interesting things to do than hang around street corners smoking and drinking too much.

Knowledge is but one step to empowerment. As described above, in Britain the whole population understands that smoking is bad for health – yet there is a social gradient in smoking. Poverty and inequality are deeply disempowering. People with little control over their lives do not feel able to make healthy choices.

Which may be part of the reason that health advice, if effective at all, can act to increase inequalities in unhealthy behaviours. So it was with smoking. A habit that did not discriminate among socio-economic positions has become increasingly distributed along the social gradient. Now in Britain only 9 per cent of adults in higher professional households smoke, compared with 31 per cent in manual households.[13] Smoking is a cause of illness and death. We must address the causes of the causes.

OBESITY AND OVERWEIGHT –
GENES OR EDUCATION?

Obesity and overweight illustrate well the interaction of individual and social determinants. Individuals make choices about what to eat and how much, what exercise to take and how much, but those choices are influenced by the environment in which they find themselves. Part of the individual propensity to obesity will be genetic. Studies of twins provide one way of sorting through the contribution of genes and environment to any condition. Identical twins are identical genetically, but they also share environments. Fraternal twins share half their genes, on average, but also share environments. Twin studies suggest that obesity is 50–90 per cent heritable – a big genetic component.[14] But note: twin studies are, in general, performed in a restricted range of environments. The assumption that fraternal twins share environments to the same extent as identical twins could also be questioned. But that is not my main point here. It is: how do we reconcile the results of twin studies with results from other types of studies?

I have been interested in the health of migrants to the UK from the Indian subcontinent. A study in West London of men of South Asian background showed a mean body mass index (BMI) of 28. BMI is a widely used measure of healthy weight and adjusts weight for height (squared). Given that the desirable range of BMI is 20–25, and that anything over 25 is defined as overweight, and over 30 as obese, an *average* of 28 means a great deal of overweight, not to say obesity. A study in rural Punjab, the area of India from which these men originated, showed a mean BMI of 18. The average was underweight. Assume an average height of 1.72 m (5 feet 8 inches) in both places. A difference in BMI of 10 corresponds to a difference in average weight of 29 kg (64 pounds). That is enormous. Unless the Punjabi men with a genetic predisposition to put on weight were more likely to become immigrants, which seems unlikely, the men in the Punjab and the men in London of Punjabi origin are likely to be similar genetically. Which means that, in this case, overweight is chiefly environmental.

A standoff. Twin studies say it is predominantly genetic. Migrant studies say it is predominantly environmental. The environmentalists can criticise the twin studies as understating the environmental component, as I have done; the geneticists can criticise the migrant studies as not controlling the genetic component adequately, and they do. The point should be that if there is a restricted range of environmental exposure, *all* the variation will be genetic. If there is the environmental equivalent of a tsunami, individual differences in susceptibility, genetically determined, will make less difference – the environment predominates. To explain emaciation in India and overweight in London we have to appeal to 'environmental' explanations. To explain the differences between identical and fraternal twins exposed to very similar environments, we appeal to differences in genetic susceptibility.

In Figure 2.1 I have copied three maps from the US Centers for Disease Control and Prevention (CDC) on obesity levels by state using the years 1985, 1997 and 2010 to show the progression. The maps show each US state shaded according to the prevalence of obesity. As the years roll on, the colours get deeper and deeper, as the rate of obesity rises. When I present these graphs, the reaction of the audience is similar to mine when I first saw them. They are jaw-droppingly shocking. As the colours go from pale blue to deep red, the audience gasps in unison. It is amazing how rapidly the genome can change in the USA! I am being ironic. Whatever genetic contributions to obesity there may be, these will be stable over two or three decades. They most certainly don't run riot within a generation. Increases in obesity such as these have to be 'nurture', not 'nature'.

Not just in the US, though. The waistline of the planet is expanding. In Egypt and Mexico 70 per cent of women are overweight. This has been labelled coca-colonisation. Rational choice, perhaps, but growth in processed foods and decline in opportunities for physical activity are more potent explanations.

For some decades in high-income countries, we have seen that, in women particularly, the lower the education the greater the prevalence of overweight and obesity – a social gradient.

Worryingly, obesity levels in children have been rising. With children the discussion about personal responsibility is more complicated. Even parents who are ideologically opposed to the nanny state will have no compunction in saying to children: don't eat that chocolate bar now, it will spoil your dinner; if you don't eat your broccoli, no dessert for you. We are probably biologically

FIGURE 2.1: GOING, GOING, GONE!

Percentage of obese (BMI>30) in US adults – 1985

Percentage of Obese (BMI>30) in US Adults – 1997

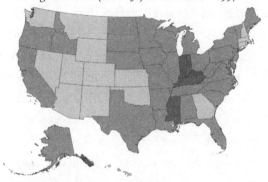

Percentage of Obese (BMI>30) in US Adults – 2010

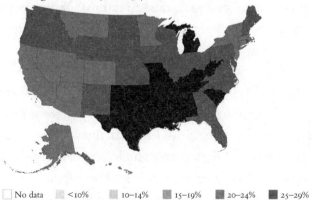

☐ No data ▓ <10% ▓ 10–14% ▓ 15–19% ▓ 20–24% ▓ 25–29% ▓ ≥30%

Source: CDC. Obesity trends among U.S. adults between 1985 and 2010. Centers for Disease Control and Prevention, 2010.

programmed to like sweet things. It is only by exerting will that we
do not subsist on a diet of sugary drinks and ice cream. Rising obesity in children, then, reflects the diets to which they are exposed,
not the likelihood that children have changed their economic
calculus and started valuing the pleasures of present consumption
more highly than future health. In England, now, the rise in childhood obesity has levelled off in children from families of intermediate and higher social position, but the rise continues in children
from less advantaged families.[15] In the future, the social gradient in
obesity may be steeper than it is now.

By contrast, in low-income countries women with more
education are more likely to be overweight than women with
less education. This may reflect two linked phenomena: women of
low education in low-income countries are simply too close to the
absolute poverty line to have sufficient calorie intake to get fat. The
obverse is that getting fat may give a public sign that you have risen
above the destitution margin.

As countries get richer, the social gradient shifts towards the
familiar pattern in high-income countries: high education, less
overweight. Amina Aitsi-Selmi, working with me, examined this
trend in Egypt and other countries. She found that richer women
were more likely to be overweight – a worrying finding. Worrying,
because I do not want to be the Jeremiah who says that rising
above absolute poverty will bring punishment in the form of obesity and its complications such as diabetes. Amina found further,
however, that the link between wealth and obesity was not seen in
women with more education. Now I display my own prejudices:
I like this finding. Women with more education are not punished
with obesity for rising out of poverty.[16]

The social distribution of obesity and overweight within and
between countries should give pause to those who think of health
only in terms of personal responsibility. Why should it be that
personal responsibility should follow the social gradient? Is personal

responsibility an exclusive preserve of the better off? The idea is absurd. Rather, as I would put it, create the conditions for people to have control over their lives – spread the advantages of education more broadly, for example – and women and men will have the tools, and concern, to do something about their own body weight.

ALCOHOL – JUST PERSONAL RESPONSIBILITY?

Alcohol is an obvious example of a health behaviour influenced by social conditions. Male mortality rates rose dramatically in Russia after the collapse of the Soviet Union. It is estimated that there were 4 million excess deaths in the first decade after 1990. It is clear that heavy alcohol consumption played a role in this increased mortality. The scale of its contribution is debated, but binge drinking was deeply implicated in the frequency of violent deaths and possibly in sudden deaths. Alcohol is a cause, but we need to ask why more Russian men than before were killing themselves with drink. Can drinking fatal amounts of alcohol be described as a rational choice to maximise utility? This would only be helpful as an approach if it helped us understand the changes and what to do about them.

Of course, I am making the assumption that 4 million extra deaths should be a concern. That we should not stand by and say that if individuals set their minds on behaving as they did, they should reap what they sow: it's their fault for behaving so irresponsibly. Rather we should say that changes in circumstances accounted for changes in behaviour on a mass scale.

These changes include sharp declines in social and economic conditions. Following the collapse of the Soviet Union there was a dramatic fall in national income (GDP), which translated into a 60 per cent drop in real incomes for average families. Faced with poverty, with difficulties finding work, with a steep rise in inequality, Russian men turned to drink, including toxic alcohol substitutes, with dire consequences.

In Britain the patterns of alcohol consumption, and harm endured, are different. Take the question of who drinks more on average in Britain: high status or low. Contrary to popular opinion, survey after survey shows that average alcohol consumption is higher in people of higher socio-economic position, and especially women. Women with more education and higher-status jobs drink more on average than those with less education. Similarly, in the US, the higher the education the more likely are people to be drinkers.[17] By contrast the pattern of alcohol-related harm shows a clear social gradient the other way: more alcohol-associated hospital admissions, and alcohol-associated deaths, the lower one stands in the social hierarchy. The mismatch between average drinking and harm is striking. It may arise because the pattern of drinking differs. If high-status people have half a bottle of burgundy with dinner each night, they may have a higher weekly consumption than someone who gets blind drunk on a Friday night. The latter may do more harm. Other factors may also contribute to the increased risk associated with being low-status: poor nutrition, risky behaviour and smoking are all likely contributors to risk of harm.

In the case both of European East–West differences in alcohol-associated harm and of the social distribution in Britain, we must not only understand the causal connection between patterns of drinking and ill-health, but the causes of the causes: what determines the pattern. Broadly speaking we understand three types of causes affecting population patterns of alcohol consumption: price, availability and cultural influences. I illustrate one of these causes of population fluctuation in alcohol – price – in Figure 2.2.

Alcohol became progressively cheaper between 1960 and 2005. As the price dropped, so consumption rose. One of my economist colleagues saw this graph and said: 'I teach this stuff – how price changes demand – and I have never seen such a clear real-life demonstration.' If as a society, we think lower alcohol consumption

FIGURE 2.2: THE THEORY WORKS: THE CHEAPER THE DRINK THE
MORE IS DRUNK

UK alcohol consumption relative to its price

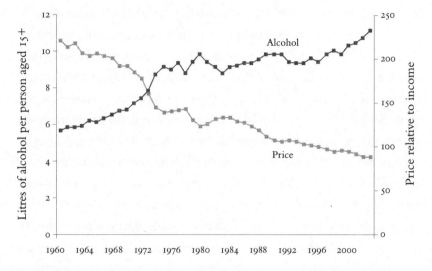

Source: Tighe A, editor. *Statistical Handbook 2003*. London: Brewing Publications Limited, 2003.

might be beneficial, we should raise the price. As I discussed earlier
in the chapter, this offends some free-marketeers.

Note that, as well as price, availability and culture influencing
population trends in alcohol consumption, there are individual determinants, which may include genetic predisposition, personal history,
personality and subculture. Individual-level determinants may need
counselling and treatment. Population determinants require social
action. It doesn't help simply to say that it is up to the individual.

WHOSE RESPONSIBILITY?

As I was cycling home after a dinner at the Royal College of
Physicians, still wearing my dinner jacket and bow tie, my bicycle
swerved and went over, and left me lying in agony and unable to
move off the road. The ambulance came promptly. The ambulance
man took one look at my fancy dress and said: "E's 'ad a few!' I'd had

one glass of wine between 7 and 11 p.m., I protested, but wondered what that had to do with anything. Was he somehow not going to look after me if he thought I had been drinking, because he would have held me responsible for my own downfall – literally?

As it was I received excellent care, including a titanium pin to hold the ends of my fractured femur in place – again, thank you NHS. But I was still mulling over the ''E's 'ad a few' when a Conservative member of Parliament said that, in his view, people who suffered from lifestyle diseases should pay for the cost of their treatment. I wonder if, in this parliamentarian's view, had I had three glasses of wine, not one, I should have been liable for the cost of treatment of my fractured femur. Was the politician suggesting that any down-and-out who fell over in a stupor and banged his head should be left lying in the gutter where he belonged, because he couldn't afford to pay? Was that the kind of society he envisaged?

I'm being melodramatic. The MP might have been referring to diabetes linked to obesity. As I described, obesity is more common the lower in the social hierarchy you are. As a result, diabetes prevalence also shows a social gradient – higher in lower-status groups. The proposal, then, is that poor people should be held liable for the cost of their diabetes treatment. There may be three reasons why this proposal has been made:

- Disincentive. Forcing people to pay for the cost of treatment would encourage them to adopt healthier lifestyles, not get obese, and thereby avoid diabetes.
- Punishment. If people behave badly they should incur a cost as a penalty for their bad behaviour.
- Cost saving. Lower the costs to the health service by offloading the cost onto irresponsible people.

The evidence to support the first argument, disincentive, is completely lacking. People become overweight and obese over a lifetime. The idea that a slice of chocolate gateau would be forgone at age twenty-five in order to avoid the burden of having to pay for diabetes care at sixty-five is completely fanciful. If there were evidence of such a deterrent effect, we could then have a debate as to whether we agreed with the principle of a sick individual having to pay – I do not – but there is no such evidence.

I speculate that most of us would deem the second view, punishment, as unworthy. The objection is a moral one. The whole principle of a universal care system, free at the point of use, is that it treats all comers according to need, not according to some third party's idea of moral virtue. Not only should we treat the drug addict who has got HIV from using unclean needles, there is a good case to be made for medicalising drug addiction precisely to reduce harm. In other words, to go out of our way to use society's resources to improve people's lives, even those labelled by some moralists as unworthy.

Given that poor people are more likely to suffer 'lifestyle' diseases than rich, but the rich pay more tax than the poor, the third argument, reducing costs in the health system, would have the effect of transferring money from poorer people to richer. That form of anti-equity redistribution, too, has no place in a civilised society.

This discussion of whether we should hold people responsible for their own misfortune leads in two directions. First is the moral case for taking action on social determinants of health and health inequity, which will be the substance of the next chapter. Second, I argue that empowerment – having freedom, in Amartya Sen's terms, to lead a life you value – is crucial to good health. The question then is how can society achieve conditions that will enable people to take control of their own lives, including fostering healthy behaviours? Or, to put it differently, how can we take action against David Gordon's top ten list, the social conditions one, with which I began this chapter? The rest of the book will address that question.

Don't people have poor health because
they don't have health care?

You might be thinking: if he is concerned with health, surely he should be discussing health care. Give everyone access and health inequalities would go away.

Here's a choice. What would you prefer: not to suffer a heart attack, or to have access to high-quality treatment when you had one? For heart attack I could substitute stroke, cancer, diabetes, mental illness. As with most of my questions, the appropriate answer is: probably both. You'd like to avoid a heart attack, but if the calamity struck you would want access to best-quality health care.

Access to high-quality health care for everyone would be a good thing, but health inequalities would not go away. Health inequalities arise from the conditions that make people ill; health care is what is needed to treat people when they get sick. Lack of health care is no more a cause of ill-health than aspirin deficiency is the cause of headache. We should not add the insult of lack of access to health care to the injury of getting sick in the first place.

It is common to equate health and health care. Ask the average person her views on health and she might talk about how wonderful the nurses were when her grandmother was in hospital, or the difficulties of seeing a doctor on weekends. You are unlikely to get the Chief Medical Officer's top ten list, and almost certainly not David Gordon's top ten. I hear people talk about investing in health when they mean investing in health care. Policy wonks discuss how much a country spends on health, when they mean health care. I would argue that most of what a country spends affects health: transport, education, social protection, environment, foreign affairs, overseas development – sometimes positively and sometimes adversely. That is in addition to expenditure on health care.

In the US much of the discussion of 'disparities' – the American term for health inequalities or health inequity – is indeed about health care. Such concern is hardly surprising given that although the US spends more on health care than any other country, about one-sixth of its population lack health insurance, and hence have had difficulties in access to care. This should change with the Affordable Care Act, Obamacare. Well-meaning US colleagues have urged me not to talk about social determinants of health in the US because it might detract attention from inequities in access to care. An example of why they might be concerned was given to me by a US colleague. Medicaid pays for health care for the poor. Its director in one US state said he was against expansion of Medicaid coverage because insurance was less important than social determinants of health like income, education and housing conditions.[18] As the colleague who sent me this remarked wryly: the devil can always quote the scriptures for his purposes.

The fact that a Medicaid director is talking about social determinants of health, and even using the phrase, is great encouragement to those of us promoting this agenda. The fact that he is using social determinants as an excuse to discourage people from having health insurance is indefensible.

The US spends 17 per cent of its gross domestic product on health care. The UK spend per person is about 40 per cent of the American spend. What does the US get for all this outlay? Not much. We compared the health of white Americans and white English men and women aged fifty-five to sixty-four and showed first, that among Americans with health insurance there was a social gradient in health, related to income and education, and second, that even though 92 per cent of Americans in our sample had health insurance, the Americans were sicker than the English.[19] Richer Americans were sicker than richer English; poorer Americans were sicker than poorer English. And in case you were wondering, in one or two cases richer Americans were sicker than poorer English.

Bad news has legs. The good news that the English were healthier than Americans caused a momentary flutter in the airwaves in the UK. The bad news that Americans had lost the health wars to the English was on US headline news for at least two weeks after the original news hysteria. The finding led to at least two National Academy of Science Reports asking why the US was doing so badly.[20]

Some US economists have argued that spending on health care is a good thing, and spending more on health care would indeed lead to better health.[21] My response is one of curiosity. The US spends more on health care than any other country, yet, as I worried in Chapter 1, it ranks 50th in the chances of a fifteen-year-old man surviving to sixty.[22] Likewise in that chapter I pointed out that the US ranks sixty-third in the world in lifetime risk of a maternal death.

In Britain we have a national health service; the evidence shows that low income is mostly not a barrier to access. Yet we still have inequalities in health.

Two lessons emerge from this contrast. First, it is likely that provision of medical care interacts with social determinants. Given how much richer the US is than Greece, for example, and how much more it spends on health care than *any* other country, maternal mortality in the US should be as low as in Greece, 2 per 100,000 live births. So we should ask why some women are not saved. It is highly likely that the women who die are poor, black, ill-educated, often migrants.[23] Women who for other reasons would be at increased risk of ill health are put at higher risk by their lack of access to health care. According to the Centers for Disease Control and Prevention, over half of maternal deaths in the US are preventable.[24] The second lesson is related: the question should not only be how much medical care there is, but how it is distributed. We need to ensure that provision of health care does not increase health inequalities due to inequitable access.

It has proved very hard to calculate the contribution that lack of access to medical care makes to health inequality. The answer will depend on context. Health inequities persist in the UK, despite a health-care system that is free at the point of use, and where cost is not a barrier to care. It is likely then that differential access to care does not make a huge contribution to generating health inequities. Likewise the fact that Americans with health insurance and their generous health-care spending are sicker than English with their more modest levels of expenditure suggests that it is not differences in health care that account for big differences in health status.

That said, there is potentially much that health and medical people can do about social determinants of health.[25]

Much of public health in high-income countries, and increasingly in middle- and even low-income countries, focuses on behaviours thought of as lifestyle. Were we told by an overweening state that we absolutely had to eat French fries and drink fizzy sugary drinks daily we would take this as an intolerable erosion of our freedom. *We* decide what we eat, whether to exercise, whether to smoke, how much alcohol to drink. It is our choice and therefore our responsibility.

But, and it is a big but, the evidence I have reviewed in this chapter shows that our choices are influenced by circumstances beyond our control: price, availability, not to mention billions spent on advertising and marketing seeking to influence our choices. Do food, drink and tobacco companies sponsor sporting events because they just happen to like sports? One way we see the operation of these forces beyond our control is the rise in obesity; another is the social gradient in smoking and obesity.

Such observations suggest two approaches to promoting healthy behaviours. First, the time-honoured 'make healthy choices the easy choices'.[26] If fresh fruit and vegetables are less readily available and cost more than fast food full of saturated fat, salt and sugar, that will act as a barrier to consumption.

A second approach is to empower people to take the decisions that will positively influence their health and well-being. In

Amartya Sen's words: to create the conditions for people to have the freedom to lead lives they have reason to value.[27] If an experienced doctor, knowing the risks, chooses to cycle home after a dinner late at night, it is his choice. If his bicycle slips on wet leaves and he injures himself, he has no one to blame but himself. But David Gordon's top ten list of tips for health is outside the control of the people it most concerns. We should be seeking to improve the social environment *and* take the steps to give people the freedom to lead lives they have reason to value.

In my view we should take the steps just summarised because it is the right thing to do – a matter of social justice. If I am arguing that we *should* act in a spirit of social justice, it is well to understand what we mean. I turn to that key question in Chapter 3.

3

Fair Society, Healthy Lives

PICKERING. *Have you no morals man?*

DOOLITTLE *[unabashed]. Can't afford them, Governor . . . What am I? I ask you, what am I? I'm one of the undeserving poor: that's what I am. Think what that means to a man. It means that he's up agen middle class morality all the time. If there's anything going, and I put in for a bit of it, it's always the same story: 'You're undeserving: so you can't have it.' . . . I don't need less than a deserving man: I need more. I don't eat less hearty than him; and I drink a lot more. I want a bit of amusement, cause I'm a thinking man. I want cheerfulness and a song and band when I feel low. Well they charge me just the same for everything as they charge the deserving. What is middle class morality? Just an excuse for never giving me anything . . .*

HIGGINS. *Pickering: if we were to take this man in hand for three months, he could choose between a seat in the Cabinet and a popular pulpit in Wales.*

DOOLITTLE. *Not me, Governor . . . Undeserving poverty is my line.*

George Bernard Shaw, *Pygmalion* (Act II)

In Puccini's opera, candidates for Turandot's hand are given a fair choice: correctly answer three riddles and gain marriage to the princess; fail and be executed. No male, however ardent or focused on the main chance, is forced into it — he can choose, so one could argue that the process is fair. The outcome, as distinct from the process, is anything but: a trail of dead suitors and one chaste princess (until, of course, the tenor arrives, which in opera usually spells the end of the soprano's chastity). On this evidence – fair process versus fair outcome – would we deem the society in which Turandot was a princess to be a just society?

Obviously not. We have become a little squeamish about executing unsuccessful suitors for the royal hand. We rig things in more subtle ways. Some philosophers argue that process is the thing. If the process is fair, the outcome is fair whatever it may be, wrote John Rawls, the doyen of liberal political philosophers.[1] To see if the Rawls thesis holds, try this experiment with two young children. You have two ice creams, one vanilla and one chocolate. They both want the chocolate. You explain carefully that they can both have ice creams but there is only one chocolate. Do they agree that a fair way to decide would be to toss a coin? Yes, they agree. The coin is tossed and Peter gets the chocolate and John the vanilla. And the first thing John says? Unfair!

You try to explain to John that we all believe in equality of opportunity. He had an equal opportunity to get chocolate ice cream. Things just didn't work out. John is totally unconvinced by such theory. It wasn't the opportunity he wanted but the chocolate ice cream. He is focused on equality of outcomes, not equality of opportunity.

I haven't done the research to know what the age cut-off is beyond which John would learn to live with his disappointment and acknowledge that although he's unhappy he had an equal opportunity and it was a fair process. But for a younger child, and I suspect for all of us, the outcome matters too. The principle of tossing a coin may be better than some other way of deciding – primogeniture for example, or who's better-looking – but in the end, they both wanted the chocolate and Peter got it and not John.

Can you imagine a politician on his soapbox declaiming: 'I am of the firm belief that we should deny some people the opportunity to succeed, simply on the basis of the accident of their birth'? No. I can't either. It would be difficult to find a social commentator or politician who is against equality of opportunity – even if their policies deny such opportunity. But our discussions of social justice should not stop there.

Certainly as a doctor I care not only about opportunities and process but about outcomes. Outcomes really matter. Not at any cost or to the exclusion of all else, but they are important. If the doctor offers you chemotherapy – that will go on for months, make you sick and leave you bald – for your disease, the first thing you ask is how it will affect the natural course of the disease. You may be prepared to put up with an uncomfortable process if there is a good prospect of your health being better at the end. Conversely, if the likely improvement in survival is marginal, you may decide that the game is not worth the candle.

Outcomes matter in many domains. One of the objections to capital punishment, not the only one, is that even though the trial may have been 'fair', whatever that may mean in a particular jurisdiction, there are well-known examples where a person subsequently shown to be innocent has been executed. There are also good examples where a 'fair' judicial process is open to question. If the accused has been killed, sorry executed, there is no redress. The outcome matters as well as the process.

In the Introduction, I described the WHO Commission on Social Determinants of Health. On the cover of the Report we declared: social injustice is killing on a grand scale. In my English Review, so as not to frighten anyone in case social justice sounded like socialism we used the term fairness, and called it *Fair Society, Healthy Lives*. Colleagues from different European countries have since told me that 'fairness' sounds like the English playing cricket.

I am going to use the terms fairness and social justice as if they amount to much the same thing.

Ethical debates about justice and health used to revolve around access to health care.[2] Recognising that health is strongly influenced by social determinants changes the ethical debate to the just organisation of society, in order to achieve better health. Amartya Sen once wrote that all moral social systems require equality of something, the question is equality of what?[3] And the philosophers really do disagree about the 'what'.

Immodestly, I think we can help the philosophers. In Chapter 1, I said that we *can* use health, and inequities in health, as a measure of how we are doing in society. I follow that approach here by exploring which approach to social justice is most likely to increase health equity. If a libertarian says that he is right, or an Aristotelian, or a Kantian, I'll ask which approach, if followed, would lead to a diminution of health inequities. That, surely, is one worthy goal on which we can all agree.

To help resolve this, I want to look at the reality of the lives of people that I have been studying and writing about – people whose health is worse because of their social conditions, worse, that is, than it would have been had they grown up and lived in more favourable social conditions.

SOCIAL JUSTICE AND AVOIDABLE HEALTH INEQUALITIES = INEQUITIES

Three examples of people at the wrong end of health inequities

We met Gita and Jimmy in Chapter 1. To repeat: Gita sells vegetables on the street in Ahmedabad in the state of Gujarat in India. She has no formal education. Gita lives in an 'informal settlement' (a slum made of makeshift housing) and has two children who sit with her by the roadside as she sells her vegetables, and an older girl who helps with the vegetable trade. To keep her business going Gita takes out short-term loans, at 20 per cent a month interest, to buy vegetables from the middle man in the wholesale market. Her husband is a migrant worker who is living in another state and sends a few rupees back each month. Gita was just about making her tight budget work, but it was time for her daughter, aged fourteen, to marry, and instead of paying off her debts she put money into a dowry and a wedding party for her daughter. Some aid workers are tearing their hair out at what they see as this 'irresponsible' waste of money, as her interest payments have gone up.

Jimmy was born in Calton in Glasgow, was in trouble in school, and delinquency problems led to trouble with the police as a teenager. Jimmy was enrolled in an apprenticeship but dropped out; he has never had a 'proper' job, but did short-term temporary manual work. As is common in his subculture, any money Jimmy gets goes into drink and drugs; his diet, if you could call it that, consists of pub food, fast food and alcohol. Jimmy has had a series of short-term girlfriends, but is liable to alcohol-fuelled violent behaviour. He is known to the police for his various gang-related violent activities.

Rachel is an executive officer in the British Civil Service. She finished high school, but university was not the done thing in her school, so she took a low-level job in the British Civil Service; it's taken twenty-five years but she has slowly worked her way up from clerical assistant, through clerical officer to low-ranking executive officer. Rachel's salary is above the national median income, just, and she will retire on a pension that amounts to half her salary. She is divorced and lives alone. She sees her daughter two or three times a year. When council housing was being sold, she bought her flat and has nearly paid off the mortgage. Given that she lives alone she doesn't bother much about preparing elaborate meals.

Rachel is not poor but she feels that her life is somewhat impoverished, in the sense of being restricted by lack of money. When she and her husband were both earning modest salaries they could go out and do more things. She does not really have the money for foreign holidays that she sees work colleagues enjoying and, while she puts a brave face on her single life, were she to admit it, she is lonely.

What Gita, Jimmy and Rachel have in common is that their health is worse than those around them in more favoured social and economic positions. All three are on the downside of health inequalities, and I am arguing that putting these health inequalities right is a matter of social justice.

There are strong and possibly irreconcilable views among political philosophers as to what constitutes social justice. If there is simply no solution to the philosophers' disagreements then I do not expect to devise one. My approach is as a doctor. I am concerned with health and avoidable health inequalities – health inequity. I want to know, therefore, which approach to social justice helps provide the framework for understanding and the impetus for action on health inequities.

My guide has been Professor Michael Sandel, although he doesn't know it.[4] He teaches a philosophy class at Harvard which apparently is regularly oversubscribed. Having seen him in action at my own university, I can see why. He uses everyday problems and controversies, examined in lucid Socratic dialogues with his audience, to draw out principles of political philosophy. He does not provide me with an answer to social justice and health but he provides a framework for thinking about it.

Sandel distinguishes three approaches to social justice:

- maximising welfare,
- promoting freedom, and
- rewarding virtue.

It illuminates the cause of social justice and health to see how each of these might apply to avoidable health inequalities.

Maximising welfare

Jeremy Bentham, a great philosopher whose auto-icon – his skeleton dressed up in his own clothes with a wax face – sits in a case outside the office of the Provost and President of UCL where I work, is the founder of utilitarianism. Simply put, he argued for the greatest good for the greatest number, where good was measured as utility, on a scale of pain and pleasure. Given that my concern is with health more than with happiness, the same utilitarian principle could be applied: the greatest level of health for the greatest number.

A big advantage of simply adding up everyone's utility, or health, is that prince and pauper are counted the same. Given my focus on health, equal utility implies that a sick prince and a healthy pauper add up to the same societal level of health as do the healthy prince and the sick pauper. Predictably, healthy prince and unhealthy pauper are more common.

What if we want to value health against some other desirable good? Economists will often choose money as a universal measure. As, for example, in the following exchange that I had with a Chicago economist at a meeting. The economist said:

'If you want to know how much people value a television set, see how much they are willing to pay for it. So it is with human life. See how much people are willing to pay for another year of life and, ergo, you have the value of a year of human life.'

Setting aside the temptation to invoke Oscar Wilde's definition of a cynic (someone who knows the price of everything and the value of nothing), and some questions about the economist's stunningly simple methodology, I wondered about the incommensurability of human life and televisions. Provoked, he said: 'What's the difference between a life and a television? You can't answer that, can you!'

I mulled over this telling point. Of course, our students are motivated to go off to Africa to improve the dire situation of suffering televisions. The continued violence to female televisions is unacceptable. We could have the Millennium Television Goals, easier to meet than the Millennium Development Goals. Interrupting this silent riff I was moved to ask: if a poor person were willing to pay less for another year of life than a rich person, did that mean that a poor person's life was worth less than a rich person's? Absolutely, was the answer. Bangladeshi lives all worthless? Pretty much. Well, at least that's clear.

About this time I read a headline in the *Financial Times*: Economists are from Mars, Europeans are from Venus. Not all economists, I should add.

It has been put to me that I simply cannot turn my back on such economic calculations. For example, is it a good idea to introduce a new health programme, say, breast screening? Tot up the life years saved in dollars, set that against the cost of the programme, and you know how much society has benefited from the breast-screening programme.

I have two problems with this utilitarian calculus: the first is that it measures life years on the same scale as television sets. It is superficially attractive to measure everything the same way, to make comparisons. With a limited pot of money, should we invest in curbing global warming or in a programme of breast screening? Measure the relevant outcomes in dollars, compare them with the costs, and the decision is made.

Except it isn't. The methods of assigning dollar values to very different benefits are problematic. Which would you rather have: a 20 per cent reduction in your risk of dying from breast cancer, the benefit of screening, or have the polar ice cap melt at a slower rate? The inherent difficulty in answering that question is not solved by the superficial attractiveness of measuring them both in terms of dollars. Many have written on this subject.[5] I have resisted translating lives saved into a price for any of the reports on health inequalities for which I have had responsibility.

The second problem, which exercises me more, is one of distribution. Think of Gita in Ahmedabad. Suppose we are part of a team that goes into two Ahmedabad communities with a programme to improve nutrition of two-year-old children. When the programme is implemented, the children in both communities grow, on average, 6 cm in height in the next year. The benefit is the same in the two communities; they are equivalent in maximising welfare.

The difference is that, in the first community, the growth of all the children was actually between 5 and 7 cm, average 6. In the second community, there was a group of children of the poorest families, Gita and her fellow vegetable-sellers, who were discriminated against and excluded from the nutrition programme, one-third of the whole, and their average growth was only 2 cm. The other two-thirds leapt ahead with an average growth of 8 cm – average for the community 6. Simply by adding up the greatest good for the greatest number, the two communities are equivalent, average childhood growth in a year 6 cm. Should we leave it there? Which community is really doing better, the one where two-thirds of the children are growing rapidly, leaving one-third behind; or the other where all the kids are growing at about average rate? What I would not conclude is that the two communities were equivalent.

The outcome of the discussion may depend on whether all the children were valued equally. If, for example, you thought that the children left behind were somehow less valuable, then the community with two-thirds of children growing at 8 cm is clearly doing better.

Are some people's lives less valuable than others?

Kevin Murphy is a much-respected economist at the University of Chicago. Widely admired within his profession, he has won prizes and is tipped for more. He and Robert Topel use willingness-to-pay methodology to work out the value of a human life.[6] They ask, as with televisions, how much is someone willing to pay for another year of life? I am profoundly uneasy at the willingness-to-pay methodology in principle, and in particular at the way they use compensation levels in various occupations to infer 'revealed preferences'. Their methodology says that the societal value of life is greater:

(i)   the higher the lifetime income
(ii)   the less illness people have
(iii) the closer in age people are to the onset of illness

As I read this: the lives of older, richer, healthier people are more valuable than the lives of poorer, younger, sicker people. If I believe that, what am I doing caring about poor, sick, Indian children? Their lives are worthless. And if you believe it, do not waste a moment more on this book.

I was invited to a meeting at the RAND Corporation in Santa Monica California with a group of economists to discuss valuation of life. The starting text was the Murphy–Topel paper. I went next. I began by saying that I had had lunch with an Indian historian recently and I told him that the news from Chicago was that he did not value his life – he was willing to pay far fewer dollars for another year of life than an American. Ergo, he didn't value his life very highly.

Some of the Chicago economists in the room had expressions on their faces that said: that *is* what we think but would rather you had not put it so bluntly. I told them, to little effect, that my Indian lunch companion told me that Indian villagers were willing to give up food for their families for two days in order to be vaccinated against smallpox, so highly did they value their lives. But dollars, man, where are the dollars! My historian colleague's point is fundamental. Where people do not have money, money is the wrong unit of measurement to assess value. And where they do have money, it still may be the wrong unit. In discussing this with one economist, who I knew was devoted to his daughters, I showed him an SMS text I had just received from my daughter: 'Happy birthday, Daddy. You are the best. Love you. xxx'. I asked him how much that was worth in dollars. He couldn't answer because of the lump in his throat.

If you use the valuation of life to make allocation decisions, you spend the money where it will yield the greatest result, measured in dollars. It is inefficient to care for the poor, the sick and the young. If social justice demanded attention to the young, the sick and the poor, I must be paying a price to do this. Economists could work out the price and then ask me if it was worth it to use the money in this inefficient way.

To say that I was uncomfortable with this approach would understate it. I was aghast. At the meeting, I showed the Whitehall mortality graph – the lower the position in the hierarchy, including low-grade civil servants such as Rachel above, the shorter the life. I understood that the high-grade civil servant, Rachel's superior, would get a higher pension than Rachel in a relatively low grade, but if they each had renal failure Rachel and her boss had an equal right to dialysis and renal transplant. The economists disputed that, vigorously and all at once. First was the Murphy–Topel argument: the senior civil servant's life was worth more. Another suggested that the high-grade civil servant contributed more to society, so society would be better off if we treated her and let the low-grade woman die. Yet another suggested that we offer Rachel some money as compensation for not getting the treatment. Not a lot of money, because if we had a lot, we would give her the treatment. That amounts to bribing someone to accept a slow, uncomfortable death, rather than treating her.

There will always be less medical care to go around than we might like. Choices will always have to be made. Rachel may be less 'deserving' of high pay than her boss, but she has the same right to treatment for her chronic renal disease as her boss.

Women tend to have more illness than men, although they live longer, and are paid less than men for the same job, so are likely to be less rich than men. Does that mean we should give priority to treating men rather than women because the women are sicker and poorer? I wouldn't vote for any government that proposed that. Regrettably, such gender discrimination is all too common in parts of the world. Social injustice kills, and the utilitarian calculus does not capture or rectify this.

Do 'we' in rich countries, owe anything to 'them' in poor countries, whose poverty renders their lives worthless? I do not pretend for a moment that the answer to that question is simple. In this book I set out what *could* be done if the global community took seriously social determinants of health and health equity. The question of what *should* be done is, in my view, not answered by taking the view that the poorer you are the less valuable your life.

If the utilitarian calculus means the greatest good for the greatest number it runs up against other principles of action that take distributions into account. This was brought home to me by a conversation with an Irish minister of health. She spoke out in favour of targeting her limited resources on the poor and the needy and said:

'I want to spend the money where it will do the most good.'

'In that case', I replied, 'spend it on the middle classes.'

She was shocked.

'The evidence shows,' I continued, 'that people of higher socio-economic position have better cancer survival after treatment than people of lower position. If you have limited resources, and who doesn't, spend it where you'll get the most health gain: on the middle classes. That would serve the principle of the greatest good for the greatest number.' (I didn't think her tolerance would stretch to my telling her that, in addition, economists say that saving a rich person's life is more valuable to society, measured in euros, than saving a poor person's.)

'But that's not what I came into politics to do,' she said, 'I want to help the poor and disadvantaged.'

'Ah, then you have an equity principle, as well as an efficiency one. I would vote for you.'

It is clear that for her, as for me, a principle of equity was more important than simply the greatest good for the greatest number. I am presenting it as if it were a straightforward choice. It is anything but straightforward. If you were Rachel's boss you would not like to be told that because of your privileged place in society your chronic renal disease was not going to be treated because poor Rachel took priority, even though she was less likely to benefit than you.

If choosing who got treatment between Rachel and her boss, I would not choose on the basis of their income or seniority. I further enraged the economists at the RAND valuation of life meeting by saying that Canadians had made the case that it was wrong for rich people to buy more health care than was available to the poor. Now the economists were really screaming at me: 'Would you not let anyone have a Mercedes unless everyone could have one?!'

As I shall say, when we get to section three on rewards, I do not think everyone should have the same income – we should reward some sort of virtue, problematic as that is – but I do not think motor cars and health care are equivalent. Rich people have more money to spend, fine, within the limits that society deems acceptable. But that should *not* mean that they get better health care than people who have less to spend.

There is no easy answer to such dilemmas, which is why there are such vexed debates about allocation of scarce resources. For many of the actions I propose in this book, the dilemmas are less

intense. For example, all over the world children from less advantaged backgrounds have less adequate pre-school education and
care and less opportunity for quality education than do children
from more privileged backgrounds. It is entirely feasible to work
towards bringing the levels of pre-school education and care up
towards the standard available to the best-off. As I shall show in the
chapter on early childhood, there is even a good economic case for
doing it. Would anyone seriously argue that it is morally wrong to
give all children the best start in life?

PROMOTING FREEDOM

In a democracy, it is not easy to find someone to argue that freedom is a bad thing, and rightly so. Barring a few authoritarians,
most people are in favour. I thought of writing a justification of
why democracy is a good thing, and then remembered that the late
Oxford philosopher G. A. Cohen wrote that in Oxford, as opposed
to Harvard, they choose their deepest normative convictions pre-
philosophically. To a non-philosopher, that means they start from
some deeply held beliefs and then reason, rather than reason their
way towards these beliefs. Democracy, then, is a good thing. If I
had to have a 'because', I would say: because it has at its heart more
freedom than other systems of government. What then is the issue?
Surely any approach to social justice that has as an aim to promote
freedom has to be the correct one.

The challenge is to rescue 'freedom' from a polarised political
debate. Commentators of the political 'right' prize the freedom of
the individual over the controls of the state. The economist Milton
Friedman called his influential book calling for free markets and
freedom from state intervention *Free to Choose*. Putting a more
negative slant on a similar idea, Friedrich von Hayek called his
book *The Road to Serfdom*. Once the state gets involved in economic
decision-making, individual liberty is eroded and we are on the

road to serfdom. When neoliberalism is looking for intellectual flag-bearers these two fit the bill.

Libertarians, articulately represented by Robert Nozick in his *Anarchy, State, and Utopia*, argue that only a minimal state limited to protecting people against force and fraud and enforcing contracts is justified. Anything else is an intolerable erosion of freedom.

What freedom do Jimmy, Gita and Rachel enjoy? On the surface you might think that Jimmy in Glasgow has the most freedom to change his situation. He could stop being a scallywag, lay off the drugs and alcohol, stop abusing his girlfriends, put away his knife, leave the gang, pull his socks up, find a job and get on with it. Beneath the surface, though, Jimmy is not simply a tearaway. There is more to his biography, which is based on a case history brought to me by Detective Chief Superintendent John Carnochan, the top policeman who was head of the homicide unit in Glasgow until 2013. Jimmy never knew his father. His mother had a succession of male partners, most of whom abused Jimmy physically, if not sexually. He and his mother moved house about every eighteen months. By the time Jimmy entered school he already had behavioural problems and difficulty concentrating, and was subject to outbreaks of aggression towards other children and teachers. As soon as he was old enough, he was in trouble with delinquency problems, and later was well known to the police for a series of possibly drug-related thefts, and for violence. At various times, psychiatrists labelled him as having personality disorder, anxiety, depression and antisocial tendencies. Jimmy has this in common with men in prisons, over 70 per cent of whom have two or more mental disorders[7] – fourteen times more than among the general population.[8]

I'll try and get inside the head of a libertarian. Jimmy is free, when he is not in prison. He has the freedom to live a life of relative poverty, be arrested and, if he survives the battles of the gangs, die at age fifty-four of heart disease, if not alcohol-related

causes or drug poisoning. The role of the state should be limited
to locking him up whenever he gets caught for one crime or
another. My response: is the freedom that allows the heads of
corporations to have multi-million-pound salaries the selfsame
freedom that Jimmy enjoys to lead a life of intermittent depression, violence, drugs and alcohol? Perhaps it is a comfort to
Jimmy to know that his miserable situation is what libertarians
call freedom.

But what if, a libertarian might ask, Jimmy chose to live this
way? My response is: 'chose' to be unemployable, fall out with his
friends, be tossed out by his girlfriends, and to be angry, depressed
or drunk most of the time?

Karl Marx said: 'Men make their own history, but they do not
make it as they please; they do not make it under self-selected
circumstances, but under circumstances existing already, given
and transmitted from the past.'[9] I do not think you have to be a
Marxist to recognise that Jimmy is a product of circumstances. To
describe him as having the freedom to change his life is to ignore
the imprint on him of his appalling conditions from early in life.
Please remember I am speaking of averages. There will be some
individuals who emerge from the circumstances that bred a Jimmy
who do well, by their own lights as well as society's.

As I shall show in the chapter on early childhood, the evidence
is clear that state-provided services such as family–nurse partner-
ships could have helped with Jimmy's early child-development. In
turn, fewer social, emotional, behavioural and cognitive problems
would have meant a better chance to flourish in school. In its
turn, better school performance means better chances of decent
employment and reasonable income. Then, I would argue, Jimmy
would have far greater freedom to make his life choices. If at
that point he chooses the Glasgow equivalent of sitting under the
yum-yum tree, rather than pursuing a more conventional route,
that is his choice.

John Carnochan, the policeman in Glasgow, said: 'When I began my career as a police officer back in 1974, I don't think anyone would have imagined one day a police officer would be standing on stage talking to a conference full of midwives about the importance of cuddling your child when it comes to preventing violence.'[10] Carnochan said that, given the choice, he would rather have more health visitors than more officers on the beat, in order to prevent violence.

What of Gita? How can she be free when she lives in dire poverty in the slums of Ahmedabad? Freedom to wallow in poverty, to see your children on the edge of starvation, and to lack both education and prospects, is not a freedom many would prize.

But freedom does give us a good way to think about Gita's life. It may not be the freedom of the libertarian, but the freedom to be and to do what she values. Such freedom does not come by eliminating social action, as the libertarian might argue. It requires social action. Let's explore this alternative concept of freedom.

A key feature of the lives of Gita, Jimmy and Rachel is that they are disempowered; they lack basic freedoms. Things have been happening to them all their lives over which they have little control. One thing that marks out relative social advantage is the opportunity to shape your life more than the Gitas, Jimmys and Rachels can do. I think of disempowerment as having three dimensions: material – if you cannot afford to feed your children you cannot be empowered; psychosocial – having control over your life; political – having a voice.

My model is of health equity being built on creating the social and environmental conditions that make empowerment a possibility. Gita's life can be transformed if she has access to the basic necessities.

The second, psychosocial, dimension of empowerment is having control over your life, and taking your place in society without

shame. Having little control over your life is central to the mechanism by which the social environment influences health. Rachel,
who spent a career in the lower reaches of the Civil Service, has
material conditions for good health, such as Gita and her fellow
slum dwellers could scarcely imagine. What she lacks is control
over her life, at work or at home. The empirical basis for my
concern with lack of control came from our Whitehall II study
of British civil servants.[11] Men and women whose work environment was characterised by little control over the circumstances
of work – what they did, when they did it, and with whom –
had increased risk of heart disease, mental illness and sickness
absence.[12] We also asked a simple question about degree of control
at home. Particularly among women, more than men, people who
reported little control at home had increased risk of heart disease
and depression.[13]

'Basic freedoms' is a concept of the inspiring economist and
philosopher Amartya Sen. He emphasises freedom to lead a life
one has reason to value.[14] Freedom to be and to do has a central
place. Sen, like most contemporary philosophers, is a great admirer
of John Rawls. His divergence from Rawls, highly significant, arises
because Sen is not searching for an ideal institutional arrangement
that would constitute the good society. Rather, he wants to evaluate social arrangements by their effects on actual lives – whether
people have the freedom to lead the lives they choose.[15] This reso-
nates with my health-centred approach. I said that if philosophers
could not settle their theoretical differences on what constituted
social justice, I most certainly could not. I want to use the impact
of our set of social arrangements on health equity as my criterion of social justice. Empowerment, freedom to choose a life you
have reason to value, would transform the lives of Gita, Jimmy
and Rachel and improve their health. How we achieve empowerment – meaningful freedoms – is set out in the chapters that
follow.

Sen's approach to human rights is that they embody important freedoms. A human rights framework has much to recommend it in seeking to promote action on social determinants of health. The British philosopher Onora O'Neill reminds us that simply claiming rights is not enough. For rights, there are corresponding duties.[16] In other words, if I claim that people have rights to good health, there is the implication that they have rights to the social determinants of health – pre-school education, good education, housing, a decent paid job, social protection. Whose responsibility is it to meet those rights? It is a good question. We cannot say simply that parents have the duty to provide good schools for their children. My purpose in bringing the evidence together is to show what we need to do. In a democracy, it is up to all of us to determine what we want to do about this evidence, and how to go about it.

Equality of opportunity?

I began this chapter by saying that the suitor for Turandot's hand who was about to lose his head because he wasn't good at riddles, little John who wanted chocolate ice cream and had to make do with vanilla, and I as a doctor were all concerned about fair outcomes as well as fair process. And Gita, Jimmy and Rachel are each on the wrong end of health inequalities that could have been prevented – unfair outcomes.

What I have said so far may sound perfectly reasonable: it is not just I, as a doctor, who believe this, but most people who care about their health. It is less reasonable than it sounds. While politicians of left and right, and the people who support them, can agree on equality of opportunity, many will argue against equality of outcome. If equality of outcome demands equality of income, of education, of living conditions, this will be several steps too far for many.

John Rawls recognised that equal opportunity was a chimera because people's basic starting conditions varied so greatly. Opportunity is heavily influenced by inequalities in power, education and resources – all socially determined – quite apart from inequalities based on the natural lottery that deals some a luckier genetic hand than others. In the Rawls schema, to achieve equality of opportunity a just society guarantees every citizen access to basic or primary social goods, including basic liberties, opportunity, powers and prerogatives of office, income and wealth, and the social bases of self-respect. For Rawls fairness rests on a fair procedure by which these primary social goods are distributed. It is the process that decides justice, not the ultimate allocation.

Rawls acknowledges that his principles for distributing primary social goods will not eliminate inequality. He is, however, concerned with the fate of those worst off. Therefore, his 'difference principle' says that, while guaranteeing equal liberties to all, inequalities in the distribution of the remaining primary social goods are allowable only when the inequalities work to make those who are worst off as well off as possible compared with alternative arrangements.

One strand of Amartya Sen's criticism of Rawls is that it is too much about process, not enough about outcome. Suppose in Ahmedabad there was a new programme of education available to all children in the slums. A child who had been malnourished from birth and was sickly would perhaps benefit less from the educational opportunity than a child who was thriving. The first child's ill-health would limit her opportunity to convert education chances into better education. For Sen, the freedom to be and to do is not guaranteed by getting the distribution of social goods right. A fair distribution of social goods that does not take account of differences in health, skills, needs and vulnerabilities will therefore not be enough.

Note that Sen is arguing that ill-health limits the conversion of opportunities into meaningful outcomes, such as more educational achievement. I agree, but am also arguing that more educational achievement, better occupational opportunities and better conditions in general will transform the lives of Gita, Jimmy and Rachel and lead to better health.

There is a particular dilemma with which Rawlsians, and the rest of us, have to deal. Going back at least to Adam Smith, economists have argued that allowing some people to have a larger slice of the economic cake may lead to the whole cake enlarging. In other words, set the wealth producers free and, although they will benefit the most, people at the bottom will be somewhat better off – trickle-down economics. I hear the distant rumble of self-interest promoting this view. What does Rawls say, given that his difference principle states that greater inequalities are fairer provided that the worst off are better off than they could be under any alternative arrangement? Does that mean that greater health inequalities might be fairer provided those at the bottom have improved more than they could have under alternative arrangements?

This is, after all, close to what has happened in many countries over recent decades. Health has improved for everybody but it has improved more for those in more privileged social and economic positions. Health improving for everybody has to be a most welcome social achievement, but so would flattening the health gradient by levelling up – bringing everyone's health up to the standard of the best.

What this suggests to me is that Rawls's focus on fair distribution of opportunity, even given his difference principle, does not provide the framework for approaching a just distribution of health. The Sen idea of freedom to lead a life one has reason to value comes much closer.

Michael Sandel's third approach to social justice, after maximising welfare and promoting freedom, is:

REWARDING VIRTUE

If you want to know what God thinks of money, just look at the people he gave it to.

Dorothy Parker

'The important thing in life is not the triumph but the struggle, the essential thing is not to have conquered but to have fought well,' said Baron Pierre de Coubertin, founder of the modern Olympics in 1896. It is often quoted as: it's not the winning but the taking part that counts.

That is not how it looks. Contests reward winners. Taking part? Yes, very worthy. But winning? Winners deserve their rewards, we think. In Britain we remember the sailor who won gold at four successive Olympics, and the rower who won gold at five successive Olympics. To keep up that level of performance over twelve to sixteen years . . . we feel they deserve all the fame, money and admiration that *is* heaped on them. No doubt each country has a similar story: praise for the wonderful winners, rather than respect for the plucky losers for turning up.

As with sportsmen, so with bankers and others: is it justified that the winner takes all? Ask the highly paid banker or hedge-fund manager why they get paid as much as they do, and the answer comes back in some version of: 'Because we're worth it.' How do we know you're worth it? 'Because that's what we get paid.' Hardly faultless logic. It is 'willingness-to-pay' methodology. How much is something worth? Whatever someone is willing to pay for it.

At the other end of the income scale, the same circular reasoning applies. Low pay is a sign of being less worthy; if people were worth more they would be paid more. When, in the English city of Nottingham in 2013, one of the coffee chains advertised eight jobs as baristas it received 1,701 applications, despite offering less per hour than the 'living wage'. By the logic of price equating to worth, people who applied presumably realised that they did not deserve to be paid enough to live a healthy life, else they would not have applied. Or might it have had something to do with the Great Recession, high unemployment in Nottingham and lack of alternatives?

It is not just the problem with what passes for logic in this argument that bothers me, it is that the level of inequalities in income and wealth has been rising in many countries. The US and UK stand out. Such inequalities may have profound effects on health in at least three ways.

First, if some people have 'too much', others may have too little. If 'rewards' to hedge-fund managers, bankers and the top 1 per cent mean that people living in the shadows of Wall Street or the City of London have too little for a healthy life, the system has gone awry. In the US it has been estimated that almost all the income growth between 2010 and 2012, 95 per cent of it, went to the top 1 per cent.[17] At the same time, 24 per cent of the population were in poverty – taking an OECD (Organisation for Economic Co-operation and Development) definition of poverty as less than 60 per cent median income, *after* taxes and transfers.[18] By contrast, in Denmark and Norway, with much lower levels of income inequality, 13 per cent of the population are in poverty, using the same definition. Despite living in a rich country some people simply do not have enough to lead a healthy life – we call that the Minimum Income for Healthy Living.

Second, if too much of the money is being sequestered at the top, local and central governments may have too little to spend on pre-school education, schools, improving services and amenities for neighbourhoods – reproducing, two generations later, what in 1958 J. K. Galbraith called 'private affluence and public squalor'.[19]

Third, too much inequality of income and wealth damages social cohesion; increasingly the rich are separated from everyone else: separate neighbourhoods, schools, recreation, fitness centres, holidays. Lack of social cohesion is likely to damage health and increase crime.[20] We used to hear that what was good for General Motors was good for America. Perhaps it was. It is a good deal harder to make the case that what is good for Private Equity Asset Strippers International, or Get Rich Quick Hedge Fund, or United Short Sellers, and the billionaires who lead them, is good for America.[21]

We will look in more detail at how communities and whole societies impact on health equity.

For these three reasons we should be concerned about distribution of income. Were you a market fundamentalist you would now be horrified, or ignore me because I'm not an economist, so what could I know. The market is a sacred thing: it allocates income according to worth. Markets are infallible, and here am I saying that if avoidable health inequalities are the result, it represents market failure.

I have been asked often: we hear your message on how inequities in power, money and resources are bad for health equity; why are governments apparently not listening? Or, if they are, why are there are such inequities in power, money and resources that health is being damaged?

Are there good reasons for the inequalities in income that we have?

There may be a sharp conflict between a distribution of income that can be justified in some other way and the distribution that is optimal for health equity. Allocating rewards based on merit or virtue goes back to Aristotle, and may be blind to the likely effect on people's lives and hence on their health. But how are we to decide virtue?

The philosopher Stuart Hampshire considers that a just distribution of society's resources might reward individual virtue and excellence and conform to the kind of society we want, but he then writes: 'Conceptions of the good, ideals of social life, visions of individual virtue and excellence, are infinitely various and divisive, rooted in the imagination and in the memories of individuals and in the preserved histories of cities and states.'[22] If conceptions of the good life and what people deserve are 'infinitely various and divisive' there will not be one answer to the question of the just distribution. Hampshire then goes on to distinguish two kinds of evils of injustice. First, the evil of injustice in the distribution of goods needs to be revealed and certified by argument as evil before it can be felt as evil. Agreeing what makes up the right way to allocate goods needs a fair process of negotiation and debate. The outcome will vary with time and culture.

Hampshire continues: 'On the other hand, the evils of great poverty, and of sickness and physical suffering, and of the misery of bereavement are immediately felt as evils by any normally responsive person.' I find that extremely helpful. There is no answer to the question of the just distribution of goods. There will and should be negotiation, probably helped by rational argument. But the 'evil' of avoidable health inequality should garner much more immediate attention and concern. To the extent that the uneven distribution of goods, including income, causes inequalities in health, it is a legitimate object of concern. Where the two questions – what is a just distribution and what kind of distribution might damage health – come together is in the question of relative inequalities and perceptions of unfairness.

If we take money as the index of how much we value someone's contribution, we think top-level basketballers and footballers are quite the most wonderful thing on the planet, and jobbing B-grade movie actors more valuable than professors of mathematics. Nurses? Worth about one two-hundredth of a banker. Unemployed single mothers? Beneath contempt.

Contempt brings out the worst in people. In the US, Governor Mitt Romney distinguished the 47 per cent somehow dependent on the state as those who would never vote for him. It was almost as if being dependent in some way on the state marked you out as a lesser person. In Britain we have had politicians dividing the population into strivers and scroungers. The scroungers are not closely defined but seem to include people on benefits of various kinds. We have the unedifying spectacle of politicians presiding over high unemployment rates and then asserting that unemployment is a lifestyle choice. One might have thought that George Bernard Shaw's sharp wit, quoted at the head of this chapter, might have skewered the language of 'undeserving poor' a century ago. My objection to this rhetoric is not only moral, it is factual. For example, in Britain, the majority of people living in poverty are in households where at least one person is working.[23] In fact of all adults in low-income working households, three-quarters were in work. For most poor people, the problem is not being undeserving, it is low pay.

The idea that the market accurately represents worth, and thus justifies the high incomes of the top 1 per cent, is a self-serving illusion. In Jacob Hacker and Paul Pierson's *Winner-Take-All Politics*, they put the convincing case that the level of income inequality that we have has more to do with grubby politics than the logic of the market and rewarding virtue.[24]

What, then, would a fair distribution of income look like? See what the population think is fair. The British Social Attitudes Survey in 2009 asked a representative sample of the population what they thought various people earned, and what they thought they should earn.[25] Averaging the answers, respondents thought that chairs of large corporations earned fifteen times as much as unskilled factory workers. Respondents thought that the big boss *should* earn £100,000 and the factory worker £16,000 – a ratio of six times.

I draw three interesting conclusions from this simple survey. First, the population is *not* egalitarian when it comes to income. It is a reasonable guess that the general public hold the view that skills, training and responsibility should be rewarded. Perhaps scarcity, too. A higher salary might be necessary to attract people who are in demand elsewhere.

Second, the public take the view that income inequalities are too big. In fact, the British Social Attitudes Survey shows that since 1983, consistently, more than 70 per cent of the population think the income gap is too large.

Third, they have no idea how big it is. The true ratio of top to bottom salaries is more like 340 than 15. I am not even for a milli-second entertaining the proposition that we set salaries by poll-ing the population on what they think they should be. It is clear, though, that the population take the view that we have a grossly unfair distribution of income. We could summarise by saying that in our democracy the majority think that 'virtue' should attract rewards, but within limits.

Will Hutton has explored this territory in *Them and Us*.[26] He reviews the interesting evidence that we are programmed, by evolution, to be sensitive to unfairness. We welcome people being rewarded for achievement, but not unfairly. Both the biological/ psychological evidence, and people's attitudes in a country like Britain, suggest that not only are we comfortable with inequalities in income, we think it is the right thing to do, provided it is done fairly. It would be hard to argue, though, that if some people are paid less than the minimum they require for a healthy life, then the distribution of income is fair.

Undeserving because it's their own fault

Are the poor architects of their own misfortune?

George Bernard Shaw has Arthur Doolittle, the dustman, claim that he has chosen his undeserving poverty, but only after a cata-logue of complaints about how demeaning he finds it – 'think what that means to a man'. Shaw's intent is clear: people do not choose their poverty. But, even if they do not choose poverty, might the decisions they make account for their poverty and the ill-health associated with it?

Given the history of Gita in Ahmedabad it would be diffi-cult to say that she is somehow poor of her own volition. She, and perhaps a billion men and women like her, are poor because of lack of both material conditions and the opportunity to do better.

Jimmy in Glasgow is different. He certainly has poverty of material conditions, compared with those prevailing in Glasgow, but as we have said, they are wonderful compared with Gita's. His poverty has more to do with his choices. Actually, that should probably be 'choices', given the disastrous family history that left him psychologically scarred. The circumstances of his background make social mobility – going up the social ladder – unlikely.

Rachel, the low-grade civil servant, is not poor, but she is relatively low in the social hierarchy, which constrains her choices. Rachel, compared with higher-status women, is more likely to be obese, and to smoke, less likely to pursue physical activities, has fewer social connections,[27] and when her daughter was young and Rachel was a single mother, she was less likely to have read to her, or to have cuddled and played with her,[28] as she juggled the demands of work, motherhood, childcare and making ends meet. These 'choices' were bad for her, Rachel's, own health and played a role in limiting her daughter's opportunities.

Two US-based researchers, Sendhil Mullainathan, an economist at Harvard, and Eldar Shafir, a psychologist at Princeton, looking at the Rachels, the Jimmys and even the Gitas of the world, asked, why do the poor appear to make decisions that are not in their own interest?[29] Summarising the evidence, they say that the poor use less preventive health care, fail to adhere to drug regimens even when the costs are covered, are less attentive parents and worse managers of their finances. In low-income countries, they are less likely to weed their plots of land even though that would increase productivity. I would add that it is not just the poor versus the rest, but the evidence shows there is a social gradient in adopting preventive behaviours or adhering to drug regimes.

So self-defeating do some of these decisions seem to be, that some speculate that it is the very fecklessness of the poor that leads to their own misfortune and ill-health. Mullainathan and Shafir's view is that this is precisely upside down. Rather than poor decision-making leading to poverty, they argue, it is poverty that leads to poor decision-making. Their book, *Scarcity*, brings together evidence that scarcity narrows a person's working memory, to use a computer analogy. Someone starving starts to focus on food, to the exclusion of other concerns; someone time-poor focuses on deadline pressures rather than on long-term planning; and, crucially, the poor focus on short-term survival rather than on more strategic decision-making.

In various experiments, they show that being relatively poor makes people less insightful, and diminishes forward planning and sense of control. The effect of poverty on cognitive function is equivalent to the effect of going without sleep for a night. Their experiments and studies show that this diminished cognitive function is not a permanent state – it gets worse as poverty worsens and improves as it lessens.

The implication of this effect of scarcity is that the poor need not only money – they do need money – but also the security of mind that allows a fuller range of mental functions to flourish. For example, if when Rachel was a single mother she could have had access to subsidised childcare, it would have reduced not only her financial burden but also her cognitive load as she juggled the tasks and the finances involved in being a single mother. In low-income countries, where employment and income are insecure and inconstant, short-term low-interest loans might be valuable in relieving intolerable mental burdens.

My entrée into political philosophy was to help understand the links between social justice and health. A simple adding-up principle, enshrined in utilitarianism, does not do it, because we need to take distributions into account.

An approach to social justice that maximises freedom is much closer to my concerns, provided that we recognise that we need to create the conditions for people to have control over their lives, to have meaningful freedoms. Such an approach to freedoms recognises human rights to health and to the social determinants of health. Understanding how to realise those rights is the task of the chapters that follow.

Rewarding virtue will be an important principle for deciding the distribution of resources. My concern is with the impact of these allocation decisions on people's lives, and hence on health inequities.

IDEOLOGY AND EVIDENCE

If everyone agreed on the meaning of social justice and there was only one conception of the good society, political philosophers would have to think of something else to do. They are kept busy because as Stuart Hampshire wrote, there is no agreement. Libertarians do not convert to Kantian philosophy, or vice versa, simply on the basis of reasoned argument. We are dealing with ideology, although the arguments are revealing.

One might have thought that, in science, where ideology has to come up against hard facts, the ideological debates would give way to debates about evidence. All too often, that is simply not the case. I described above my debate with utilitarian economists at the RAND meeting. Their views were anathema to me. I admired the intellectual coherence of putting a dollar value on people's lives and apportioning care only to the most worthy, but wanted no part of it. The culmination was what I called bribing people to die. And I would certainly speculate that not a one of them changed his mind – I think they were all men – as a result of my point of view. I am guessing now, but they may have thought that my concern for human suffering led to an intolerable degree of intellectual sloppiness. Heart getting in the way of head. What we have though is conflicting principles, ideologies, one of which is efficiency versus equity.

As I will also say later, there is great disagreement among economists when it comes to discussing macroeconomic policy. There are devotees of austerity and Keynesians, and they argue their positions with religious fervour. My own view, as a non-economist, is that data really should settle it. In practice, it does not. Alan Blinder, a self-declared liberal Keynesian economist at Princeton, quoted a Chicago economist, John Cochrane, as saying that Keynesian economics is 'not part of what anybody has taught graduate students since the 1960s. [Keynesian ideas] are fairy tales that have been proved false.' Blinder comments: 'The first statement is demonstrably false; the second is absurd.' Blinder then goes on to call this dismissal of Keynes's ideas ideological. That said, and despite the heavy interplay of ideology and evidence, economic evidence is important.[30]

When I come to discuss early child development I will touch on the long-standing debates on nature and nurture. Here, I think that thought and evidence can help penetrate the ideological positions, even if it does not change them completely. Environmental determinists will not issue a mea culpa and convert to genetic determinists; nor vice versa. But evidence matters.

Economists and public health people disagree, too. Recently, I proposed a screening test to detect an economist: if someone comes across the social gradient in health and assumes that health leads to socio-economic position, rather than social circumstances lead to health, then he is an economist.[31] Like all screening tests there are false positives and false negatives, but the typical economist starting position is that people's health determines what happens to them. The public health starting position is that what happens to people affects their health. When economists analyse birth cohort data they find evidence that health in childhood influences adult socio-economic position. When public health people analyse the same data they find evidence that childhood socio-economic circumstances influence adult health. Each concludes that their pathway is more important.

One economist was furious with me for pointing out this alleged bias. He said that any sensible person would conclude that the pathway can go both ways – from wealth to health *and* from health to wealth; I give too little credence to the possibility that ill-health causes low social position. I agree. I do give too little credence to it. Not because it cannot happen. For example, ill-health can lead to inability to work. Particularly where there are no safety nets, of the type described in Chapter 9, inability to work will, of course, lead to lack of income. But, in my view the evidence is overwhelming that social condition, acting through the life course, influences health and health equity. No, my concern is the tendency of many economists to emphasise this health-to-wealth pathway – I would call it reverse causation – to the exclusion of a focus on the social determinants of ill-health of the type that this book has addressed. That is not prejudice on my side, it is an empirical observation. More or less every time I have given a lecture and someone has asked if I have considered the possibility that everything I have said is wrong, because ill-health leads to low social position, that some-one has been an economist.

This is not just a polite, or even testy, academic debate. The policy implication of these two positions is quite different. If the main causal direction goes from health to wealth the appropriate intervention is to control illness in order to improve an indi-vidual's social and economic fortunes or, indeed, eradicate illness to improve the economy of a whole country. If, as I conclude, the main causes of health inequalities reside in the circumstances in which people are born, grow, live, work and age – the social determinants of health – then action to reduce health inequali-ties must confront those circumstances and the fundamental drivers of those circumstances: economics, social policies and governance.

When we published *Fair Society, Healthy Lives*, the Marmot Review of health inequalities in England, *Social Science and Medicine*, an academic journal, invited eight commentators to give their reac-tions to our report.[32]

Six of the commentaries are in little doubt that we have enough evidence to take action, although all, like us, want a stronger evidence base. Some commentators thought we put too much emphasis on income, some said too little. Some thought we had made great strides politically, some that we were not political enough. Absolutely fine with me. Exactly what you expect when you ask for comments. The comments were a constructive contribution to the debate.

What of the other two commentators? They were economists. As expected, their starting position was that people's health determines what happens to them. The Marmot Review's starting position was that what happens to people has a cumulative effect throughout their life course, progressively affecting their health.

This issue of reverse causation has been examined extensively in the epidemiological literature. The debate has been around for a long time. I reviewed it, *in extenso*, in my book *Status Syndrome*,[33] where I concluded that there was strong and conclusive evidence for social causation – social conditions cause health. When the *Social Science and Medicine* debate surfaced I happened to be reading Dickens's *Hard Times*. Here is Dickens on housing: 'In the hardest working part of Coketown, . . . where Nature was as strongly bricked out as killing airs and gases were bricked in.' He also describes the terrible working conditions in Coketown.

Should we really assume that these dark satanic mills and airless places, rather than causing terrible illness and shortened lives, selectively employed and attracted as residents sick people and those whose backgrounds accounted for all their subsequent illness? That subsequent improvement in living and working conditions, thus abating Victorian squalor, and associated improvements in health, were correlation, not causation? That while medical care improved health, housing also got better, and an intellectually slack public health profession mistook the improvement in housing and working conditions for causes of improved health?

If proponents of this set of assumptions dropped their guard for a moment and accepted the evidence that air pollution, crowded living space, ghastly working conditions and poor nutrition were causes of ill-health in Victorian times why, a priori, do they start from the position that living and working conditions are not a cause of ill-health in the twenty-first century?

Of course, this disagreement between commentators is not just about evidence. It is also about ideology. Talking to a senior economist, Anton Muscatelli, Principal of Glasgow University, I said that you can explain why we in public health may emphasise the wealth-to-health pathway. We want to improve health and the evidence suggests that improving social conditions is an important way to get there. Why do economists take the reverse position, I asked, do they not want to improve society? Professor Muscatelli's response: economists are taught that health is a contribution to wealth, rather than the other way round, because it is easier to model in their equations. Not a very exalted ideology, then.

What I can say is that not all economists take the same view. Amartya Sen was a member of the Commission on Social Determinants of Health, and Sir Tony Atkinson was a Commissioner of the Marmot Review. Each signed up to the conclusions in the respective reports. Jim Smith, whose work showing how health affects income is quoted, also showed elegantly the powerful influence of education on health; such that income drops out of the model.

The fact that ideology, of various degrees of fervour, infuses debates about evidence does not dim my respect for the evidence. All of the conclusions and recommendations in this book are based on evidence. But I will assert that I do have an ideology: avoidable health inequalities are unjust. We need the best evidence that will help us take steps to make society more just, and reduce health inequity.

4

Equity from the Start

*So we beat on, boats against the current, borne back ceaselessly into the
past.*

F. Scott Fitzgerald, *The Great Gatsby*

In Aldous Huxley's dystopia *Brave New World* there were five castes.
The Alphas and Betas were allowed to develop normally. The
Gammas, Deltas and Epsilons were treated with chemicals to arrest
their development intellectually and physically. The result: a neatly
stratified society with intellectual function, and physical development, correlated with caste.

That was satire, wasn't it? No relation with real life. We would
never, surely, tolerate a state of affairs that stratified people, then
made it harder for the lower orders, but helped the higher orders,
to reach their full potential. Were we to find a chemical in the water,
or in food, that was damaging children's growth and their brains
worldwide, and thus their intellectual development and control of
emotions, we would clamour for immediate action. Remove the
chemical and allow all our children to flourish, not only the Alphas
and Betas.

Yet, unwittingly perhaps, we do tolerate such a state of affairs.
The pollutant is poverty or, more generally, lower rank in the social
hierarchy, and it limits children's intellectual and social development.

We should want that removed as if it were any other toxin so that children can develop their potential, to flourish across the whole social gradient, not only at the top.

What happens to children in the early years has a profound effect on their life chances and hence their health as adults. At the heart of it is empowerment, developing the capacities to enjoy basic freedoms that give life meaning; and early child experiences have a determining influence on that development. Early child development is influenced in part by quality of parenting or caring from others; which in turn are influenced by the circumstances in which parenting takes place.

Perhaps the thought crossed your mind that removing the toxin of poverty or social disadvantage would still leave some children with greater intellectual and social flourishing than others. Of course. Which is why I use the words 'develop their potential' and 'flourish'. If we remove the damaging effects of social disadvantage, the fact will remain that individuals vary in dexterity, chess-playing, mathematics, creativity, athletic potential, sociability. There are many ways to flourish. Long live diversity. Recent books address this question.[1] Nor would I call this diversity unfair, other than in the ironic sense that the gods are unfair. The unfairness comes if children, by dint of circumstances acting over years, are deprived of the opportunity to flourish.

There is a great deal to celebrate in the revolution in child survival. All over the world, child mortality has been coming down, albeit there are still huge inequalities, as shown in Chapter 1. In its way there is an even bigger tragedy that is the subject of this chapter: for each child that dies unnecessarily, there are twenty-five or more who survive but do not develop to their potential.[2]

As I shall show in this chapter, social conditions in which parents bear and raise their children have a big influence on the quality of their development. And children who survive and develop to their potential will become healthier adults with reductions in inequalities in health. The case for social action is compelling.

Not in the minds of some. It was put to me by one minister of health in Europe that the whole notion of social determinants of health is wrong-headed. It is no business of governments, health practitioners or the World Health Organization to meddle with society. Health is a matter of personal responsibility.

My response was: you might blame adults for their absent-mindedness in being poor, let alone what you see as their disgraceful behaviour in risking their health by eating cheap food and being too ground down and poor to join a gym or Pilates class. Fecklessness, it has been called, or being one of the undeserving poor – but don't blame the children! They do not choose their parents; they do not choose to be born in poverty.

Holding adults responsible for their own misfortune is one thing. Condemning children because of their parents is to take a rather primitive biblical approach: the parents have eaten sour grapes and the children's teeth are set on edge.[3] Ensuring the health and well-being of children, regardless of how blameworthy you judge their parents to be, might even cut across prior political beliefs. Once, a bit overwrought, I declared to colleagues at the American Medical Association: Republicans, Democrats, I couldn't care less. This is our children we are talking about. Would there be a politician in America who said they didn't care about the children? 'You'd be surprised,' was the response.

This chapter will lay out the evidence that position on the social gradient affects parenting, which in turn affects cognitive, social and emotional, as well as physical development of children, which in turn is related to inequities in mental and physical health in adulthood. We have then a model of causation. There are at least two pieces missing from this model. First, what goes into the mix I have summed up as 'position on the social gradient affects parenting'; second, how do these social and psychosocial influences affect bodily processes, how do social influences get under the skin?[4]

But first, let's look at why it matters. Experiences in childhood are vital for adult health, and for crime. We can then go on to examine the causes of the social gradient in early child development, and see how equity from the start is strongly linked to health equity at later ages.

CHILDHOOD EXPERIENCE AFFECTS
ADULT HEALTH . . . AND CRIME

Two great Canadians, Fraser Mustard and Clyde Hertzman, did as much as anyone to emphasise the relevance to adult health and health inequities of the circumstances in which children are born, grow and develop. Fraser Mustard, a charismatic figure, was a cardiovascular scientist whose research led to the recognition of aspirin in preventing cardiovascular disease, an innovative medical educator at McMasters University, and founder President of the Canadian Institute for Advanced Research (then CIAR, now CIFAR). His mission at CIAR was to bring the best people together, regardless of discipline, to work on a particular topic. He got the medical scientists to engage with economists, educators, psychologists and sociologists in pursuing population health.

Fraser Mustard turned up in my room at UCL in about 1986 because he wanted to hear about the Whitehall studies of British civil servants. The Whitehall II study had just been launched as a study of men and women in the Civil Service aged 35–55 at entry to the study. As Fraser told it, the Whitehall social gradient in mortality from cardiovascular disease, and a range of other diseases, convinced him of the importance of social determinants of health. I was simply trying to do good science, but Fraser wanted to focus on the profound policy implications of the gradient.

'There are no policy implications,' I told him. 'Mrs Thatcher has declared that there is no such thing as society. And the Department of Health has ruled that health inequalities are not a matter for discussion. All of which means that I am doing pure science with no policy implications.' Fraser assured me that there were policy implications in Canada.

He then asked if I had considered early life influences on the social gradient in health in adults. I tried to explain that I was studying civil servants. They sprang into adulthood, fully formed, clutching umbrellas. They had no childhood. Fraser was totally persuaded by the evidence that early life experiences shape children's development, and indeed their brains, and change the development of health and ill-health in adult life. Civil servants and others, he said, come to their adult lives with the experiences of early childhood impressed upon them. Now, I am persuaded too. There is abundant evidence. Hence this chapter.

Clyde Hertzman was – he died tragically early, aged fifty-nine – a young doctor spotted by Fraser at McMasters as a future star. He picked up on the importance of early life, both synthesising the science and taking out into the community measures of early child development and what can be done to improve them.[5] I invited Clyde to convene the knowledge network on early child development for the WHO Commission on Social Determinants of Health. Clyde's inspiration runs right through the relevant chapter of the final report of the commission, *Closing the Gap in a Generation*, and this chapter.

Clyde, and his collaborator Chris Power, identified ways that childhood experience can influence adult health. We can group these into two. First is accumulation of advantage and disadvantage through the life course. Poor early child development leads to worse performance in school, which means a lower-status job, less money, worse living conditions in adult life – all of which can damage health. Not only can where you start off influence where you end up, but advantage and disadvantage accumulate. Second are the effects of events in early life on health in later life: events at one time of life exert bad effects on health later on – latency effect.[6]

Accumulation of disadvantage through the life course leads both to ill-health and to crime

The City of Baltimore in the US state of Maryland is marked by stark inequalities. A young man, let's call him LeShawn, has grown up in the Upton/Druid Heights neighbourhood in Baltimore's inner city. Bobby has grown up in Greater Roland Park/Poplar. Life expectancy in Upton/Druid is sixty-three; in Roland Park, eighty-three. This is of the same order as the gap we now see in Glasgow.

LeShawn's was a single-parent family, like half the others in Upton/Druid Heights. Their household income in 2010 was $17,000, the median for the neighbourhood. At school, in common with four out of ten of his classmates, he scored under the 'proficient' mark in reading in the third grade; and in high school he was one of the more than half of his neighbourhood who had missed at least twenty days of school a year. LeShawn completed high school, but like 90 per cent of his neighbourhood he did not go on to college. It was during the school years that he gave his mother the most worry. It seemed as if everyone his age was getting arrested. In fact, each year, in Upton/Druid Heights, a third of youngsters aged ten to seventeen were arrested for some 'juvenile disorder'. A third every year means that there is little chance that LeShawn would get to the age of seventeen without a criminal record, with everything that means for the future. In Upton/Druid, in the period 2005 to 2009, there were 100 non-fatal shootings for every 10,000 residents, and nearly forty homicides.

You can write the script for the contrast with Bobby in Roland Park. Bobby, and all but 7 per cent of his neighbours, grew up in two-parent families, median income $90,000. Bobby was one of the 97 per cent of his neighbourhood to achieve 'proficient or advanced' in the third grade reading. He was not among the 8 per cent who missed at least twenty days a year of high school, and he was one of the three-quarters who completed college. When it comes to juvenile arrests, there are no guarantees of immunity, but the figure for Roland Park is one in fifty each year, compared to the one in three in Upton/Druid. Another stark contrast with Upton/Druid: there were no non-fatal shootings in 2005–2009, and four homicides per 10,000 – one-tenth of the Upton/Druid rate.

Writing from England, I cannot help but comment that had guns not been freely available there would have been far fewer non-fatal shootings and homicides in either area. Deprivation leads to crime, but without ready access to guns, at least your violent behaviour toward your neighbours does not end up with someone getting shot. As a reminder, the differences in lifetime experiences between neighbourhoods are not just in crime. LeShawn and others like him from the deprived part of town face twenty years' shorter life expectancy than Bobby and his neighbours from classy Roland Park.

I have ignored the fact that the population of Upton/Druid is almost exclusively black and that of Roland Park nearly uniformly white. The determinants of health, and crime, are not blackness or whiteness, but accumulation of disadvantage through the life course. The perspective of the 'causes of the causes' recognises that advantage and disadvantage are, in the US, closely linked with race, largely because of widespread and institutional discrimination.

The link between crime and ill-health was brought home by the riots that scarred London in the summer of 2011. The year before, I had been citing Tottenham as containing a ward, Tottenham Green, that had the worst male life expectancy in London, eighteen years shorter than Queens Gate Ward in Kensington and Chelsea. No surprise that the riots should have started in Tottenham, and not in Kensington and Chelsea.

As just shown in Baltimore, there is a close correlation between the geographical distribution of ill-health and of crime. Not that one causes the other, but that they have common causes. A British newspaper pointed out that in the Tottenham riot one handler of stolen goods had a job, and another parked his VW round the corner. Hence, the paper concluded, there was no link between poverty and urban unrest. A politician said that this was criminality pure and simple. To misquote Oscar Wilde, the riots were not very pure and their causes are certainly not simple. But relative poverty and disadvantage play a role. The *Guardian* newspaper reported that of 1,000 rioters going through the magistrates' courts only 8.6 per cent were in employment or training, i.e. 91.4 per cent were not. Nationally, NEET (Not in Employment, Education or Training) is about 10 per cent. No link between social disadvantage and being hauled in for crime in the rioting? The link is astonishingly strong: 91 per cent of rioters were NEET versus 10 per cent of non-rioters. With a few exceptions, people in jobs or education did not take part in, or strictly were not caught for, committing crimes during the riots.

That which does not kill us makes us . . .
more vulnerable. Events in childhood influence
adult health – latency effect

There is a second way in which early childhood may matter for adult health. The thrust of physician David Barker's work was to show that growth *in utero* and in the first year of life was important to the risk of heart disease and diabetes when these infants became adults.[7] Poor nutrition in this early period can change subsequent risk of disease. The risk will be affected by later events, but an episode or period of malnutrition can have a lasting effect.

What David Barker showed for the effects in adult life of poor nutrition in infants may also apply to social and psychological – psychosocial – experiences. We should have long known this, but a study that put it on the map in 1998 was done in California and is known as the ACE, Adverse Childhood Experiences, study.[8] Just over 8,000 people living in San Diego were asked if, during their first eighteen years of life, they had experienced any of three categories of childhood abuse: psychological – being frequently put down or sworn at, or in fear of physical harm; physical; and sexual – four questions about being forced into various acts. They were also asked about four categories of household dysfunction: someone they lived with a problem drinker or user of street drugs; mental illness or attempted suicide of a household member; mother treated violently; criminal behaviour in the household.

The first striking finding is that if people reported one of these adverse experiences they were likely to report at least one other; and more than half reported at least two others. Adverse experiences tend to cluster. The question is what happens when these individuals reach adulthood.

People love to quote Nietzsche: that which does not kill us makes us stronger. Well, it doesn't actually. It makes us more likely to get sick. If we think of those who report no adverse experiences as the reference group, compared with them, the more different types of adverse experience a person had, the greater the risk of depression and attempted suicide. People who had four or more different types of adverse childhood experience had nearly five times the risk of having spent two or more weeks in depressed mood the previous year, and twelve times the risk of having attempted suicide.

In general, the more types of adverse childhood experience, the more likely people were to describe themselves as alcoholic, to have injected drugs, to have had fifty or more partners in sexual intercourse.

When I first read this study I objected that perhaps people with mental illness or behavioural problems as adults were more likely to 'recall' adverse childhood experiences – memory of such things is notoriously unreliable. In other words, the relation with mental illness might not be causal but be biased by people with mental illness searching their background for reasons and coming up with blameable events in their childhood. But – and this is a big objection to my objection – the more adverse experiences, the higher the risk of diabetes, of chronic obstructive pulmonary disease (bronchitis or emphysema), stroke and heart disease. It is a good deal less likely that people with physical illness were spuriously blaming their childhood for their diabetes or heart disease.

A notable feature of the ACE study is that the study participants were all enrolees in a prepaid Health Maintenance Organisation (a type of health insurance) in San Diego. They were not a down-and-out population. As well as having health insurance, 94 per cent had graduated from high school, and 43 per cent were college graduates.

The ACE study was not a one-off. A review of 124 studies confirmed that child physical abuse, emotional abuse and neglect (they did not study sexual abuse) are linked to adult mental disorders, suicide attempts, drug use, sexually transmitted infections and risky sexual behaviour.[9] The authors of the review concluded that this is more than simple correlation but represents causation.

The graded nature of the relation between abuse and adult mental, and perhaps physical, ill-health – the more types of abuse the worse the adult health – suggests that we should not be looking only at exceptional episodes of abuse but, more generally, at quality of early child development. Indeed, further evidence supports this. Britain has been blessed by a series of long-term studies of people born at a particular moment and followed through their lives. One of these, the 1958 British birth cohort study, followed a national sample of people born in the first week of March 1958. It showed that children who were not read to daily by their parents, who did not adjust easily when first attending school, and whose height increased slowly, an indicator of poor nutrition, were far more likely to have poor health at age thirty-three than people who were more 'advantaged'. This impact on adult ill-health was independent of all other influences from subsequent periods of their lives that could be studied.

It all sounds like common sense. Childhood experiences matter. But the fact that it sounds reasonable does not make it true – as I argued with Nietzsche's evocative declaration. Geneticists would argue that nurture matters little, it is nature that determines outcomes – I will come back to this idea a little later in the chapter. Of course, genes matter. But the evidence shows that what happens in early childhood has a powerful effect on health and disease in adult life through the causal pathways discussed. The long-term effects of early exposure and the accumulation of advantage and disadvantage through life, whereby childhood experiences determine education, employment, income and, more generally, empowerment in adult life, are responsible for determining inequalities in health.

INEQUALITIES IN EARLY CHILD DEVELOPMENT – THE SOCIAL GRADIENT STARTS EARLY

Here is a novelist's perspective on socio-economic differences in attitudes to rearing young children, contrasting a low-income area of North West London (Caldwell) with its 'other': 'Caldwell people felt everything would be fine as long as you didn't actually throw the child down the stairs. Non-Caldwell people felt nothing would be fine unless everything was done perfectly and even then there was no guarantee.'[10] I would add, and there is a gradient between these two extremes. The evidence shows that what happens to children does make a profound difference, and it differs by social circumstances.

With that in mind, let's consider four children: Alex, Beth, Claire and Debbie, or A, B, C and D for short. When measured at twenty-two months, Alex and Beth, A and B, are in the top 10 per cent on a measure of cognitive performance, something akin to intelligence; Claire and Debbie, C and D, are in the bottom 10 per cent. If we follow these four children until they are ten years old, what is likely to happen to their cognitive scores?

Figure 4.1 gives the answer, and it is one that should give us pause. Looking first at A and B, the 'clever' ones, Alex is raised in a family of higher socio-economic position and her scores remain high over the period up to ten years of age. Beth's family is of lower socio-economic position, and her relative ranking on cognitive scores plummets over time. Now look at Claire and Debbie, the 'not-so-clever' ones at twenty-two months. Claire is raised in a family of higher socio-economic position, and her scores shoot upwards as she approaches age ten. Debbie is raised in a family of lower socio-economic position and her scores remain low. These four children are emblematic of what occurs on average in Britain and in other wealthy countries.

(The convergence of the curves between time one and time two – the first and second measurements – results from regression to the mean and need not detain us here.)

FIGURE 4.1: JUST HANG IN AND NORMAL SERVICE RESUMES

Distribution of cognitive scores. Relative positions.

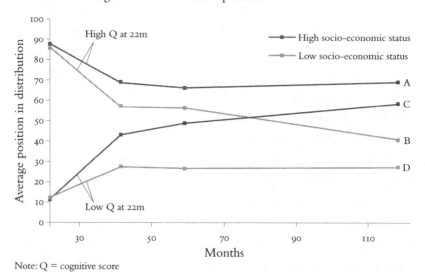

Note: Q = cognitive score
Source: 1970 British Cohort Study.

Returning to our four children, the effects are dramatic. Assume for a moment that all the differences in cognitive function at twenty-two months are biologically determined – genetic endowment, experiences *in utero*, nutrition – and that all the changes that occur after twenty-two months are to do with social environment, broadly conceived. The social trumps the biological! Beth may be clever at twenty-two months, but her family is low-status; her cleverness will diminish as she approaches ten years of age. Claire may not be the brightest at twenty-two months; she just needs to hang in and her scores will go up, as she is blessed with a family of high socio-economic position. Debbie loses both ways – low score at twenty-two months and having a family at the low end, socially.

I have simplified. Not all the differences at twenty-two months are biological in origin; not all the differences associated with social level of family will in fact be social – genetic effects may make a late appearance.[11]

What are LeShawn in Baltimore and Jimmy in Glasgow missing out on? Quite a lot, it would seem. The political right would say that they suffer from poor parenting and the left that it is poverty. They are both correct. What is not correct is to conclude that there is nothing we can do about the social gradient in early child development.

Figure 4.2 is my gift to both the political left and right. It shows the proportion of children in each local authority in England rated as having a 'good' level of development at age five. Local authorities are ranked on their degree of deprivation, or lack thereof, from 1, the most deprived, to 150, the most affluent. First, then, is the gift to the left. The graph shows that the greater the degree of deprivation the smaller the proportion of children who have a good level of development at age five. It is a gradient. One message from the graph is that if the more deprived areas had their socio-economic circumstances improved, there would be a higher percentage of children with a good level of development. Reduce poverty and you reduce inequalities in early child development. Poverty is important.

FIGURE 4.2: A GOOD START? BETTER FOR SOME

Children achieving a good level of development at age five, local authorities 2011: England

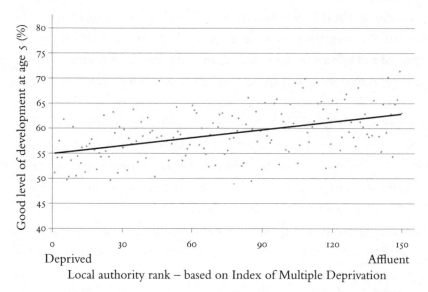

Local authority rank – based on Index of Multiple Deprivation

Source: UCL Institute of Health Equity, London Health Observatory. Marmot indicators for local authorities: indicator data 2012 and including data for 2011. London: London Health Observatory, 2012.

But poverty is not destiny. A second message derives from the variation around the line. At any given level of deprivation, some local authorities are doing better than others. If we can find out what is happening in the 'good' areas to weaken the link between deprivation and poor early child development, there is the potential for great advance.

There is actually a third message contained in Figure 4.2: the median is under 60 per cent. Translated, that means that fewer than 60 per cent of children nationally, in England, were rated as having a good level of development aged five. Our most recent figures, 2013, put the figure at 52 per cent of children having a good level of development.[12] Can it really be true that in an advanced country like England, more than 40 per cent of children do not have a good level of development?

Well, yes it can. Periodically, UNICEF (the UN children's organisation) publishes a report card, the results of which are shown in Figure 4.3.

When UNICEF examined four measures of child well-being, the UK ranked sixteenth out of twenty-one. I tease my US colleagues that I do like visiting the US – it's the only big country that makes me feel better about my own. The US ranks bottom of twenty-one

FIGURE 4.3: THE PROBLEM WITH RANKINGS IS THAT SOMEONE HAS TO BE BOTTOM

Country comparison on average rank in four dimensions of child well-being – material, health, education, behaviours and risks, in early 2000s and late 2000s

Rank	Early 2000s	Rank	Late 2000s	Change in rank
1	Sweden	1	Netherlands	+2
2	Finland	2	Norway	+2
3	Netherlands	3	Finland	-1
4=	Denmark	4	Sweden	-3
4=	Norway	5	Germany	+2
6	France	6	Denmark	-2
7	Germany	7	Belgium	+1
8	Belgium	8=	France	-2
9=	Czech Republic	8=	Ireland	+4
9=	Poland	8=	Switzerland	+3
11	Switzerland	11	Portugal	+5
12	Ireland	12	Poland	-3
13	Spain	13	Czech Republic	-4
14=	Canada	14=	Canada	no change
14=	Italy	14=	Italy	no change
16=	Greece	16	United Kingdom	+4
16=	Portugal	17	Austria	+1
18	Austria	18=	Greece	-2
19	Hungary	18=	Hungary	+1
20=	United Kingdom	18=	Spain	-5
20=	United States	21	United States	-1

Source: UNICEF. Innocenti Report Card 11. Child well-being in rich countries. A comparative review: UNICEF; 2013.

rich countries. The poor performance in child well-being in the US and the UK underlines the importance of improving it across the whole of society, for the whole social hierarchy (or gradient), not just for the poor.

There is another message from Figure 4.3, and that is that rankings can change relatively quickly. Between the early and late 2000s, Sweden slipped from 1 to 4. The UK went from equal 20th to 16th. The US languished at the bottom. Changes in ranking suggest that changes in policy and practice can have effects relatively quickly. We see this in local areas where concerted action can change rankings in early childhood development.

The challenge

The evidence shows us clearly the importance of the mind. It is not that the material conditions of life are unimportant, but those conditions shape the input children receive from parents and other carers.

We want our children to be bright, to be good at language, to learn how to get on with other children and adults and control their emotions, and of course to develop normally physically. Put more formally, we want children to achieve their potential on cognitive development, development of and use of language, social and emotional development, and physical development. The chances of children achieving healthy development in all these domains diminish progressively the lower their parents' income. Why is this? And what can we do about it?

Some parents do more

By the time children get to school, those from lower-status backgrounds have fallen behind in their language development. In a remarkable study in Kansas, researchers went into a number of family homes at set times over the first four years of a child's life and counted the amount of speech addressed to the child.

The results are staggering. The higher the socio-economic level of the family the more words were addressed to the children over the first forty-eight months of life. Children of professional parents had *30 million* more words addressed to them than children of families on welfare.[13] That's more than an extra 20,000 words a day. Even if the absolute numbers are exaggerated, it is not a surprise that children of professional parents possess more highly honed verbal skills than children of parents on welfare.

When the researchers studied the type of comments addressed to the children, they found that discouragements were more common in the families on welfare. It is not hard to paint the picture. In the US as in Britain, welfare is hardly sufficient to eke out a living. Frazzled parents, possibly a single parent, juggling multiple demands, perhaps depressed, ground down, and, in the language of the authors of *Scarcity*, with reduced band width, are more likely to scold their children and to want to keep them under control.

To test out the contribution of parenting to the social gradient in child development a group of us at UCL, led by Yvonne Kelly, analysed data from the Millennium Birth Cohort Study, a national study in England. We asked mothers of children aged three: was it important to talk to and to cuddle their children? About 20 per cent of mothers denied that these activities were important. We asked about reading, singing, playing; and found that the lower the income the lower the scores on these parenting activities. In fact, our analyses suggested that about a third of the social gradient in linguistic development and about half of the social gradient in social and emotional development could be attributed to differences in parenting.

So who won the political argument?

Earlier in this section, I implied that worse child development scores among the poor could serve as a political litmus test. The political left would blame poverty, the right would blame individuals for their poor parenting. The evidence shows that they are both correct, in part. 'Good' parenting is not randomly distributed. It follows the social gradient – there is less of it lower down the social hierarchy. When we see regular patterns such as these it is hardly a complete explanation to blame individual parents. To be sure, it is individuals who make the decisions whether to read to their children, or engage them in conversation or play. But the freedom of those individuals to make those decisions is shaped by the influences on them. For example, maternal depression also follows the social gradient, more frequent lower down. I would not blame a depressed woman for not having the energy to read to her children. Short of depression, if a parent lower in the hierarchy is ground down by misery, poverty and living in cramped conditions, playing with children may become a luxury too far. The nature of parenting is shaped by the context in which it takes place.

This is tricky terrain. It was reported to me that one woman living in poverty complained: 'That man Marmot is accusing me of being a bad mother just because I'm poor.'

Difficult. My response is threefold, which means I'm almost certainly bound to lose the public argument – a good sound bite would be better – but it is based on the evidence I have just presented. First, good parenting *is* important and *is* less common among the poor. Second, blame is unhelpful. The context in which parenting takes place is really important. Third, poverty is not destiny. The message of Figure 4.2 is that for a given level of deprivation some children are doing better than others.

The general message from the scientific evidence is that there are good grounds for intervening at two levels: reduction of poverty and supporting parents in their parenting activities. We shall come to the policy implications in a moment. First, though, if parents matter, how do they deal with the work–life balance? Should they be home addressing an extra 20,000 words a day to their offspring, or should they be grinding maize so the family can eat, toiling in a factory to eke out a living, or pursuing an interesting career which might also be of benefit to their children? It is hard to make those choices sound neutral.

EARLY CHILD DEVELOPMENT –
WHERE SHOULD PARENTS BE?

Two answers to that question are supplied by heart-felt testimonies from mothers. The first is from England, but it could come from any rich country:

> There is a presentation of women who look after their own chil-
> dren full-time as air-headed, spoilt and dowdy. However, there is
> also a prejudice against women who look after their children but .
> aren't dowdy (yummy mummies); women who go back to work
> after having had children; women who stay out of work but also
> employ nannies; women who work part-time and look after their
> children the rest of the time.
>
> I think the only way you could gain approval for your time-
> management, as a mother, would be to look after your children all
> the time as well as working full-time but for some socially useful
> enterprise (ideally voluntary work), while never relying on a man
> for money, yet never claiming benefits either, but God forbid that
> you should have a private income.[14]

The second is from Ahmedabad, India, from the Self Employed Women's Association (SEWA):

> According to the mothers, the immediate benefit of the crèche
> service is they can go to work at ease and with peace of mind. For-
> merly, if there was no one at home to care for a young child and
> the 'khali' or tobacco factory owners did not allow them to bring
> younger children to work, the mothers would remain at home and

forfeit the day's wages. Only the husband would go to the 'khali' [tobacco factory] and a single salary of Rs 8 to 10 per day was not enough for covering daily household expenses. In such circumstances, the families could not afford to buy even the basic necessities like food and just had to do without.

Mothers said that the crèches had resulted in increase in income because they could go out to work. One of the mothers in Vanoti village expressed her satisfaction lucidly: 'First, sister, we had "rotlo" [thick bread] to eat only once a day. Now we can eat twice a day and have enough money to buy vegetables also. I pray that this crèche will remain – it has been such a support to me and my family.'[15]

It is difficult being a mother. Whether you are ten rupees away from starvation or struggling with work–life balance in a rich country, it is not an easy ride – the poorer you are the tougher the ride. The SEWA experience makes it clear that, if the alternative is destitution, it is better for mothers to work. Being able to feed your children is not bad compensation for missing time with them.

In richer countries there has been much debate, and no little angst among mothers, on whether the family is better served by a mother being in paid employment or staying home with her children. In the UK, there has been a problem for women on low pay that the economic benefits of work do not make up for the cost of childcare. The economic incentives to work are not there.

In focusing on mothers, I am not diminishing the role fathers might, or even should, have. I am simply reflecting the usual.

Facts do not always count with ideologists, but it may be helpful to know if there is evidence that young children are damaged by their mothers going out to work. The Millennium Birth Cohort, as its name suggests, was started in 2000. Colleagues of mine at UCL, led by Anne McMunn, noting the controversy over mothers of young children combining work and childcare, examined the impact of different household arrangements on social and emotional development of children aged five.[16] The most favourable outcomes for the children, the best scores on socio-emotional behaviour, are in families where both mothers and fathers are living in the same household and in paid work. This outcome was evident even after taking account of parents' education and of family income.

The worst situation for children was to be in a household with no parent working, particularly a single mother with no paid employment. Much of this is because of poverty and maternal depression. Grim findings. Girls, in particular, seem to suffer from their mothers *not* being in paid employment. A tantalising finding that was not explained by the study, it sparks speculation about gender roles. I am not sure what it means.

The finding that for parents to be working is, at the very least, not bad for the child is not to deny the importance of maternal and paternal bonds with the child. As we saw above, they are vital, particularly in the early months of a child's life. Paid maternity (and paternity) leave enables these bonds to develop while reducing financial disadvantage. Jody Heymann, at UCLA, has looked at the arrangements for paid maternity leave globally.[17] The USA stands out as providing no – I repeat no – state-guaranteed paid maternity leave. It is not alone, however: neither Surinam nor Papua New Guinea provide state-guaranteed paid maternity leave. Every other country does.

DO PARENTS REALLY MATTER OR ARE THEY JUST BYSTANDERS?

I do have one piece of advice for worried parents. Read the literature on behavioural genetics.

Behavioural geneticists believe that what parents do with or for their children matters little for their children's cognitive and behavioural development.[18]

If you believe this, all that reading to children, all the love, warmth and attention that you bestow on them, is for naught – it makes little difference. That does seem to be in direct contradiction to the evidence of profound effects of parenting, and the circumstances in which parenting takes place, on the physical, cognitive and linguistic, social and emotional development of children. Above, I only touched on a vast scientific literature that shows parental effects on children's development.

How do we reconcile the research I reviewed above with the research of behavioural geneticists? One answer, not the only one, is that we are asking different questions. My primary concern is the regular patterns of differences between countries and between social groups – why children from the families of insecurely employed unskilled workers are less likely to do well than children from the families of well-paid professionals. Behavioural geneticists ask the question of why one person differs from another – why, if you have two children, they are so different, the one from the other.

Surely this is a false debate. To think that genes do not count in children's development would be to think nonsense. To deny the importance of environment would be to turn a blind eye to the evidence. The balance between genes and environment, and how they interact, will differ for different characteristics. How tall you are is largely genetic – tall parents have tall children, on average. Genes, however, do not explain why Dutch men in 1858 had an average height of 163 cm (5 foot 4) and 140 years later had reached 184 cm (over 6 foot).[19] Improved nutrition accounts for that. In other words, in a given environment where most people have good nutrition, genetic differences will play a big part in determining why one person is taller than another. Where there is marked environmental variation, over 140 years in the Netherlands for example, genetic differences will not tell us why there has been such spectacular growth in average height.

The same principles apply to early child development. In twin studies, for example, genetic variations are important for IQ and a range of other characteristics. If the environment is largely controlled – twins come from the same family – what else is there but genes? Twin studies do not address the question of why you and your partner, both with university education, are more likely to have children who go to university than is a couple neither of whom graduated from high school. Genes may play a role here, too, but so may the kinds of input that I review above.

When we turn to differences among countries, those in Figure 4.3 for example, let alone differences between those OECD countries and countries of South Asia, Africa and Latin America, it is very unlikely that we can explain differences in early child development on the basis of genetic variation. These country differences arise because of the different circumstances in which children are raised.

HOW THE SOCIAL GRADIENT GETS UNDER
THE SKIN — BIOLOGICAL EMBEDDING

Early in this chapter I sketched out a causal pathway: position on the social gradient affects parenting, which in turn affects cognitive, social and emotional, as well as physical, development of children, which in turn is related to social inequalities in mental and physical health in adulthood. I said that there are at least two pieces missing from this model of causation. First, what else goes into the mix I have labelled as 'position on the social gradient affects parenting'. I have attempted to fill in that gap. Second, how do these social and psychosocial influences affect bodily processes – or, as Clyde Hertzman and others have put it, get under the skin?[20] The two are linked. By understanding biological mechanisms we may get a better grasp of what it is in the environment that influences the social gradient in children's development and subsequent health.

The brain has proved to be an active battleground for theories of how we humans got to be as we are. The acclaimed evolutionary psychologist Stephen Pinker wrote a whole book critical of the idea that the brain – actually the mind, but you can't have one without the other – was a blank slate to be written on by experience.[21] Of course. The way we see, speak, exercise executive functions, think, feel emotions, and behave with others, and the neurological pathways by which these happen, are similar for all of us. Patterns of neurological wiring are common to us as a species. And we share some of these wiring patterns with other primate species. Disorders in the genetically determined wiring pattern can lead to psychological disorders. Most experts who study autism, for example, think it can be traced to biological inheritance of some form. Parents are not to blame.

However, the brain can be sculpted by experience. The word 'sculpted' is important. If one child is easily distractible and another concentrates with a fixity to be admired – this too follows the gradient: more distractibility in more deprived children – it is hardly surprising to find that there may be different neurological pathways involved. But sculpting implies changes to the brain's architecture, consequent upon experience.

Clyde Hertzman has summarised the elegant neurological research on critical periods.[22] The idea is that the developing child needs to be exposed to the appropriate environmental inputs during the critical period. If not, certain pathways never get developed.

Hearing, vision and emotional control all need appropriate input in the first two to three years of life to develop normally. Language, numbers and peer social skills can all start to develop a little later. You can learn a foreign language after age ten or so, but you may never quite speak it with the same accent-free facility that you would if you learnt it earlier. The key point is that the environment needs to provide the right input.

The lower down the social hierarchy are children's families, the less likely are the kids to get the right input. Poor nutrition, both before birth and after, stress, and appropriate cognitive stimulation are *all vital*. We have dealt with cognitive stimulation above. Stress affecting the mother, which becomes more common with increasing social disadvantage, has demonstrable effects on the function and structure of the developing child's brain. Part of the effect of stress may be that it limits the parents' cognitive stimulation of their child. But there may be other pathways too.

Clyde Hertzman and his colleague Tom Boyce identify four biological systems by which social disadvantage may get under the skin. First, the HPA axis (hypothalamic pituitary adrenal cortex), by regulating the output of the stress hormone cortisol, is one way the brain communicates a response to stress to the rest of the body. Second, the autonomic nervous system is an essential part of the body's fight-or-flight mechanism. Third, the development of memory, attention and other executive functions in the prefrontal cortex of the brain may underpin the cognitive development that we discussed above. Fourth are the systems of social affiliation involving other parts of the brain, amygdala and locus coeruleus, mediated by serotonin and other hormones.

There are exciting and rich pickings here for scientists investigating the impact of social environment on mind and body, treated together. One of the best worked out comes from the studies of Michael Meaney at McGill University in Montreal. He has been peeling back the layers of incomprehension to reveal a remarkably coherent picture, not only of how the environment influences the brain and stress pathways, but how it changes the function of genes – epigenetics.[23]

Mother rats nurture their pups in not so very different ways from those enjoyed by human infants. The rats do it by licking and grooming their offspring. One way to increase mother rat's attentiveness is to handle the rat and remove the pup from

Mum for a brief period. On her pup's return, mother engages in extra licking and grooming. It turns out that this especially attentive licking and grooming programmes the pup's HPA axis. The pup produces cortisol on cue when faced with a stress, but for the rest of its life, the rat that has had this extra attention puts out less cortisol, on average. Less cortisol, on the whole, is thought to be linked to less stress-related illness. This conditioning effect has to take place in a short time window, a critical period, in the first few days of life. Outside that window, all the extra maternal attention has little effect.

It gets more interesting. The chronic overproduction of corticosterone, the ratty equivalent of human cortisol, damages neurones in the brain of the rats who did not get the mother's special attention, leading to cognitive deterioration. People are not rats, but some of the potential parallels with humans should be intruding themselves. Over time, the rats who got less attention from their mothers had faster deterioration in memory and in other cognitive performance tasks.

For too long, we have been arguing over nature versus nurture; genes versus environment. I was at it again a few moments ago. It's the wrong debate. Nurture can sculpt nature, and nature can influence the environment. The long-term effect of maternal licking on the HPA axis is an elegant example of environment affecting genes. DNA is the material that constitutes genes. Simply put, genes dictate the production of proteins, which do just about everything. Maternal attention during the appropriate window of opportunity modifies DNA, and thus affects its function and subsequent manufacture of proteins. A region of DNA that regulates HPA axis function is altered (it is methylated), and that changes its function.

Over the next few years this already growing scientific literature is set to expand rapidly. It is likely to provide a richer understanding of how the social environment acting through the brain has long-term impact on development, bodily function and disease risk.

WHAT CAN WE DO ABOUT PROBLEMS OF
EARLY CHILD DEVELOPMENT?

I described Figure 4.2 as a gift to both the political left and right. It suggested there were two strategies to improve early child development: reduce deprivation; and, for a given level of deprivation, apply knowledge as summarised above to improve early childhood development.

Reducing deprivation

Poverty is neither simply an act of God nor something people do, or don't do, to themselves. The level of child poverty in a society is under a great deal of political control. It is a choice made by the political system. Figure 4.4 looks at child poverty in different countries before and after taxes and social transfers.

Child poverty is a relative measure. For each country, the cut-off is less than 50 per cent of median income.

Before social transfers, the levels of child poverty in Spain and France were 19 per cent in each country. After taxes and transfers, child poverty was reduced to 17 per cent in Spain but to 9 per cent in France. In Slovenia, not a rich country, it is even lower at 6 per cent. The minister of finance, by deciding what the level of child poverty should be, is probably having a bigger effect on child development than the minister of health.

In the US, after taxes and transfers, child poverty is higher than in Lithuania – 23 per cent compared with 15 per cent – despite having similar levels of poverty pre-tax. I challenge my American colleagues: you live in a functioning democracy. This must be the level of child poverty you want, otherwise you would do something about it. Once again, I argue that this should be above party politics. We are talking about our children, and their future blighted by poverty.

We can see why it might be part of a consistent world view for the political left to blame poor early child development on poverty

FIGURE 4.4: THE MINISTER OF FINANCE COULD REDUCE CHILD
POVERTY IF SHE WISHED

Child poverty rate before taxes and transfers (market income) and after taxes
and transfers (disposable income)

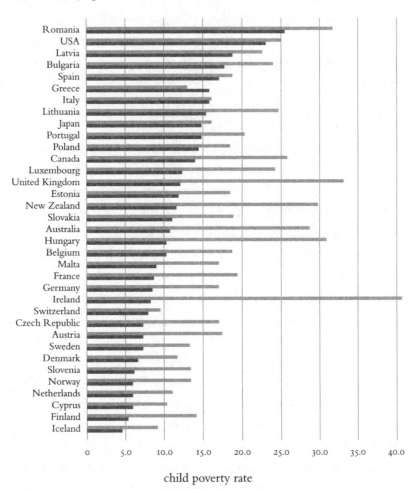

child poverty rate

(% of children living in households with income lower
than 50% of the national median income)

■ before taxes and transfers   ■ after taxes and transfers

Source: UNICEF Innocenti Research Centre. *Measuring Child Poverty: New League Tables of Child
Poverty in the World's Rich Countries*. Florence: UNICEF Innocenti Research Centre, 2012.

and the right on parenting. If you are of the persuasion that tax is theft, you will be intolerant of using the tax system to reduce poverty. But if you are of that persuasion you might find it uncomfortable to acknowledge that your tax preferences are damaging children's lives by failing to reduce poverty.

The evidence that early child development follows the social gradient cannot be disputed. In my view, the evidence is persuasive that the material conditions in which children grow up have a profound effect on how their minds develop. While the precise contribution of parents or others can be debated, it is a reasonable conclusion that poverty reduction will be good for children's physical, psychological, social and emotional development.

Breaking the link between poverty and poor early child development

I was invited to visit the English city of Birmingham. They have a set of plans to implement my English Review, *Fair Society, Healthy Lives*. Birmingham is more deprived than the average for England as a whole. As expected from everything shown above, the proportion of children aged five who were ranked as having a good level of early child development was worse than the English average. That was in 2007. By 2010 they had closed the gap. In only three years they had closed it. They could not have abolished deprivation in that time, but they broke the link between deprivation and poor early child development.

'What did you do?' I asked. They focused: they made good early child development a priority. There are some well-evaluated programmes for improving early child development, with the input of trained staff: Family Nurse Partnership, Incredible Years Parenting Programme, Promoting Alternative Thinking Strategies (PATHS), Triple P Parenting Programme.[24] Children's services applied these programmes and in three years they closed the gap. When parents need help, providing it can make a huge difference. What I have described is not a carefully controlled experiment.

One should be cautious of over-interpreting. The data do show, however, that rapid improvement is possible.

More generally, provision of high-quality services for early childhood makes a huge difference. Evidence suggests that after two years of age, spending some time each week in stimulating and high-quality group care benefits all children, and helps children from poorer backgrounds to gain more. Provision of high-quality services is also a major poverty-reduction strategy, enabling parental employment and so increasing family income. Ideal provision includes multiple uses for childcare centres, such as advice and support on parenting, health and diet. In the UK, wider community use is supposed to occur in children's centres, but often does not.[25]

The idea that provision of universal services helps to reduce the gradient, by helping the worst-off more, is supported by evidence from France. Pre-school has existed in France since the 1880s but enrolment rose dramatically in the 1960s and 70s so that around 90 per cent of three-year-old children are enrolled. An evaluation found that all children had some benefit in cognitive scores, but poorer children benefited more, thereby narrowing the gap with children from better-off families in subsequent school performance.[26]

EQUALITY OF OPPORTUNITY?

In Chapter 3 I posed the question of whether it is enough to aim for equality of opportunity in society, which must include the opportunity for children to grow and develop to their full potential. I said that, as a doctor concerned with health equity, outcomes mattered, too.

It's easy enough to be in favour of equality of opportunity; doing something about it is a good deal more challenging, especially as, in the US, UK and other countries, increasing inequalities that are affecting adults are also influencing life chances of the next generation. A telling illustration is given by the Great Gatsby

Curve. In 2012, Alan Krueger, Chairman of the President's Council of Economic Advisors, demonstrated the correlation between inequality and social immobility between generations, which has been dubbed the Great Gatsby Curve – perhaps not only referring to accumulation of great wealth, but to the influence of one's past history on present circumstances (see the quote at the opening of this chapter). The graph in Figure 4.5 shows that the growth of income inequality is not just inequitable for the present adult population, it diminishes life chances for the next generation – it diminishes equity between generations (intergenerational equity).

The term 'intergenerational earnings elasticity' plots the resemblance between the earnings of parents and the earnings of their adult children. To explain: if the next generation's earnings were exactly the same as their parents – rich parents → rich children,

FIGURE 4.5: INEQUALITY IS NOT JUST BAD FOR MUM AND DAD

Higher income inequality associated with lower intergenerational mobility

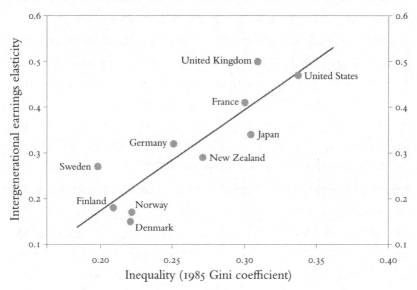

Note: The Gini coefficient is a measure of income equality in which 0 = everyone has the same income; 1 = one person has it all.
Source: Corak (2011), OECD, Council of Economic Advisors estimates.

middle-income parents → middle-income children, poor parents → poor children – then a country would score high on intergenerational earnings elasticity and would have low social mobility between generations. For example, in Denmark there is only a relatively small relation between the earnings of parents and the earnings of their offspring – rich parents are only a little bit more likely to have rich children than are poor parents. There is a great deal of social mobility, so Denmark scores under 0.2 on this metric. By contrast the US and UK have scores in the 0.45–0.5 range. How rich your parents are has a profound influence on how rich you will turn out to be. Poor parents tend to have poor children – social mobility is much lower.

The graph shows that the greater a country's income inequality the lower the social mobility. In other words, the greater the distance between the rungs of the ladder, the harder it is to get from one rung to the next. Going by the curve, Finland, Denmark and Norway experience high social mobility between generations and low inequalities within generations. The US and the UK are up at the other end. We might conclude that there is genuine equality of opportunity in the Nordic countries, and a good deal less in the US and UK. For the US, the Great Gatsby Curve is damning evidence of the decline of the American dream.

The message of this chapter is that early child development matters hugely for subsequent health and health equity, and that good early child development is shaped by the environment in which children grow and develop. Equity from the start is possible, but it will take action at all levels, from the magnitude of income inequalities and social mobility, to levels of poverty, to the quality of services and the care parents and others give to their children. The developing mind of the child is key. He or she will benefit more from school if he or she has had a better early child development. It is the issue of education to which we turn next.

5

Education and Empowerment

We want to provide only such education as would enable the student to earn more. We hardly give any thought to the improvement of the character of the educated. The girls, we say, do not have to earn; so why should they be educated? As long as such ideas persist there is no hope of our ever knowing the true value of education.

Mahatma Gandhi

You are a young girl sitting outside a rude shelter, humble but home, in a Bangladeshi village, watching your baby brother play in the dirt – your parents are both at work – and daydreaming. The fairy godmother appears and asks: 'How would you like a more secure future, better nutrition, a paid job, control over the decision if and when to get married, defence against being beaten by your husband, control over your sexuality and childbearing, increased chance that children you choose to have survive and grow in good health? Oh yes, and you can have an inside toilet, too – none of the embarrassment and indignity your mother has of having to "go" outdoors.'

No belief in fairies is required. The remedy is called education. Not only would it deliver all the good things the fairy godmother promised, it would enhance your capacity to live an informed life, enable you to learn the values of your culture and society,

to participate in the wider community and in the political decisions that affect your life, to exercise your freedoms and claim your
rights.[1] There's more: education can be fun; more fun than starting
a life of back-breaking menial toil at age ten or eleven, and being
married off to an older man at thirteen.

Sitting outside the hut, minding your little brother, you may
give little thought to public goods. You may not, but we should.
Education is not just good for the individual; it is good for all
of us. A more educated society is likely to be a healthier society.
Education can do all that. In rich countries as well as poor.

When we published the report of the Commission on Social
Determinants of Health, *Closing the Gap in a Generation*, with its
list of recommendations through the life course, I was asked by one
journalist: 'What's the one thing you would recommend to the US
President?'

'One thing? . . . Read my report.'

Annoying perhaps, but had I thought we only needed to make
one recommendation, I would have made only one. That said, if
I had to choose one among all of our recommendations about
daily life and social and economic inequalities, it would be education, and in a global context, education of women. It is central to
women's empowerment. Of course, by education I don't mean just
years spent in a classroom, but the outcome of education: knowledge, skills, opportunity and control over your life, and gender
equity and social inclusion. Were I Dickens, I would add: 'graces of
the soul' and 'sentiments of the heart'.

Education is at the centre because it captures so much of
everything else that is in this book. Looking backwards through
the life course, inequalities in education are caused, in part, by
inequalities in early child development. Looking outwards from
the individual to the society, inequalities in society cause inequalities in education. Schools matter too – radical thought. And good
education in its turn leads on to all the good things promised by

the fairy godmother. It is worth repeating: at a stroke, a focus on educating girls is the best single contributor to empowerment of women, with improvements in national and community development and health for women and their children.

EDUCATION IS GOOD . . . FOR CHILD SURVIVAL

Rightly, there has been much emphasis on improving access to primary education, globally. It is scandalous, in any country, that children of either gender should be deprived of the opportunity to attend primary school. That problem is on its way to being solved. Crucial, now, is secondary and tertiary education. Figure 5.1, with data from low- and middle-income countries, shows how beneficial secondary education of mothers can be to the next generation's chance of taking up the struggle of life.

Figure 5.1 shows three things: first, the dramatic differences in infant mortality between these low- and middle-income countries, from just over 120 per 1,000 live births in Mozambique to just over 20 in Colombia. Second, within each country, women with secondary education, or higher (the lower end of the vertical bars), have babies who are more likely to survive than those of women with no education (the top end of the vertical bars). Not shown is the gradient within countries, the fact that women with primary education are in the middle: their babies have a better chance of survival than those of women with no education but worse than those of women with secondary education. Third, having a secondary education reduces dramatically the disadvantage of having your baby in a poor country with a high toll of infant deaths. In Mozambique, for example, the infant mortality of the offspring of the educated women is a good deal closer to the Colombian level than is the figure for those of uneducated women.

In Chapter 4, when discussing the social gradient in early child development, the data suggested to me two strategies: reduce

FIGURE 5.1: GET EDUCATED OR MOVE

Inequity in infant mortality rates between countries and within countries by mother's education

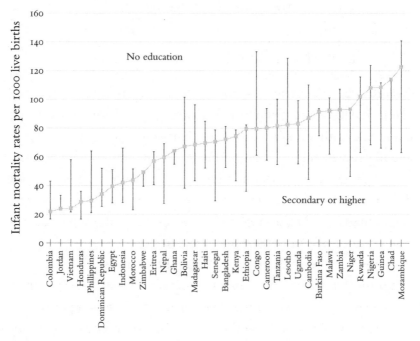

Source: Commission on the Social Determinants of Health. *Closing the gap in a generation: health equity through action on the social determinants of health. Final report of the Commission on Social Determinants of Health.* Geneva: World Health Organization, 2008.

deprivation, and break the link between deprivation and poor outcomes. So it is with these data. Mozambique is more deprived than Colombia. One strategy for reducing the high infant mortality in Mozambique is to reduce deprivation: improve nutrition, sanitation and provision of medical care. A second strategy is to educate women. Being educated will reduce the disadvantage associated with living in a country with high average levels of deprivation and infant mortality. And the effect is really big: in Mozambique going from no education to secondary education is associated with infant mortality falling from 140 to 60 per 1,000.

The effect of education of women in overcoming the disadvantage of having babies in a poor country is so potentially worthwhile that we have to ask if it is education itself that is so beneficial, or something correlated with it. This question will recur, as we look at the link between education and adult mortality in high-income countries. In the case of infant mortality, education is almost certainly causal for all the reasons the fairy godmother promised: better nutrition and sanitation, and mothers know more about what to do to protect their children. The mother's education is a much stronger predictor of infant mortality than is household income or wealth.

So convinced by these findings are the authors of the United Nations Human Development Report, that they conclude that development policy should be focused more on education of women than on household income.[2] Two propositions overlap: that one way of increasing household income is education of women, and that one way of making education more likely is to increase household income. All of this is made more possible with good policies.

In rich countries, now, infant mortality rates are under ten per 1,000 live births. It is a dramatic result of strategy one: improving conditions and access to care for all in society. But even here, we find that mothers with more education have better child survival than mothers with less. The differences may be 2.5 compared with 7.5, rather than 60 compared with 140 in Mozambique; but they remain important.

. . . AND FOR REDUCING FERTILITY

In high-income countries, we stopped worrying that if all babies survive their entry into our chaotic world we would suffer over-population. France has had a long concern with fertility below replacement rate. In Italy, too, the number of children per woman is 1.4. I tease my Italian colleagues: 'Italy is a Catholic country, contraception is proscribed, if you're not having babies it must mean you've given up sex.' They reassure me they like sex, but in Italy women are educated and know how to exercise the choice of when, and how often, to reproduce.

So it is in low-income countries. Birth rates have not fallen below replacement, at least not yet, but educated women are in control of their reproduction. There have been welcome declines in child mortality rates globally. Fewer babies dying does not necessarily mean an overstocked planet. Fertility rates, the number of births per woman, have been declining, particularly for more educated women. Figure 5.2 shows that in action.

I have only shown four countries, but could show one hundred and the point would be the same. Women with more education have fewer children. In Ethiopia it is particularly dramatic. The more educated women have two children, compared with an average of more than six for their uneducated sisters.

The problem for Ethiopia is shown in the 'overall' column. The country as a whole has a fertility rate of 5.4 births for each woman – higher than the fertility for women with primary education. Why? Because very few women in Ethiopia have secondary education. No education or primary is the norm. The likelihood is that if all women in Ethiopia had secondary education, the fertility rate would be nearer to two births for each woman rather than more than five.

FIGURE 5.2: KNOW WHEN TO SAY NO?

Total fertility rate (births per woman) according to mother's education

Country	No education	Primary	Secondary or higher	Overall
Bangladesh	3.0	2.9	2.5	2.7
India	3.6	2.6	2.1	2.7
Ethiopia	6.1	5.1	2.0	5.4
Nigeria	7.3	6.5	4.2	5.7

It is precisely lack of education that has led to fertility rates actually rising between 1970 and 1990 in Sub-Saharan Africa, when they declined in *every* other region of the world. A great deal has been written about structural adjustment programmes.[3] The International Monetary Fund (IMF), when asked for help by countries in dire economic straits, had a formula which required structural adjustment. That sounds neutral, but in practice it meant the state spending less on public services and putting things out to the market.

In Africa in the 1980s large cuts in public expenditure may have satisfied those who equate government expenditure with waste and economic failure, but such cuts meant that real expenditure on education per person fell by nearly 50 per cent on average in Sub-Saharan Africa.[4] In some countries there was an actual decline in school enrolment; in others the previous growth in the proportion of girls being educated slowed down.

This 'natural experiment' – that is being kind to structural adjustment: others would use sharper descriptions – disempowered women. Cuts in education meant that more women were denied the possibility of having the knowledge, the skills, the freedoms to control their own reproduction. This effect on fertility of reductions in education spending is a clear example of damaging a public good: education does not only help individual women, it is good for society. Because fertility rates went up in the 1980s, the number of people reaching childbearing age twenty years later is high, so that population increase will continue for longer than it might have done, putting huge strains on already poor countries.

How does it work? Education leads to lower fertility rates in many of the ways the fairy godmother promised. A more educated woman has access to information, she can get access to contraception and service, and is more likely to be an economic participant in the wider economy. So is her husband, which reduces the incentive to have more children. They have jobs and careers to pursue and will be less likely to see children as insurance for their old age. Education gives women more control of both their sexuality and their reproduction. And, of course, if education leads to more babies surviving it reduces the incentive to have more, just in case.

. . . AND FOR YOUR OWN HEALTH

The US is an attractive destination both for highly qualified people, and for those who are desperate, economically or politically. It has many good features. Good health is not among them. In Chapter 1, I drew attention to the US's remarkably poor health for men and women – worse than would have been predicted by that country's income and wealth. A study by the US National Academy of Science reaches similar conclusions, and points out that the health disadvantage in the US, compared with so-called peer countries, is biggest for Americans who are most disadvantaged.[5]

One group who are disadvantaged is African Americans. Another is people with little education. They overlap. Black Americans have shorter life expectancy than do white Americans, by 4.7 years for men and 3.3 years for women.[6] The US reports much of its health statistics by race. My own view is that skin pigment has little to do with health. So-called racial differences in health are related to degrees of social disadvantage and discrimination.

If the argument about social disadvantage is correct, we might see that Black Americans have worse health than whites because of less education. This does seem to be largely true for women, less so for men. Figure 5.3 gives figures for life expectancy by education for blacks and whites.[7]

Much of the health disadvantage among black women is linked to the fact that they have less education, on average, than do white women. Among men, there are two ways to describe what we see. Either white men get more health advantage from their education than do black men – six years' black–white difference for men with a bachelor's degree or higher – or something is going badly

FIGURE 5.3: IT DOESN'T JUST SEEM LONGER...

Life expectancy at birth for men and women in the US, 2008

Years of education	White women	Black women	White men	Black men
<12	73	73	67	66
12	78	74	72	68
13-15	82	80	79	74
16+	83	81	81	75

Source: Olshansky SJ, Antonucci T, Berkman L, Binstock RH, Boersch-Supan A, Cacioppo JT, et al. Differences in life expectancy due to race and educational differences are widening, and many may not catch up. *Health Aff (Millwood)*. 2012; 31(8): 1803–13.

wrong for white men with little education. In fact, it is likely to be the latter. White men with little education have seen their health decline over the last two decades.

I cannot resist drawing attention, yet again, to the gradient. It is not simply that people with little education have poor health – they do – but there is a graded relation between years of education and length of life. We see it even at the top. People with less time in college have shorter life expectancy than those who went even further with sixteen or more years of education.

Explanation for health disadvantage must include the gradient. We have to explain not only why it is bad for your health to be uneducated in a poor country, and to be relatively uneducated in a rich country, but also why the more education you have the better your health.

We also have to explain why the strength of the link between education and health varies. My colleagues and I at UCL in London were invited by the European Commission to put together a group report on health in Europe, focusing mainly on the European Union. Figure 5.4, from that European Report, shows how dramatic are the health inequities both within and between countries.[8]

It can be read in a similar way to Figure 5.1, which shows infant mortality. Look, for example, at Estonia. The average life expectancy for men at age twenty-five is only forty-five more years, ten years fewer than Sweden. Now look within Estonia. Twenty-five-year-old men with the lowest level of education have life expectancy of another thirty-six years, a staggering seventeen years fewer than for men with the highest level of education, at fifty-three more years. Adding the figures, that means that if today's death rates applied, a twenty-five-year-old with the lowest educational level could only expect to survive to sixty-one, on average. By contrast the twenty-five-year-old who has been to university or other tertiary education can expect to be alive at seventy-eight. In Sweden, everyone is doing better and the gap in life expectancy between the least and most educated is about four years – not seventeen as in Estonia.

In general, all the countries with the largest inequalities in life expectancy are in central and eastern Europe. They are the poorer

FIGURE 5.4: EUROPE: NOT ALL THE SAME THEN

Life expectancy in Europe at age 25

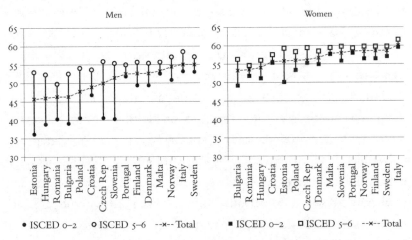

Note: ISCED = International Social Classification of Education, where 0-2 = none to lower secondary; 5-6 = tertiary and advanced research

Source: Eurostat. Life expectancy by age, sex and educational attainment (ISCED 1997) 2012 [updated 2012/07/27].

countries of the region, with lowest national income, and they also tend to be those with the lowest average life expectancy. But we see something else – another gift for those who think that our health is mainly determined by the choices we make. If you are going to have the lowest level of education you'd be well advised to have it in Sweden, Italy or Norway, rather than in Estonia, Hungary or Bulgaria. Putting it the other way: if you have the lowest level of education, it really matters which country you live in. For those with the highest level of education, it matters far less. We saw something similar with infant mortality and mothers' education in poor countries in Figure 5.1. I call this 'choice'. It is a grim mockery of choice. People have no control over where they are born, and only some control over how much education they get.

I hasten to add that length of life, life expectancy, is not all there is to health. In our comparison of European countries, we also looked at whether people felt themselves to be in poor health, and whether they had a long-term illness. We found clear social gradients in these measures of ill-health too – the lower the level of education the worse the health.

I started this book by emphasising that a combination of material deprivation and disempowerment is responsible for many of the health inequalities we see within and between countries. At lower levels national income is important as a guide to material deprivation; and education is not a bad proxy for empowerment. Are these really two separate influences or can the apparent link between education and health shown in Figure 5.4 be accounted for by the fact that less educated people are more likely to live in deprived conditions?

In order to answer that question, we have to think what deprivation means in Europe. In Sub-Saharan Africa and South Asia deprivation means lack of basic conditions for health: water and sanitation, food and shelter. More or less everyone in Europe has those things, yet we still see dramatic inequities in health. To measure

European deprivation we have used an index constructed from responses to questions on the ability to afford:

- to pay rent or utility bills
- to keep the home adequately warm
- to face unexpected expenses
- to eat meat, fish or a protein equivalent every second day
- a week's holiday away from home
- a car
- a washing machine
- a colour TV
- a telephone

The data show clearly that for individuals in Europe the greater the material deprivation, in terms of the list above, the worse their health.[9] It is an interesting list. Deprivation in Bangladesh means having no bathroom, watching your little brother grow too slowly because of too few calories to eat, or catching infections because of having to drink dirty water. Deprivation in Europe means no holiday, no car or colour TV, as well as having to choose between eating and heating.

What happened to education? Education and material deprivation overlap: in general, the less the education, the greater the deprivation. They only overlap. They are not measuring all the same individuals. Both material deprivation and education, independently, are linked to the social gradient in health.

In sum, then, it is likely that even in rich countries the fairy godmother got it about right. We can build a life-course picture. Inequalities in early child development lead to inequalities in education. Educational outcome is related to the kind of job you get, or whether you have a job at all, if you have enough money to get by, and the choices you make about smoking, drinking and lifestyle. All of these will have an impact on health and health inequalities.

. . . AND FOR PROTECTING YOURSELF

I find these next figures almost too awful to contemplate. Demographic and Health Surveys are conducted in many low- and middle-income countries. One question asked women if they agreed that it was acceptable for a husband to beat his wife if she refused to have sex with him.[10] What would be your guess as to how many women would endorse that proposition? The answers for two countries are shown in Figure 5.5.

In Mali, just over half of women with primary education agreed that it was all right for the husband to beat his wife. It had been higher. The glimmer of hope is that the proportion agreeing was under 40 per cent among women with secondary or higher education. In Ethiopia, 33 per cent of women with primary education thought a beating was acceptable in return for exercising control over their bodies; down from 45 per cent. The figure was 11 per cent for women with secondary education or higher. And so on, in country after country, education makes a difference. One interpretation of these figures is that lack of education renders women more vulnerable. Those in power, be they husbands or dominant ethnic groups or tyrannical authorities, prey on the vulnerable. Education reduces women's vulnerability.

FIGURE 5.5: HE CAN DO WHAT?!

Proportion of women agreeing that it is acceptable for a husband to beat his wife if she refused to have sex with him

Country	Year	Total (%)	No education (%)	Primary (%)	Secondary or higher (%)
Mali	2001	73.5	75.8	74.5	51.6
	2006	56.8	59.9	53	37.5
Ethiopia	2000	50.9	56.2	44.8	17.1
	2005	44.3	51	40.4	14.5
	2011	38.6	48.9	32.8	11

Source: Demographic and Health Surveys, 2011.

The first lesson when getting involved in global health is to be culturally sensitive, to respect the reality that 'they' do things differently 'over there'. Very important, but respect does not supersede women's rights. It is wrong for one half of humanity, men, to have licence to batter the other half. Women's right to control their own bodies must surely trump cultural sensitivity. If that is how 'they' do things, then they are wrong. The fact that education of women makes this clear underlines the message. The improvement over time, i.e. declining percentages, fuels my evidence-based optimism.

Education may play a further role in women protecting themselves. It helps women to gain paid employment. Being economically self-sufficient reduces the chances of intimate partner violence.

. . . AND FOR YOUR COUNTRY'S DEVELOPMENT

'Development' is an evocative word. We used to talk about 'developing' and 'developed' countries. Was that supposed to imply that developed countries had done it – it was all over, finished? Someone once defined an optimist as one who thinks the present organisation of society is the best that could possibly be. A pessimist is one who fears that that may very well be true. Most of us would probably want our societies to continue to develop, in the sense of getting better. Even those who think everything was better before, and progressives wrecked everything, probably want 'development' in the sense of going back to a better time, whenever that was. I cannot muster too much enthusiasm for a rose-tinted past.

The United Nations has a whole agency devoted to Development, the UNDP. I find their reports invaluable. Pioneered by Mahbub ul Haq, and influenced by Amartya Sen, UNDP recognises that development involves much more than economic growth. It uses a Human Development Index, HDI, that includes measures of national income, of education, and of life expectancy. Further, rather than divide the world into developed and developing it ranks countries on their HDI. In the 2013 Report Norway ranked number 1 on HDI, and Democratic Republic of Congo and Niger ranked joint bottom at 186.

Health and education are vital components of lives that people value. A fundamental assumption underlying this book is that people value health. The fact that the UN privileges these, and does not rely solely on national income as the measure of development, is excellent.

While questions might be raised as to whether the planet could stand continued growth in national incomes, putting sustainable development under threat, improvements in health and education are considered by most to be good things. Therefore, on the whole, growth in HDI is a good thing. Such growth is damaged by inequality. According to analyses presented in the UNDP's 2013 Human Development Report, it turns out that inequalities in education and health have a big impact on the HDI, but inequalities in income do not. In fact more equal achievements in education and health counteracted increases in income inequalities in their effects on human development.

Even taking a narrower approach, and considering economic growth as an outcome, public education was vital to economic development in Japan in the Meiji era (1868–1912), and latterly to South Korea, Taiwan, Singapore, Hong Kong and China.[11]

The fairy godmother might take note: improving equity both in education and health is vital not just for a young girl in a village but for development of the whole society. I don't find any need to believe in fairies to believe that the world can be made a better place, is being made a better place, by improvements in education. Progress is never without its hitches and glitches, inequalities chief among them, but the evidence is clear. When we make a difference in improving education, improved health equity is likely to follow.

Understanding and addressing
inequalities . . . by learning from Finland

All Finnish primary school children seem to look particularly fresh-faced, healthy and actively engaged – a bit like their teachers, actually. The head teacher tells me that the pupils at Ressu comprehensive school in Helsinki are not from particularly privileged backgrounds. The catchment area has three groups: academics, artists and working class. The head teacher is polite, well informed, generous with her time, and very indulgent, given that I am not the first to come to pray at the shrine of Finnish education. Ever since the PISA (Programme of International Student Assessment) showed Finland's fifteen-year-olds scoring particularly well compared with other European countries on standard tests, people have been wondering how they do it. PISA is a study conducted regularly by the OECD, the rich country club. It tests fifteen-year-olds on mathematics, science and literacy using standardised tests – in so far as such things are possible in cross-country research. Its results are pored over when they come out, as countries examine how they fare.

The UK made a reputation as being a brainy country – a great many discoveries, wonderful creative arts, brilliant universities. Despite that, we don't do very well on PISA tests. The US is no slouch either, when it comes to innovation and skills. Why do the Finns do so brilliantly and the British and Americans so badly on internationally standardised tests? It's quite a neat natural experiment, because the UK and Finland do things so differently.

The current approach in the UK to improving education for our children is for the relevant government minister to take central control, abolish meddlesome local authority control of schools, set the national curriculum, set out a programme of school visits by inspectors to make sure they are up to scratch (the schools, that is, not the inspectors), and lay down the criteria for what children should be able to achieve at various stages of their school career. Central government will examine at each of these stages, publish league tables of school performance to name and shame schools, and abolish minimum qualifications for teachers so as to stimulate creativity. Education and standards of education have become intensely political.

Finland has followed pretty much the reverse. There is a national curriculum but teachers have a great deal of autonomy in deciding what they teach; schools are under the control of local authorities; and there are no tests to see if children have reached the relevant competency at various ages. There is one national test at the end of nine years of basic education in comprehensive schools, but the results are not published, not fed back to pupils, and are used by the schools for statistical purposes so that they can see how they are doing alongside other schools. All teachers have a master's degree – unthinkable to have less; teaching is highly prized and teaching jobs are much sought; teacher training is research-based, so teachers are encouraged to develop an enquiring approach to sort out solutions for children who are having difficulties.

The Finnish system is based not on managerial control of teachers but on both teachers and students taking responsibility. The lack of emphasis on national exams represents a judgement not only that they are not necessary for high levels of performance – witness the high PISA scores – but that they represent too narrow an approach to education. Finland is interested in educating future citizens who know how to work with people from diverse backgrounds, are educated in music and culture, have learnt traditional Finnish skills such as working with wood and textiles, and know how to cook.

I put two contradictory hypotheses to my hosts – the head teacher and an official from the teachers' union. One is that school reduces the effect of social disadvantage on educational performance. The other is that school amplifies the effects of social advantage and disadvantage because the kids from more stimulating backgrounds are better placed to take advantage of what schools have to offer. No question in the teachers' minds: Finnish comprehensive schools reduce the effect of social disadvantage on educational performance. Children who are having trouble – up to 30 per cent of pupils – get special attention. Equality is the most important word in Finnish education.

I suggested that if educational performance follows a bell-shaped curve, their special attention to the children in trouble may have reduced the prevalence of dumb-bells, but it may also have reduced elite performance, fewer Nobels.* They were not having any of that. The teachers work not only at helping the slower kids, but at challenging and extending the more able.

Might it not be the case that Finland's good performance educationally may have less to do with schools and more to do with a relatively homogeneous population with low levels of child poverty? This was a typical academic's question, wanting to isolate relevant variables. They chided me gently. You cannot separate the performance of the schools from the society and culture in which they are embedded. Schools are influenced by culture and society, and their mission is to contribute to society and culture in a positive way.

There are lessons to draw from the Finnish experience that are applicable globally.

. . . AND, ALTHOUGH THERE ARE SOCIO–ECONOMIC DIFFERENCES IN EDUCATION, POVERTY IS NOT DESTINY!

In Finland, as in all other countries in the PISA Survey, the higher the socio-economic and cultural level of the family, the better their fifteen-year-olds perform on standard tests. Examples are shown in Figure 5.6. Please forgive me if I remark, yet again,

---

* I am grateful to Helena Cronin for this terminology.

FIGURE 5.6: GETTING IT ALL TO ADD UP... FOR EVERYONE.
KEEPING UP WITH THE CHINESE.

Within country maths results by quarters of ESCS (economic, social and
cultural status)

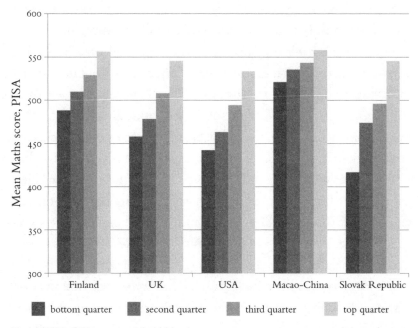

Note: ESCS is PISA's measure of social level.
Source: PISA, 2013.

that it is not just children from poor families that do poorly, but
it is a social gradient in all the countries shown here – shallow-
est in Macau and Finland, steepest in the Slovak Republic and
intermediate in the US and UK. Given everything in the first
part of this chapter, it is entirely reasonable to suggest that if we
in the US and UK, and much of Europe, want to catch up in
educational performance with the Chinese and the Finns, we
have to take active steps to reduce the social gradient in educational performance.

I presented results such as these at a meeting convened to
discuss growing up in Tower Hamlets, a particularly deprived area

of East London. The Director of Education in Tower Hamlets challenged me:

'Your results are out of date,' she said.

That was hitting me where it hurt. What did she mean?

'We tell ourselves every day, poverty is not destiny. We have broken the link between deprivation and school performance.'

She sent me their results and, indeed, they had broken the link between deprivation and outcome of education. That too is what the PISA results show. Poverty, or more accurately, low scores on PISA's measure of economic, social and cultural status (ESCS), is not destiny. While all countries show the socio-economic gradient, many young people perform better than predicted by their ESCS background, and some perform worse. PISA talks of resilient people who do well despite their social and economic disadvantages. Schools and families matter. The Tower Hamlets case shows that dedication on the part of teachers can make a huge difference, making Tower Hamlets schools more like Finnish ones.

Disadvantage can be destiny, under the wrong circumstances. A particularly telling, and upsetting, example of how economic, social and cultural background can influence educational outcomes comes from India's caste system. Researchers for a World Bank Report on Equity gave Indian children aged ten to twelve a set of puzzles.[12] They had to solve mazes in a fixed period of time, and were rewarded on the number of mazes they solved. The children were from high-caste and low-caste backgrounds. In the first part of the experiment, their caste background was in no way made obvious. Under these conditions the lower- and higher-caste children performed equally well on the intellectual task. It is the next part of the experiment, when the children's caste was revealed, that is upsetting. Under these conditions, the lower-caste children performed significantly worse than those from more privileged backgrounds – the lower-caste children solved 25 per cent fewer mazes compared with when their caste was not announced. One interpretation is that this is disempowerment in action. Once the lower-caste children knew that the authority figures knew about their background, they knew the game was rigged. No matter how hard they tried, no matter how well they did, they would not get due reward for their efforts.

There is a clear message: create the conditions so that caste is not destiny, and children will do better regardless of their background. After one lecture in the US, in which I featured these results, an African-American member of the audience came up and gave me a big hug. 'Now you know what it is like to grow up black in the ghetto in the US,' he said.

Putting these results together, we see socio-economic gradients in educational performance more or less everywhere. The magnitude varies. Evidence suggests that there are three sets of influence on these gradients: the family, the wider socio-economic conditions and the school. One of the predictors of school success is the readiness for school when children start. As was laid out in the previous chapter, early child development, and hence readiness for school, is influenced in part by parenting. Parents may have a continuing influence in the school years. Peer effects, connected with the socio-economic environment, will also be important. We saw in Baltimore that in the more deprived part of the city the absence rates from school were dramatically higher than in the ritzier parts of town – if everyone is at it, why not me? The Finnish and the Tower Hamlets experiences suggest that schools can really make a difference.

. . . AND FOR MOVING TO GENDER EQUITY

In Finland, now, not only has gender equity been achieved in primary and secondary education – participation of girls and boys is 100 per cent – but more women than men go on to tertiary education. Finland is not alone. The figures suggest that there is a threshold globally for this phenomenon, and it is related to national income in a clear-cut way (no gradient here). Below a national income of around $10,000 (adjusted for purchasing power) fewer women than men participate in tertiary education. Above that level, in most countries, more women than men go on with their education. Gender isn't destiny either.

We see this in PISA scores. Study after study reports that girls are better at language, boys at mathematics. Not in Finland. Girls are better at reading, as they are in all countries, but girls do better at maths than do boys – likewise in Sweden and Iceland.

Gender equity remains a problem for the rest of the world. The good news, really good news, is that enrolment in primary education has increased dramatically in all parts of the world in the last forty years, despite hiccups, with improvements in gender equity. As Figure 5.7 shows, the last forty years have also seen dramatic increases in enrolment in secondary education.

FIGURE 5.7: SCHOOL'S OUT EARLY... IN SOME REGIONS

Upward trend in secondary gross enrolment ratios seen in all regions and for both sexes, 1970–2009

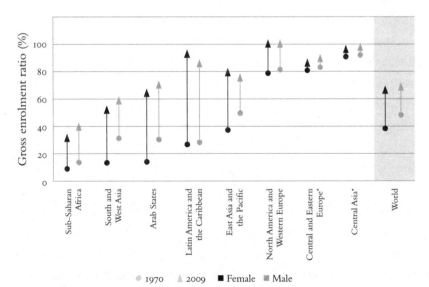

*1970 data for Central and Eastern Europe refer to 1971. Data for Central Asia go back to 1993.
Source: UNESCO World Atlas of Gender Equality in Education UNESCO 2012.

Continuing the good news, in Latin America, and East Asia and the Pacific, girls' participation overtook the boys'. But as Figure 5.7 shows, gender equity remains a huge problem for secondary education in Sub-Saharan Africa and South Asia. As we shall see in a moment, this should be an intensely soluble problem. Put simply, gender equity in education is likely to be a reflection of gender equity in society.

WHAT CAN BE DONE TO IMPROVE EDUCATION?

A great deal, it would seem. The problems are clear. In low-income countries there are too few children in school, standards are indifferent, and absentee rates are high. In countries poor, middle and rich, there are social gradients in educational performance.

Don't start from here

The best intervention to improve education is to start before school age. All over Europe, children who were enrolled in formal pre-school programmes have better performance on PISA scores at age fifteen. Important as it is to increase participation in primary, secondary and tertiary education, we should not forget pre-school. The principles of what constitutes good pre-school education are well understood and were reviewed in the previous chapter. It is not necessary to live in a rich country to have access to quality pre-school. For example, the Mwana Mwende project in Kenya involves the whole community in providing support, education and child-care for the youngest children. The project trains parents in child and youth development, community development and participatory processes. The Mwana Mwende Child Development Centre, which set up the project, also trains pre-school teachers to a professional level.

In Latin America the countries that have high enrolment in pre-school are the same countries that do well on reading at school. Cuba and Costa Rica have nearly 100 per cent attendance at pre-school, at ages three to five, and have top reading scores in Latin America in sixth grade. Paraguay and the Dominican Republic have low pre-school participation and low reading scores in sixth grade. Argentina and Peru are somewhere in between. I should beware of jumping to conclusions, but I do note that people in Cuba and Costa Rica have remarkably good health (life expectancy at birth over seventy-nine); Dominican Republic and Paraguay relatively poor health (around seventy-three); and Argentina (seventy-six) and Peru (seventy-four) come somewhere in between.

Money matters but is not everything

Education brings money and money brings education. This seems to work for both poor countries and families within those countries. To be more precise, among low-income countries, the greater their national income the more they spend on education. For low-income families in those countries, in general the higher their income the more they spend on education. But it works the other way as well. Education of individuals, in general, brings higher incomes; and education, as we have seen, has proved one route for economic growth of countries.

Breaking into this cycle has proved quite possible. Many countries have done it. In India 63 per cent of adults are literate. By contrast, in Vietnam and Sri Lanka – the first a little poorer than India, the second a little richer – more than 90 per cent of adults are literate. India's economic growth at 6–8 per cent a year is the envy of the rich world, but it is likely that the benefits of that growth would reach further if education were more widely spread.

One way countries have helped families to break out of the cycle of low income→low education→low income is with help from outside. Conditional cash-transfer schemes, first in Mexico and Brazil, were developed as a way of reducing poverty AND producing long-term change. Poor families are targeted and

receive regular cash subsidies, provided they meet certain conditions such as taking young children to nutrition and health clinics,
and keeping older children in school. The Mexican scheme, origi-
nally known as *Progresa*, subsequently as *Oportunidades*, covered
5 million low-income households by 2004.[13] The largest part of
the cash transfer came for children in school; more for older children and more for girls.

I visited one *Oportunidades* location in a rural area outside
Mexico City. One young member of our party commented that
the people queuing to receive their benefits were all women, short,
and looked 'Indian'. Accurate observation. Women, because giving
cash to women is a more reliable proposition than giving it to men.
The money is more likely to be used to support the family than if
men chose its uses. Short, because poverty is linked to malnutrition
and hence to short height. 'Indian', because indigenous groups are
more likely to be in poverty.

These schemes work. In general, participants in a conditional cash
transfer scheme are more likely to have their children in school.[14]
The conditionality element makes some of us uncomfortable. In
effect, the government is saying to poor families: we'll give you cash,
provided you do what we tell you; take young children for check-
ups and keep older children in school. A recent review of seventy-
five reports from thirty-five studies compared schemes that gave
cash without conditions with those that imposed conditions. The
unconditional schemes did increase school enrolment, but the more
the conditions were applied and monitored, the greater the positive
impact on school enrolment.[15] That said, there are examples, Malawi
is one, where unconditional cash transfers had as big an effect on
girls staying in school as transfers with strings attached.[16]

The report highlighted the obvious but vital point. Keeping children in school is one thing. Teaching them something is another.
There was no evidence that conditional cash transfer schemes
improved test scores. The implication is clear. You cannot get the

benefit of school if you don't turn up, but real effort has to be put into improving quality of education as well as the mere fact of it.

Improving quality is a concern for all countries, whether low-, medium- or high-income. That a country does not have to be rich to get there is shown by the staggering results on PISA scores by Macao-China, shown in Figure 5.6, and similarly excellent results from Shanghai China.

Delivering good education

I have had my differences with economists over the years, but as my economist friends tell me, they pale compared with the differences economists have with each other. Two MIT economists, Abhijit Banerjee and Esther Duflo, have carried out a programme of research on reducing poverty.[17] They use hard evidence to adjudicate the arguments among their fellow economists. In particular, one set of views suggests that top-down provision of education, from central or local government, will deliver good education. The opposing view is leave it to the market: people will demand good education and be willing to pay for it; the private sector will come in and provide it.

Beware of ideology here. If one suggested to Finland that what they most needed was a private sector in education with parents paying school fees, rather than having schools funded from taxation, they would (politely, because they are Finnish) show you the door. They have among the best results outside Asia because of the way they run their affairs. On the other hand, as Banerjee and Duflo point out, people do not trust state provision of education in India, with some good reason based on experience. The private sector is mixed in quality and the fees are out of reach of the poor. But certain non-governmental organisations are providing high-quality education that is making a difference. The message is that simple nostrums such as public good/private bad or vice versa are too limited. We need to take account of circumstances.

Countries like South Korea show us the way. It is possible from a standing start to make dramatic improvements in educational performance. In South Korea, success is due in part to significant investment in education. The budget for the ministry of education is six times what it was in 1990, and now represents 20 per cent of central government expenditure. Teaching in Korea is a respected and competitive occupation – teachers are well paid (ranked tenth in the world), and are rewarded after fifteen years of service. The curriculum has been significantly revised over the last fifty years, and now emphasises individuality, creativity and knowledge of Korean and other cultures. There is a 93 per cent high-school graduation rate, compared with 77 per cent in the USA.

Education is an important part of the life course, which highlights education's importance but also shows the difficulties in isolating its effects on health. The picture so far is that the circumstances in which children are born and grow have a profound effect on what happens to them in school. The 'outcome' – skills, knowledge, ability to control their lives – will determine what happens next in the world of work and in general living standards as adults. Both the effects from earlier life and what happens when young people leave school are important for health equity.

Improving education will take good schools, of course, but as the Finns taught me, education takes place in a context. To achieve good educational results, we also need action to reduce poverty and socio-economic inequality and to improve the family and community context in which children's education takes place. One aspect of both redressing socio-economic inequalities and improving family lives is work, the subject of the next chapter.

6

Working to Live

. . . all the melancholy-mad elephants, polished and oiled up for the day's monotony, were at their heavy exercise again . . . Every man was in the forest of looms where Stephen worked to the crashing, smashing, tearing piece of mechanism at which he laboured.

Charles Dickens, *Hard Times*

Alan was a picker. In a vast warehouse. You order goods online. Alan goes to the shelf where they are stored, 'picks' them, places them in a trolley and takes them to the packer, who puts them in a box, sticks on a label, and you have them a couple of days later. It's so neat: you click, he picks, she packs and sticks. It's convenient for you; less so for Alan. Alan *was* a picker. He was fired for collecting three penalty points, which he explained to me when we met as part of a BBC *Panorama* programme.*

When on nights, a typical shift lasted ten and a half hours, punctuated by two fifteen-minute breaks and one half-hour break – i.e. nine and a half hours of work. On arrival for his shift, Alan was handed what was in effect his controller and conscience: a hand-held electronic device that directed him to Row X to pick up item Y and put

---

* I met 'Alan' (not his name) as part of this programme broadcast in 2013.

it in his trolley; then to Row P to pick up item Q, and so on. When his trolley contained about 250 kg his device would direct Alan to the packers. Then he'd be off again for another load. His target was 110 large items an hour (more for smaller items), two a minute. That was the job, for nine and a half hours, plus the hour of breaks.

His hand-held electronic gizmo was not just his controller, it also fed back what he had done, so his performance could be monitored to see how he did against his target. He was warned when he did not keep up the pace. If he fell too far behind he would incur half a penalty point; more, a whole point. 'Did you ever,' I asked Alan, 'in all the time you worked there, meet your target and finish a shift with a sense of achievement?' Not once, was his answer. Hour after hour, day after day, and feeling always that he had fallen short.

'Did you feel that once you got used to it, at least you knew that you had secure employment?' No, he always felt he was on borrowed time because of the penalty points.

'How did other employees feel about the job?' Alan didn't know. He rarely spoke to anyone but his line manager, whose job it was to warn him about his failure to meet targets. There was no time to talk to other employees while the shift was on. During the break, the walk from one end of this aircraft hangar of a warehouse to the canteen took so long, plus the security going in and out of the warehouse, that there was simply no time to chat with anyone while taking a few minutes to eat and drink.

Alan told me that he used a pedometer one night and he clocked up eleven miles (18 km). Bone-weary, his feet blistered, he had never felt more exhausted in his life. When, on one shift, he went off sick he incurred another penalty point. Doing a job like Alan's, the employer is at some pains to ensure you do not take work home with you – security at the door. What Alan did take home with him was the beeping of his miniature malevolent gizmo that echoed through his mind.

One day he turned up late for a shift, about three minutes, and added to his penalty points. It took about eight weeks to accumulate the three penalty points, but he did, and was summarily dismissed.

My reaction to Alan's experiences was that it was as if his employers had taken everything we know about damaging aspects of work, concentrated them in a syringe and injected them into Alan. Added to the heavy physical demands, Alan's work was characterised by high demand with no control over the work task, by high effort and little reward, by social isolation at work, by job insecurity, by organisational injustice, and by shift work – all of which, as I will lay out below, have been shown to damage health. About the only 'good' thing about Alan's work was that it wasn't sedentary. That would have been fine had his activity not involved physical strain and heavy lifting.

In the 1930s film *Modern Times*, Charlie Chaplin pitted the little tramp against the implacable will of the production line – to the detriment of the little tramp. What's changed since then is that we now have much more evidence as to when, and under what circumstances, work is bad for health. People in high-status jobs do not have working conditions like Alan and the little tramp. People in low-status jobs don't have to have such working conditions either but, all too commonly, they do. Poor working conditions make a major contribution to inequities in health.

Charlie Chaplin and Alan both illustrate the key theme of this book: inequities in power, money and resources are the fundamental causes of inequities in health. All three of these inequities stand out in the workplace: the lower the position in the hierarchy, the more disempowered, the less the money, and the worse the physical, psychological and social resources. Worse health ensues. Work is a breeding ground for disempowerment.

Let's expand on the disempowerment. Not only was Alan's work full of the bad things work can do to your health, it lacked the positives that we look for in work. We go to work to get money – he was not well paid. Work helps define our social status and identity, who we think we are and what society thinks we are – Alan said he felt like a drone; the only reason he was not actually replaced by a drone is that he was a little more flexible – his intelligence had little to do with it. Work can provide opportunities for self-fulfilment and personal growth – not so for Alan in his work as a picker. Work is a place for developing social relationships – not if your target is 110 heavy items an hour, up to 240 small items, and you are averaging 80. Work and life have to be in balance. Alan's shift work and sheer exhaustion were hardly conducive to work–life balance.

Work is fundamental to security and to empowerment. Without work we can be lost, insecure, restricted and in poverty. If your reaction to Alan's experience is that, bad as it is, he would be worse off without work, you may well be right. Unemployment is bad for health. But we should not simply contrast work with no work: the quality of work really matters. All of which means we need to consider not only working conditions but also employment status – the nature and existence of employment contracts. Both have an impact on health.

Work like Alan's does not come about by accident. It is planned and requires certain general societal conditions: low unionisation – or else working conditions would be better; lack of alternative employment – people would go elsewhere; relentless attention to the profit margin; and tolerance, or even fostering, by the society of this type of employment. If work and employment can be a cause of ill-health, we need, as elsewhere, to look at the causes of the causes – why work and employment are the way they are. Is Alan's work a grim predictor of the future of work, divided into high-paid, high-skilled work at the top, drone-like work at the bottom, and a diminishing middle?

We will examine the evidence on work and health in a moment, but first . . .

IF YOU THINK ALAN HAD IT BAD . . .

Lalta was a human scavenger. Her occupation, and that of a million or so others like her in India, was to clean human excrement out of dry latrines by hand, pile it in a reed basket, carry it on her head to a dumping place and deposit it. Can you imagine a line of work more foul? Lalta couldn't either. As she said: 'All I missed was my dignity . . . I felt like the dirt I carried on my head.'[1]

Lalta lived in Alwar in Rajasthan in India, but she might have been in one of several states. Most of the latrines built in India in the twentieth century were of the dry type, largely because of water shortage. The tradition of this most demeaning of work was passed down through Dalit (outcaste) families for centuries or, in Lalta's case, she married into it at age seventeen. Parenthetically, about one-sixth of India's vast population are Dalit. There are a lot of people in demeaning occupations.

The scavengers had to reach in through a tunnel and retrieve the human waste by hand. The problem with work like Lalta's is a double burden: as well as the physical and biological hazards, there is the gross lack of dignity, the threat to self-worth, the appalling stress of such an occupation. Lalta felt there was no way out. She was told this was her fate. Not that there was calm acceptance of it: 'There was no happiness in our lives. It actually had no meaning. All the time it was either people's filth on the head or its thought in the heart.'

I have never been more inspired by toilets than when I heard someone from Sulabh International, a non-governmental organisation set up to deal with this issue, describe what happened next. Lalta herself could not solve her problems, but an organisation could. There were two parts to the solution. Sulabh International installed low-cost, safe sanitation systems in villages. Public toilets replaced dry latrines. Villagers had to pay a small cost to use the public toilets, so that the enterprise of installing toilets paid for itself. Since 1970, Sulabh International has installed more than 1.4 million household toilets and maintains more than 6,500 public pay-per-use facilities.[2] They even set up an international museum of toilets.

More interested in people than in porcelain, I am inspired by what happened to the scavengers in the areas where Sulabh has been working. They were retrained. In the case study I was shown, they were retrained as beauticians. Wonderful image. Instead of toiling beneath the surface of human dignity, dealing with the waste we would all rather not acknowledge, they were working to enhance others' dignity and their own, by working to help women look more beautiful. Pictures of these graceful former scavengers in white saris gladden the heart. Other scavenger women have also been trained to make pickles, have various jobs in food processing, do office jobs, and have received micro-credits for small businesses.

Lalta saw her pay go from 600 rupees a month to 2,000 rupees. More, she says: 'From a heap of humiliation to the heights of self-respect and self-confidence, I believe life has turned out miraculously for the good. I don't ask for more, for today I can stand and face the world with respect.'

When I hear people in rich countries lament appalling working or living conditions with no apparent way out, I remind them of Lalta and people like her in demeaning work all over the world, and the power of group action and vision to transform people's lives. It is worth bearing in mind, as we examine the evidence on work and health, that if the working conditions of India's scavengers can be improved by concerted action, all working conditions can be improved wherever we find them.

WORK AND HEALTH

We owe a great deal to a great Italian

Our understanding of the influence of work on health owes much to Bernardino Ramazzini. When I meet Italian colleagues I soon turn the conversation to Ramazzini. The usual reaction is: who? Bernardino Ramazzini was the father of occupational medicine. Born in Carpi in northern Italy, near Modena, he became professor of medicine in Modena, where he published his great book *De Morbis Artificum Diatriba*, Diseases of Workers, in 1700. Ramazzini instructed the physicians of his day that if they wished to understand what made workers ill they had to stop holding their noses and enter the workplace: 'I hesitate and wonder whether I shall bring bile to the noses of the doctors . . . if I invite them to come to the latrines.'[3]

Doctors belonged to one class, sufferers from occupational diseases to another. Ramazzini attracted the derision of other physicians by suggesting they might learn something from crossing the class barrier: 'and have not thought it beneath me to step in workshops of the meaner sort now and again and study the obscure operations of the mechanical arts'.[4] He suggested actually talking to people of the humbler orders to find out about their work, and hence their health. Talk to patients? Whatever next!

I would like to think that with modern epidemiological and toxicological science we know more now about work and health than Ramazzini did in 1700. Not a lot more, I have to admit. He observed, he recorded, and he linked workers' ailments to their work. His concern with working conditions did not imply neglect of the influence on health of other things in workers' lives.

INEQUITIES IN POWER, MONEY AND RESOURCES COME TO THE WORK PLACE – NOT JUST PHYSICAL AND CHEMICAL EXPOSURES: THREE WAYS WORK CAN DAMAGE HEALTH

Inequities in power, money and resources as causes of health inequity – it was the language we used in the report of the Commission on Social Determinants of Health. With only a little adaptation, it is a good description of how work can affect health. In general, the lower the social position, the greater the hazards – hence the contribution of work to inequities in health.

Ramazzini drew attention to physical and chemical hazards of work. Regrettably such hazards still prevail in many parts of the world, in agriculture, in mines, factories and construction sites, and in service work. We could, with a touch of poetic licence, call these inequities in physical resources. As the nature of work has changed in a post-industrial world, of even more concern are inequities in power in the workplace – the psychosocial conditions – features of Alan's workplace, but also rife in office-based and service work. And third, work can influence health by the obvious mechanism of money. Work can make people rich or keep them poor, and much in between. Both how much money you have in absolute amounts and how much relative to others affects health and health inequalities. The tragedy of Lalta's work as a scavenger was that she was subject to all three at the same time – inequities in power, money and resources.

Physical

It is tempting to believe that we have sorted out the first type of hazard, physical and chemical, in high-income countries with their high standards of occupational health. Tempting, but wrong – especially if we include ergonomic hazards. Here's the testimony, via an email to me, of someone from the US, I'll call her Emily, working in a job similar to Alan's:

> I was injured many times in the warehouse but was forced to con-
> tinue working or risk losing my job . . . My friend and many others,
> including myself warned safety personnel that the weight of totes
> [the goods the picker carried to the packer] were exceeding the
> limit according to safety standards. This was ignored and people
> were expected to meet the same rate [number of goods per hour]

by lifting totes that were three times heavier than safety standards. My friend bent down to grab one off the bottom shelf of a cart when she felt something snap in her back. She now suffers from a crushed disk in her back.

A European-wide panel survey on working conditions indicated that in 2005, every sixth worker was exposed to toxic substances at their workplace and many were subject to noise, at least intermittently.[5] Twenty-four per cent reported exposure to vibrations, 45 per cent were working in painful, tiring conditions and 50 per cent were confined to repetitive hand or arm movements, mainly due to computer work. Clear social gradients were observed in these adverse conditions.[6]

Don't we have occupational standards to deal with these kinds of hazard? Here's Emily's answer to that question, in the same email:

I have many friends who still work there because there are very little jobs to be found here. They feel trapped and therefore will keep subjecting themselves to the harsh conditions because they have no other choice. These people want a UNION and want to be heard, but fear if their names are released that they will either lose their job or be relocated to harsher conditions until they can't take it anymore and just quit.

No alternative employment; no union to represent workers' interests; inadequate or poorly enforced health and safety regulations. The history of improving working conditions makes it abundantly clear: trade unions and health and safety regulations played a vital role. Do you want the pilot of your commercial flight falling asleep over the controls, or drinking on the job? We expect entirely reasonable health and safety regulations to be followed. (As the grim joke has it: I want to die in my sleep like my dad; not

screaming in terror like his passengers.) Yet, read certain sections
of the press, and favourite hate objects are trade unions and 'health
and safety gone mad'. It is certainly true that in Britain in the 1970s,
had the trade unions hired public relations people with the explicit
instruction to ensure a bad press, they could hardly have trumped
what actually happened. In Britain, we have only to remember the
so-called 'winter of discontent' of 1978–9, when one trade union
after another struck to the great discomfort of the public, to think
that we do not want a return to unbridled power of trade union
bosses. But that does not mean that we should revel in unbridled
power of corporation bosses. It is entirely possible, and desirable, to
run profitable companies that do not pursue profit at the expense
of the physical and mental health of employees. Experience shows
that it is not wise to rely on the altruism of company owners. Both
health and safety regulations and effective trade unions make a
difference.

Difficulty enforcing health and safety standards in high-income
countries is as nothing compared with the problems in low-
and middle-income countries. It should not take the collapse of
a garment factory in Bangladesh with the death of more than
1,100 workers to remind us of lax standards.[7] In large parts of the
world most workers are in 'informal' employment, which means
it is extraordinarily difficult to impose standards of occupational
health.[8] But, do not despair. If Lalta's life can be improved, so can
Alan's and Emily's.

Psychosocial

One way to describe Alan's work is disempowering. More specifically, I described it in six ways: high demand and low control,
imbalance between effort and rewards, social isolation, organisational injustice, job insecurity, shift work. Each of these increases
risk of illness. Together they are a toxic cocktail.

These concepts, each backed by evidence, change the way we think about stress at work. Conventional wisdom had it that the demands work placed on high-status people increased their risk of heart disease and other ailments. Conventional wisdom is not always wrong, but it should not always be automatically trusted, especially if it asks us to reserve our sympathy for highly paid, high-status individuals. There are not vast numbers of high-status individuals striving to swap the boardroom for a quieter life in the open-plan office.

If you were going to study stress at work your first thought might not be the British Civil Service. It turns out it is quite a good real-life laboratory to study the effects of stress on health. Several years ago, the government's tax office (now Her Majesty's Revenue and Customs) was concerned because higher-grade tax officers had a high rate of suicide. Men and women doing this job told us that their in-tray was not their friend. On arrival at work, the first thing was to see quite how unfriendly the in-tray looked. The challenge of work became not to detect tax avoiders but to stem the in-tray tide that threatened to engulf them. The greater the height of the in-tray, the greater the threat of feeling like you could never get your head above water. They would start on the in-tray pile, work all day, and at the end of the day the pile was higher than it was at the beginning. Holidays made them unhappy because the tidal wave of paper would build up so that, on return, they would be engulfed. It wasn't just the ineluctable flow of work that did them in, but the lack of control. No matter how steadily, how hard, they worked, they fell further and further behind.

To make matters worse, the better they did their job, the more they were hated and the worse they felt. No member of the public thanked them for having been assiduous in pointing out 'mistakes' in their tax return. High effort, low reward and lack of control have the same effect in the office as they do in the warehouse.

My colleagues and I at UCL looked at the question of stress at work in a systematic way in the Whitehall II study of British Civil Servants. In the introduction I described the social gradient in death rates from heart disease and other diseases – the lower the grade of employment the higher the mortality – that we observed in the Whitehall study.[9] I think of it as 'life and death on the social gradient', and we saw similar gradients in the Whitehall II study of more than 10,000 men and women working in the Civil Service in and around London.[10]

In the Whitehall II study we showed that men and women whose work was characterised by high demands, low control and imbalance between efforts and rewards had increased risk of heart disease,[11] and of mental illness.[12] Further we asked a few questions about how fairly they felt the organisation treated them. We called this organisational justice. People who reported a lack of organisational justice had high rates of mental and physical illness.[13]

Just in case the thought occurred that there might be something atypical about civil servants, think about your own life. When does work, or life in general, feel most stressful? When you lose control. Most people can cope with being busy. If they are working parents, usually mothers, they can cope amazingly well with juggling work and life. When it all gets too much is when one cannot control what is happening. Trouble paying bills, pressure at work when you are worried about a sick child, demands from the landlord that cannot be ignored, then the heating fails, and the partner gets laid off and becomes morose. All contribute to a feeling of being unable to control events.

There have been several reviews of the evidence on what has been called the job-strain model: high demands, low control. A review of twenty-one studies of many thousands of people working in a variety of conditions shows that people whose jobs are characterised by high demands and low control have a 34 per cent increased risk of developing coronary heart disease compared with people without job strain.[14]

The second source of stress at work is effort without appropriate reward. To me, one of the most distressing aspects of Alan's work as a picker is that day after day his rewards were minimal – whether financial, or in terms of self-esteem, esteem in the eyes of others, promotion, or just about any form of reward one could think of. It is not only people low in the industrial food chain who need rewards; we all do. I was once in a meeting with a Nobel Prize winner, justly feted as one of the world's great thinkers. I quoted sentences from his work, and said how it had changed thinking. The great man grinned with pleasure. Even he, garlanded with recognition, needed the reward of knowing his contribution had been recognised. Rewards give life meaning, and help make the effort worth it.

Am I really alleging that failure to have someone say 'Thank you', and mean it, when you put in effort could increase risk of disease? That is to oversimplify. The reciprocal exchange of effort for money, status, recognition and self-esteem is vital. Its lack is stressful. Indeed, the evidence shows that effort–reward imbalance is associated with increased risk of heart disease, mental illness and sickness absence.[15] Similarly, organisational injustice and shift work increase the risk of ill-health.[16]

I could call this section the loneliness of the long-distance ware-house picker . . . and bureaucrat. Work can connect us socially, or isolate us, and everything in between. Social isolation is bad for health. It is one more indignity that follows the social gradient – not just more adverse things happening, but fewer potential social supports coming from a variety of sources. Whitehall II is but one example of several studies that show the lower the social position, the fewer social ties people have with friends, with co-workers, with neighbours, with clubs and organisations. The only category of social contacts that was more frequent at the bottom of the gradient was contact with family. This seems not to make up for lack in the other spheres.

My colleagues at UCL, Andrew Steptoe and Mika Kivimaki, conducted a review of nine studies, each of which followed people free of disease at the start of the study. Summarising all the data, they showed that men and women who were socially isolated and/ or lonely at the beginning of the study had a 50 per cent higher risk of developing coronary heart disease during the subsequent follow-up compared with those who were not lonely or isolated.[17] We cannot, of course, lay social isolation at the door of work. But work is one way people develop their social relations. Isolation at work cuts off one route to relief from loneliness.

Financial

During the Second World War the British economist William Beveridge produced a report with the unpromising title *Social Insurance and Allied Services*.[18] It is no exaggeration to say this report had a worldwide effect. It laid the basis for the welfare state in Britain, and influenced its development in many countries. Beveridge identified the importance of lack of income, which he called 'want', and then wrote: 'Want is one only of five giants on the road of reconstruction and in some ways the easiest to attack. The others are disease, ignorance, squalor and idleness.'

We are still dealing with Beveridge's five giants, in countries of low, middle and high income. Translating Beveridge into modern concerns: ignorance we can say is lack of education; squalor is the kind of destitution that causes babies to die in low-income countries, or people to live in cold homes in rich countries; idleness is lack of work. Given that I am concerned with the causes of health inequalities, my perspective is that four of the giants – want, ignorance, squalor and idleness – can lead to the fifth, disease. But the giants are interrelated. Lack of education can lead to unemployment; lack of employment to poverty.

Regrettably, work may not be the way out of poverty if the rewards of work are unequally distributed. In Britain, for example, Figure 6.1 shows alarming trends.

Poverty is defined as having income less than that needed for a healthy life. The number of people in poverty in workless households, including retired people, has declined. Good. But there has been an increase in poverty among those who work: by 2011/12 the majority of people in poverty were in working families. Not good.

In Britain, as elsewhere, our politicians speak in clichés that often are a barrier to both thought and communication. The simple account of economic trends is that the world is divided into hard-working families, strivers, and those dependent on state handouts of various forms, scroungers. One of the many problems with this rhetoric is that it clouds the fact that most of the people who do not have enough money to live on are in work.[19] In fact

FIGURE 6.1: WORK IS NO LONGER THE WAY OUT OF POVERTY

In-work poverty, UK 1996–2012: there are now more people in poverty in working families than in workless or retired families combined

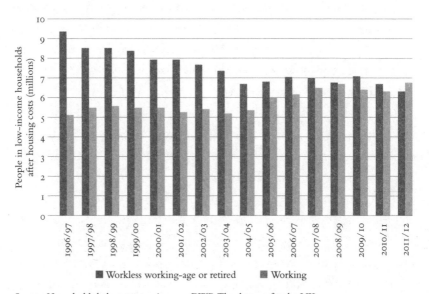

Source: Households below average income, DWP. The data are for the UK.

about three-quarters of working-age adults in low-income working households are in work. If work were the route out of poverty,
state handouts would be unnecessary for these households. The
problem is not lack of interest in work, it is low pay.

In the US, we have seen something similar. Figure 6.2 shows
what has been happening to incomes of men and women in full-
time employment.[20]

Men and women are sorted according to their income: P10 is
the bottom 10 per cent of earners; P90 is the top 10 per cent (the
90th centile). Over a twenty-five-year period incomes for men and
women in the top 10 per cent of incomes, P90 on the graph, grew
handsomely. But the lower the starting income the lower the growth
in incomes. In fact for men in full-time employment, the lower 50 per
cent of earners had a fall in real income (i.e. adjusted for inflation).

You won't have forgotten that I am concerned with the gradient, as well as with poverty. The fortunes of the middle groups are
therefore also of concern. The US is getting richer but the benefit

FIGURE 6.2: TO THEM THAT HAVE SHALL BE GIVEN...

US real earnings growth (%) for men and women working full-time by decile,
1980–2005

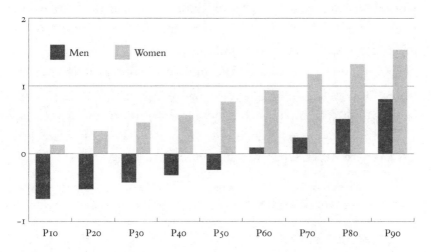

Source: OECD 2008.

is going overwhelmingly to the richest 10 per cent. As Figure 6.2 shows, not much of it reaches the bottom 80 per cent.

Simplifying and summarising, there are three ways to address low incomes of people of working age: improve the incomes of the working poor, get more people into work, and improve the incomes of people who for whatever reason are unable to work. Each of these is likely to reduce health inequalities.

Before we move from conditions in the workplace to employment conditions, we should ask an important question: is it work or the worker that is damaging health?

I argued in the previous two chapters on early life and education that it was not genes that determined the quality of early child development and educational achievement, but the nature of the social environment. But what if I were wrong, and it was the genes? What if it was genetic differences between people that decided who left education for an interesting well-paid job, and who ended up in work hell as Alan did; who found a good stable job and who went to no job at all? Even if all that were true, genes would not let work and employment off the hook.

It is the work that determines health outcomes, not just the worker. Whatever the process of getting into the job – whether fixed by the connections of your rich parents, earned by the sweat of your brow, allocated randomly by a throw of the dice by the great gambler in the sky, or determined by your genetic endowment – it is still reasonable to ask whether the nature of work, and of the employment contract, influences health.

Improve Lalta's working conditions, or Alan's, and their health is less likely to suffer, whatever their genetic makeup.

EMPLOYMENT CONDITIONS AND HEALTH

We have just been considering what happens at work and what it means for health. There are two aspects of what we may call employment conditions that are also relevant for health: unemployment and job insecurity. Let's start with unemployment.

Young people have been out on the streets of Madrid. They are angry and have styled themselves *indignados*. They are angry with good reason. Society's implied promise to them has been broken – grow up, go to school, study, prepare, and then it will be your turn to embark into the world of work, earn your living and do what every generation has done before. But not for them, it would seem. Unemployment among fifteen- to twenty-four-year-olds in Spain is 58 per cent. This figure may look worse than it is, as some young people might be in 'informal' employment – registered as unemployed but working in the grey or black economy. Even so, there is still a major issue of youth unemployment. In Greece the figures are even higher, 60 per cent of young people unemployed; in Italy more than 40 per cent.

This youth unemployment does not strike randomly: the higher the level of qualifications a person has, the more probable that they will enter employment when they leave education. So we can see the life course operate: the lower the level of early child development, the worse the educational attainment, and the greater the likelihood of unemployment.

Globally, the great recession has been disastrous for employment. The International Labour Organisation (ILO) estimates that in 2013 there were over 200 million people unemployed in the world. The global recession that began in 2008 has led to an increase of unemployment of more than 60 million over and above an already large figure.[21] As in Europe, so around the world young people aged fifteen to twenty-four are disproportionately affected – the unemployment rate in the young is three times higher than in older working-age people. An economic crisis begun in Wall Street and the City of London is depriving young people of work in North Africa and the Middle East, parts of Latin America and the Caribbean, as well as Southern Europe.

Elsewhere, the real unemployment is hidden. In a country like India, more than 80 per cent of working people are in the 'informal' sector. If the economy turns down, they do not go and register with their unemployment office – there is no such thing. They pick up rubbish, clean latrines, take whatever demeaning work is available. The alternative to work is not unemployment benefits. It is starvation if they do not do whatever it takes to earn a tiny amount of money.

Not usually given to hyperbole, I have described this youth unemployment as a public health time bomb. Unemployment is bad for health and it blights lives. Young people who leave school for the scrapheap are in danger of never getting the habit of work – potentially, they face a lifetime on the margin. Bad work may be bad for health; unemployment may be worse.

In the economic downturn in Britain in the 1980s, unemployment rose sharply. There was debate at the time as to whether this was bad for health.[22] Some economists argued that sick people are more likely to become unemployed, not that unemployment leads to sickness. The debate generated some heat, because there was little argument that government policy had put people out of work. If putting people out of work damaged their health, killed them even, then it was tantamount to saying that government policy was killing people. One British chancellor of the exchequer said: 'Rising unemployment and the recession have been the price that we have had to pay to get inflation down. That price is well worth paying.'[23] It is somewhat less likely that he would have said: rising unemployment and consequent damage to people's health have been the price we have had to pay to keep inflation down. That price is well worth paying. Not even a minister of finance would say that. At least, not publicly. Hence the government's desire to play down the links with ill-health.

It is scarcely credible when the number of unemployed goes from under 1 million to more than 3 million in about three years to claim that sickness is causing unemployment. My colleagues Peter

Goldblatt, Kath Moser and John Fox were centrally involved in that debate. In the end, the evidence settled the issue. They followed a 1 per cent sample of people identified in the 1971 national census in England and Wales and showed the same social gradient in mortality that we had seen in civil servants: the lower the social class, based on occupation, the higher the risk of dying. But for each social class, those who were unemployed in 1981 had about a 20 per cent higher mortality rate than those who were employed.[24]

Among other studies that confirm that unemployment damages health are those grouped under the acronym HAPIEE (Health, Alcohol and Psychosocial factors in Eastern Europe) which my colleague at UCL, Martin Bobak, and I set up with partners in the Czech Republic, Poland and Russia; Lithuania joined subsequently. The purpose of these studies was to investigate the reasons why health in the former communist countries of central and eastern Europe has been lagging far behind that in 'western' (using the term loosely) Europe. The hypotheses under test are contained in the title of the study, HAPIEE. We did medical examinations of nearly 30,000 people in the first three countries and have been following them since. After six years of follow-up the risk of dying in men and women who were unemployed at the start of the period was more than double that in the employed. Some of the reasons for this higher rate of mortality are that unemployed people are more likely to drink and smoke than those in employment. What else is there to do? Allowing for the fact that the unemployed had lower socio-economic positions, and were likely to have markers, such as smoking and poor diet, that put them at higher risk of dying, there was still a 70 per cent increased risk of dying.[25]

Unemployment is particularly bad for mental health. Some of our politicians claim that unemployment is a lifestyle choice. If so, it is an odd one as it puts people at increased risk of depression and suicide.

One way of examining the effects on health of unemployment is to follow employed and unemployed individuals and compare them. A different, more complex way is to see what happens to a country's health when the unemployment rate goes up.

David Stuckler from Oxford University looked at figures for Europe and showed that a rise in a country's unemployment rate was correlated with a rise in that country's suicide rate.[26] For me, a dramatic finding was that the size of the effect varied according to how generous a country was in its spending on social protection – which included unemployment benefits, active labour market programmes, family support and health care. If there were no spending on social protection a 3 per cent rise in unemployment would be associated with a 3 per cent rise in suicide. Eastern European countries spend on average US$37 a head on social protection. In these countries, a 3 per cent rise in unemployment was associated with a 2 per cent rise in suicide. In Western European countries, which spend on average about US$150 a head on social protection, a 3 per cent rise in suicide was associated with less than 1 per cent rise in suicide.

The conclusion from such complex analysis is straightforward: unemployment damages mental health so severely that it can even lead to suicide, but government policies can make a difference. The toxic combination is what Eastern European countries have done and what Southern European countries are being forced to do: have a high rate of unemployment *and* reduce spending on social protection.

To be clear about this, I do not know anyone who thinks Greece managed its finances well before the great recession. When I heard a figure that few Greek doctors in private practice declared an annual income greater than 10,000 Euros, I asked a Greek medical colleague: are the Greek tax officials corrupt or incompetent? His reply: in Greece it's hard to tell the difference. Greek government officials were either cooking the books or not keeping them, and the Greek population was practising tax avoidance on a grand scale. All that said, the policies thrust on them by the troika of the

European Commission, the European Central Bank and the IMF are damaging the health of the Greek population.

Job insecurity and health

Job insecurity is supposed to be a good thing. It's called labour market flexibility. Jobs for life? Stultifying, for the individual and the firm. At least that is the conventional wisdom. If workers are insecure they will be kept on their toes, work harder. I saw a cartoon at one workplace: 'The beatings won't cease until morale improves.'

When I presented evidence at a meeting that, in Spain, workers in insecure jobs had higher risk of mental illness than those in secure jobs I was greeted with the inevitable question: have you thought about causation? That is code for: it may be that people with mental illness are more likely to find themselves in insecure jobs. In other words, mental illness is causing job insecurity, not the other way round.

I do have an answer and it comes from the European Review on Social Determinants of Health and the Health Divide, which I led on behalf of the WHO Regional Office for Europe. Among the task groups we set up to review the evidence on social determinants of health was one on employment and working conditions. This task group summarised sixty-five studies of job insecurity with overwhelming evidence that it damages health, particularly mental health.[27] Particularly convincing are those cases where job insecurity is thrust on people by circumstances, by threatened closure or downsizing of an activity.

MAKING THINGS BETTER . . . BY GETTING CONDITIONS OF EMPLOYMENT RIGHT

Fair employment implies a just relation between employers and employees that requires that certain features be present: (1) freedom from coercion; (2) job security in terms of contracts and safe employment conditions; (3) fair income; (4) job protection and the availability of social benefits including provisions that allow harmony between working life and family life, and retirement income; (5) respect and dignity at work; (6) workplace participation; and (7) enrichment and lack of alienation.[28]

What world am I living in? you might think. I want employers and employees to treat each other with dignity. Before you dismiss me as living in some fairyland, let us return to India for a further example of how, with squalid starting conditions, change is possible.

In Ahmedabad, more than 30,000 women worked picking paper and rubbish from the roads. For working in the dirt of the streets, carrying loads of paper of up to 20 kg for twelve hours a day, they received 5 rupees. They had no legal protection, no control over the unsanitary nature of their working conditions, and no job security. The Self Employed Women's Association got involved in organising these women. Several organisations were formed. One example was the Soundarya Cleaning Cooperative, which negotiates contracts with clients, individual households, residential tower blocks, offices and institutions including academies. There is now control over working conditions, more job security, and the pay is better: 5,000 rupees a month rather than 5 rupees a day. For weddings and Divali festival it is 300 rupees a day.

To repeat what I said when discussing the pickers in the warehouse: one way of improving working conditions is to have organised labour. There was a time when 'trade union' was a respectable label, rather than a term of derision, as it now is in some circles. Another is to enforce health and safety regulations.

... AND PURSUING POLICIES THAT CREATE JOBS, NOT DESTROY THEM — THE CAUSES OF THE CAUSES

I implied above that the worldwide problem of unemployment in the wake of the Great Recession, particularly of young people, was first caused by irresponsible behaviour of whizz kids in financial institutions whose greed led to financial collapse. If in doubt read Michael Lewis's book *The Big Short*.[29] Second, I stated that policies of austerity put in place in the wake of the Great Recession made unemployment worse. If the second is true, why would governments pursue policies of austerity?

In fact, faced with the economic problems of the Great Recession economists and politicians seem to have taken up one of two positions. One side thinks we have to reduce the national debt to get economic growth; the other that we have to get economic growth in order to reduce the national debt. Amplifying a little, expansionary austerians believe that imposing policies of austerity, reducing the annual deficit and paying down national debt will enhance the confidence of the private sector and restore economic growth. Keynesians are of the view that with demand depressed, households and businesses are reluctant to invest and consume – Keynes's 'paradox of thrift'. Government must step in and, despite high levels of public debt, spend to stimulate the economy – counter-cyclical investment. Paul Krugman, Nobel Prize-winning Keynesian, characterises expansionary austerianism as belief in the confidence fairies. Austerians sneer that the Keynesian solution to high debt is more debt.

Before asking who's right, it is worth noting that views about the economic remedy appear to be correlated with positions on the ideological spectrum: austerians to the right, Keynesians to the left (although Keynes himself was not of the left and was concerned to save capitalism). Why is this so? Naively, one might have thought that it was an empirical question as to which policy 'worked'. It is likely, however, that austerians tend to be more suspicious of government solutions and less concerned with distributive effects of policies – harming the poor. Keynesians have a readier acceptance of the importance of government policies and practice, and are more concerned with inequality – more so, perhaps, than was Keynes himself. Because of this political alignment, it is hard to debate about the evidence. As so often, what should be an informed debate about evidence is a none-too-veiled contest about prior political beliefs, or short-term low-level politics.

It is difficult for a non-economist to penetrate the argument and form an independent judgement. It can be noted that the intellectual case for austerity has suffered a couple of recent blows. Austerians have cited, among others, the Harvard economists Carmen Reinhart and Kenneth Rogoff, who set out to show that when national debt climbs above 90 per cent of GDP, economic growth slows.[30] They showed it, except that a graduate student checking their figures found elementary errors that cast considerable doubt on their conclusions.[31]

Second, the IMF, which arguably has wreaked great havoc globally with its universal prescription to cut government spending, has published new estimates that austerity has a bigger effect on slowing economic growth than it used to think.[32] In Britain, the Office of Budget Responsibility says that it subscribes to the widely held assumption that fiscal contraction damages growth. The intellectual argument is under threat, but austerians are still winning the political and public relations argument across Europe and in the USA.

There is another objection to this debate: the main criterion of success of economic policy appears to be growth of GDP. But what if we had a wider set of considerations? We want economic and social policy to do more than deliver economic growth. Policies should also be evaluated for their impacts on people's lives. An important way of doing that is to look at the health impacts of policy. My entry into the debate is that if austerity leads to unemployment, particularly of young people, it has to be tempered by judicious investment and active labour market programmes.

Working locally

Earlier in the chapter, I agonised over the huge problem of young people leaving school to go straight to the unemployment scrap-heap, of being 'not in employment, education or training' – NEET. Think what that means to a young person, now and in the future. In the previous section I concluded that answers to the big macro-economic questions will have an important influence on the avail-ability of jobs. While these debates are happening, what should the young people on the streets of Madrid or Athens be doing?

It turns out that local action can make a difference. Consider these two examples from the Welsh city of Swansea.

Gareth and Derek are typical of young people growing up in the less affluent parts of Swansea. They went to their local state schools. School was not much to Gareth's liking. He had been in trouble for bad behaviour, had some minor truancy problems, and he and his teachers engaged in mutual disregard, but he got 5 Cs in his General Certificate of Secondary Education exams. To explain, at age fifteen–sixteen every young person in Britain takes so-called GCSE exams. The benchmark of success the government uses is the proportion of young people who gain five GCSEs at C or above. Nationally, the average is 68 per cent. But five Cs is not outstanding. The average scores of people who go on to Oxford or Cambridge is eight A*s and two As.

Gareth, then, was a just-average student, hadn't found a subject he wanted to pursue, and he left at age sixteen rather than trying to get into the local sixth form college to do A-levels. He would have liked to find employment, but wasn't sure where to go or what to do. He applied for a couple of jobs but they went to people who had more experience or better qualifications. When he turned eighteen he signed up for unemployment benefits, and as a conse-quence, after six months got enrolled in some short-term training courses. These didn't lead to sustainable employment. By the time he was twenty-one, Gareth had spent most of the last four years not in employment, education or training. He wanted to leave home, but could not afford rent. He tried living with a girlfriend but that didn't work out. She was employed in the local supermarket and did not appreciate paying rent for Gareth. He was back home with his parents, who he regularly argued with. He claimed unemployment benefits and supplemented this income with small-time drug dealing. Gareth's story is typical of those termed NEET.

Derek went to a different but similar school in Swansea. He was also on track to get mostly Cs in his GCSEs. However, before he sat his exams, at the start of Year 11, he was identified by the school as someone at risk of becoming NEET. As a result, he was offered a range of support by Careers Wales, the local council and his school. While he was still in school, Derek was offered a work experience placement at the local authority. He was also assigned a personal adviser with whom he could discuss the options and opportunities open to him, and the school worked with him to reduce his truancy. Derek did not particularly like school, so it helped that his adviser was not a member of the school staff, and they met outside school. Derek left school at sixteen, but support was maintained, particularly over the summer right after he finished. This helped him to enrol in a six-month training course starting in September, which included employability skills and placements in a local manufacturing company. The training course also included a discretionary fund for staff, some of which they allocated to Derek to enable him to buy tools and interview clothes. At the end of his six-month training course, the local company interviewed Derek and then offered him a one-year apprenticeship. Now he has a permanent full-time position at the company as a technician.

Derek's experience is typical of what Swansea and another Welsh town, Wrexham, achieved as shown in Figure 6.3.

By focusing on the problem in a strategic way, working with young people, giving them access to information, and perhaps

FIGURE 6.3: GETTING INTO WORK IN SWANSEA AND WREXHAM

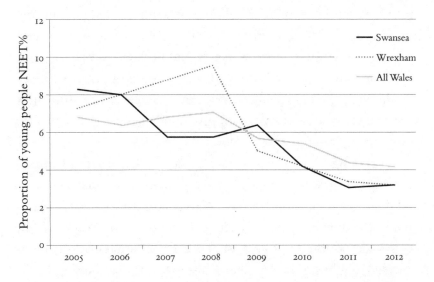

Note: NEET = not in employment, education or training
Source: UCL Institute of Health Equity. *Reducing the Number of Young People Not in Employment, Education or Training (NEET)*. Public Health England, 2014.

above all, caring, authorities in these towns lowered the toll of young people not in employment, education or training.

There was an unexpected benefit. Youth offending in Swansea fell from over 1,000 incidents a year to fewer than 400.[33] Correlation is not causation. One cannot say that the reduction in NEETs was responsible for the reduction in youth offending, but it is certainly possible.

Unemployment harms health and work is vital. When work is of 'good' quality it is empowering. It provides power, money and resources – all essential for a healthy life. The 'good' characteristics of work tend to follow the social gradient: greater empowerment and better conditions go with higher status. Not always, but the highly paid lawyers and hedge-fund managers have considerable compensation for the ridiculous hours that they work. Bond traders, who Tom Wolfe called 'Masters of the Universe', may feel stressed, but they are in control.[34]

In low-income countries, the nature of working life too often resembles the Dickensian conditions that high-income countries have put behind them. Further, with the export of undesirable jobs from high-income countries to low, the problem is not so much solved as transferred. Solutions to improving working conditions should be applied globally, but examples of local action show how working life can be transformed – witness the scavengers of India or the young unemployed of Wales.

A worrying trend is that work will increasingly be stratified into well-paid empowering work for people with education and skills and the reverse for those without. Global competition can lead to a race to the bottom. Worse working conditions and cheaper labour costs make a country more attractive for transnational corporations. Highlighting the problem is a step towards addressing it.

I said in Chapter 5 that education was central because it provided the key connection between early life and the grown-up world of work. I could say the same here. Work is central because it provides the crucial link between earlier life and those older years, beyond working age, that are stretching ever further. It is those years of later life that claim our attention next.

7

Do Not Go Gentle

Fool: If thou wert my fool, nuncle, I'd have thee beaten for being old before thy time.
Lear: How's that?
Fool: Thou shouldst not have been old till thou hadst been wise.

William Shakespeare, *King Lear* (Act I, Scene v)

Older age is a terrible time. Poverty, misery, social isolation, declines in intellectual and physical function, no social role and, old age being a kind of evolutionary accident, there is little wonder that older people get all kinds of illnesses. As well as being a misery to themselves, older people add to everyone else's misery by being a drag on society.

Like most stereotypes the description I have just given is not completely wrong, it is simply inadequate and misleading. It does not capture the rich variety in the lives of older people as they are actually lived in different countries and, given my central theme, in people living in different social circumstances. The inevitable declines that come with age pose challenges for health and social care. It can be done well, and it can be done badly. The Harvard surgeon and writer Atul Gawande asks, in a sensitive way, what the appropriate response of a caring, compassionate health-care system should be – neither neglect nor heroic over-treatment in attempting futilely to stave off the inevitable.[1]

Important as it is, health and social care for the elderly is not my topic here. I want to explore what happens before people need their final episodes of care. Consistent with my general theme, I will look at inequities in the conditions that lead to health and effective functioning. For some, older age is one stop before the scrapheap. But it does not have to be. For others it is a time of personal flourishing and contributions to family and the wider society. Here is the testimony of Maria, a ninety-year-old Brazilian woman:

> The situation has changed for older people in my country since the Law for the Rights of Older People [*Estatuto do Idoso*] was approved [in 2003]. Even after the Policy for Older People was adopted, older people abandoned their sandals and their rocking chairs and started having a life. Now we are supported by the law. We can demand our rights.
>
> Overall, there has been a change in the way society sees older people ... Now what we need are jobs and respect in the streets. Holes in the street are the biggest enemy of the older person. That is why falls prevention classes are so important. I used to have terrible falls, I even bruised my face. After going to classes I've never fallen again. Another thing is that the bus drivers are not prepared. The buses should always stop at the kerb but they don't – the companies are not worried.
>
> Now we are better respected. It is good to be able to buy half-price tickets for the theatre and concerts. Before, we couldn't go because it was too expensive. Now it is affordable and the bus pass is free too. Even buses between cities are free. I feel fortunate to have this life, I realize not everyone is so fortunate.
>
> I used to avoid going to the bank. I kept my money at home. We older people did that because we couldn't face waiting at the bank for hours. Sometimes we just gave up and went home because the lines were too long, but now there are priority lanes for older people.

We need to end the separation between older and younger people. We can share experiences with each other, which is very exciting. Younger people are starting to better understand older people. They are learning that we also have the right to sing, to dance, to talk.

There are still many things left to do, but a lot has improved.[2]

Obviously, this woman was misinformed – she didn't realise that older people, stuck in their misery, destitution and sickness, were supposed to be grateful for whatever crumbs a charitable society bequeathed them. She thought that older people should have enough money and resources to be able to do things – material empowerment. She wanted the conditions to enable her to control her life and participate, be they repairing the holes in the street, accessible transport, affordable tickets or respect and jobs – psychosocial empowerment. She demanded rights and support of the law – political empowerment.

Her lucid prose makes me wonder whether she is no ordinary older person. But then, should that not be the message: recognise that older people, just like people at all other ages, have the capacity to be extraordinary as well as ordinary. Social action will further that capacity. Recognising the rights of people of all ages will improve all our lives.

My theme through the book is that inequities in society lead to inequities in health. In this chapter, I will focus on inequities in health and functioning of older people between countries and inequities between social groups within countries. By doing so, I hope to address a further challenge to a moral society: inequities between older people and the rest of society. Year on year, as age creeps on, I become less tolerant of these age-based inequities. Maria from Brazil is my heroine, along with the novelists, orchestra conductors, the Rolling Stones, charity organisers and local volunteers who in their later decades make society just a little better.

Old in the global north, young in
the global south?

Perhaps the question should be, not what is Maria aged ninety in Brazil doing demanding her rights, but how come there are Marias aged ninety in a middle-income country like Brazil, part of the global south? Isn't the issue that there are lots of young people in the south, lots of older people in the north? It was, but it is changing very rapidly.

In France in 1865, 7 per cent of the population were aged sixty-five or over. By 1980, 115 years later, that proportion had doubled to 14 per cent. By contrast, what took France 115 years is predicted to take Brazil twenty-one years – going from 7 per cent elderly in 2011 to 14 per cent in 2032 – and South Korea about eighteen years.[3] As my Brazilian colleague Alex Kalache, retired head of ageing at WHO Geneva, says: the North grew rich before it grew old, the South is growing old before it grows rich. Put simply, rich countries have the money to enable people beyond working age to have a reasonable standard of living, if they are so inclined. By 'they', of course, I mean the countries. It is a reasonable bet that most older people would themselves be inclined towards a reasonable standard of living. Increasingly, in democracies, that inclination is becoming a powerful political force.

The world is indeed ageing rapidly, as shown in Figure 7.1. By 2020 the balance will have shifted from young to old. There will be a higher percentage of people aged sixty-five or above than children aged younger than five.

An ageing population is a reason to rejoice, to celebrate, for two chief reasons. First, populations are ageing because people are not dying young. In low-income countries the probability that a child will survive into adulthood has improved dramatically. How many adjectives may I be permitted: this achievement is astonishing, wonderful, remarkable, and its speed was probably a great deal more rapid than most experts predicted. In short, it is a cause for celebration.

FIGURE 7.1: MULTIPLE SHADES OF GREY

Young children and older people as a percentage of global population,
1950–2050

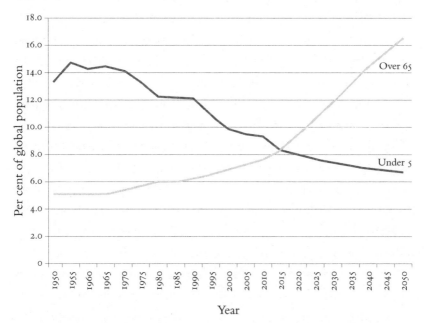

Source: United Nations Population Division. World Population Prospects: The 2012 Revision.
File POP/9-1: Percentage total population (both sexes combined) by broad age group, major area,
region and country, 1950-2100. 2013 [04/06/2014].

The second reason to celebrate an ageing population is that older
age can be a wonderful time of life – just think of the testimony of
Maria from Brazil. People over sixty-five can be creative, produc-
tive, carers, lovers, voters, citizens, consumers and enjoyers of what
a society has to offer. They receive, certainly, but they contribute a
great deal, too.

We cannot think about ageing without thinking about gender.
Sex, too, probably, but here I am concerned with gender. As the world
ages, it grows more female. Towards the end of his life, close to his
ninetieth birthday, my father voluntarily moved from his apartment

into sheltered accommodation – his own apartment with communal meals. Having lunch with him there one day I watched an elderly lady, white hair beautifully coiffured, shuffle past with her Zimmer frame. My dad smiled and said: she is one of my favourites. The elderly lady looked wistful, with just a touch of mischief, as she said: he has a lot of favourites here. Indeed, there was a choice for the men in this residence for elderly people: three men and forty-five women.

Women are hardier than men. Unless there is egregious discrimination against them, women can expect to live longer. As a result, today, for every hundred women over sixty worldwide there are eighty-four men. For every hundred women aged eighty and above, there are sixty-one men. The implications are that the greater the discrimination against women in education, jobs, owning property, receiving financial assistance, and general place in society, the worse will be the lot of the older population.

There is ample reason to adjust our angle of vision when concerned with inequities in global health. We know how to prevent child deaths and, increasingly, that knowledge is being applied. But globally the much bigger problem is going to be deaths at older ages. By 2025–30, the UN predicts, 62 per cent of all deaths globally will occur among the over-sixty-fives.[4] Of course, dying at a great age is a good deal more socially acceptable than deaths in childhood. It is the inequities in death at older ages that concern me here.

GREAT INEQUITIES IN LENGTH OF LIFE . . .
BETWEEN COUNTRIES

Here's a question: you have reached age sixty and want to know your prospects for further survival. Are they better if you had to fight off all sorts of hazards to survive to age sixty and could therefore class yourself as a hardy survivor? Or are they better if you had a cushy ride to age sixty, most people in your society get there, and had little to contend with?

I can make the choice more tangible. In Japan 92 per cent of fifteen-year-old boys and 96 per cent of fifteen-year-old girls can expect to reach the age of sixty. By contrast, in Russia, only 66 per cent of boys and 87 per cent of girls will get to sixty. Who will have better prospects for survival after sixty, Japanese or Russians?

The Japanese win it by a large margin: healthier before age sixty, they can expect to live many more years after that age.

Figure 7.2 gives the figures plus a few more examples. It is a remarkably close fit. I have listed the countries in order of the healthiest male survival to age sixty. There are exceptions, but in general, the worse the survival before age sixty, the fewer years you can expect to live after sixty. It is staggering that men in Russia should have worse health than men in India, but we will take that up in a subsequent chapter.

To remind you, a few years of life expectancy may not seem much, but it matters a lot. Japanese women have the longest life expectancy in the world. A Japanese woman of sixty can expect, on average, to live a further twenty-nine years. An American woman can expect to live a further twenty-four years. Is the difference between eighty-nine and eighty-four much to write home about? First, it is if you're eighty-four, and have tickets to hear Bob Dylan next month. Second, we calculated that abolition of coronary heart

FIGURE 7.2: HEALTHIER BEFORE 60, HEALTHIER LATER

	Probability (%) that a 15-year-old boy will survive to 60	Probability (%) that a 15-year-old girl will survive to 60	Life expectancy at 60 in years (men)	Life expectancy at 60 in years (women)
Japan	92	96	23	29
UK	91	94	22	25
USA	87	92	21	24
Brazil	79	89	19	22
India	76	84	16	18
Russia	66	87	14	20

Source: World Health Organization. *World Health Statistics 2014*. Geneva: WHO, 2014.

disease from the population, removing it statistically, would add just under four years to life expectancy. If I said that we were moving to abolish the major cause of death, that would sound revolutionary. That is what four years of life expectancy means. One year is impressive and worth having. Four years is enormous. And nine years, the difference between Russians and Japanese, is, well, staggering.

In Chapter 4 I took up the question of whether what does not kill us makes us stronger. I said that was not true when it comes to the adverse effects of early child experiences. What does not kill us harms us. That, I think, is what is going on here. There is no hardy survivor effect to be seen: less healthy on average before age sixty, fewer years of life still in store. The two likely explanations are first that similar hazards affect each age group. Drinking dirty water or sleeping on the street is bad for your health whatever age you are. So too are relative deprivation, social disadvantage and unhealthy lifestyle. Second, health at older ages is affected by the prior life course. Health and well-being in later life is affected by experience along the way. By no means does this mean that it is all over for today's older people if their mothers didn't cuddle them when they were babes in arms. Both life-course influences *and* contemporary circumstances, the kinds of things that Brazilian Maria finds so important, are linked to health inequities in later life.

. . . AND WITHIN COUNTRIES

Here is a remarkable finding. You finish your education in your teens or early twenties and the level of education you achieved predicts your chances of surviving four, five or more decades later. Figure 7.3 shows a set of figures for life expectancy at fifty – in Chapter 5 we saw something similar for life expectancy at twenty-five.

The figures shown are for the lowest and highest education, but intermediate levels of education have intermediate levels of life expectancy. It is a gradient.

FIGURE 7.3: CAN EDUCATION HAVE SUCH LONG-LASTING EFFECTS?

Life expectancy at age 50

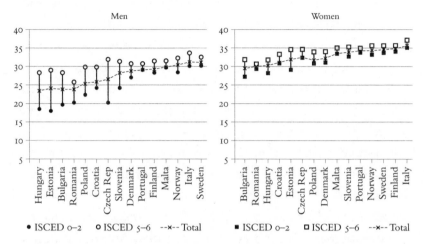

Countries are ranked by life expectancy at the specified age of the sex-specific total population.
ISCED 0–2: pre-primary, primary and lower secondary education.
ISCED 5–6: tertiary education and research
Source: Eurostat. Life expectancy by age, sex and educational attainment (ISCED 1997) 2012
[updated 2012/07/27].

There are, though, big differences between countries, particularly for those with the lowest level of education, ISCED 0–2 (ISCED is the international social classification of education). As a result health inequities are much bigger in Hungary and Estonia than they are in Sweden, Italy, Norway and Malta.

Suppose you were in Hungary and were trying to use these figures to convince your child to get serious about school – evidence-based parenting. The following conversation might take place:

YOU: You must work harder in school.

CHILD: But I'm having fun being a child, nourishing my soul and gladdening my heart, smelling the flowers and revelling at the crisp blue of a sparkling spring … [a very lyrical child]

YOU: If you go to university you'll have a longer life.

CHILD: I am a child. Why should I care about a longer life?

YOU: A longer life is not just good in itself, it is an indicator that you have enjoyed better social conditions throughout your life.

CHILD: If you were so concerned about my having a long life, or a better life, why didn't you arrange for me to be born in Sweden instead of Hungary? People with little education in Sweden have a better chance to survive after age fifty than people with tertiary education in Hungary.

YOU: Be quiet and eat your Brussels sprouts.

CHILD: Pulling rank is the last refuge of a scoundrel.

YOU: OK. We *are* in Hungary. Not too much we could do about that. But look at the figures in 7.3. Remember, we are using life expectancy not just as a good thing in itself but as an indicator that life has treated us better. It is worse to be in Hungary than in Sweden, true, but you can reduce the disadvantage by having more education. The gap between Sweden, Italy and Norway on the one hand, and Hungary, Estonia and Bulgaria on the other, is much bigger for people with little education. Go to university and you get closer to closing the gap.

CHILD: Hmm. So, education is important everywhere, as a predictor of a longer and, if you say so, a better life. But knowing what a subjunctive clause is can't be everything. Why should being good at grammar make a bigger difference to life in Hungary than in Sweden?

YOU: Good point, well made. Education probably is good in itself. It gives you life skills, puts you more in charge of what happens to you in life; but in addition, in most countries, more education gets you a better job, more income, a better place to live. If social conditions are pretty good for everybody, in Sweden for example, then having the special advantage of more education perhaps matters a little less. In Hungary it will matter more.

CHILD: So, having more education in Hungary gets me metaphorically halfway across the Baltic to Sweden, while staying right here in Hungary.

YOU: You're there already!

INEQUITIES IN QUALITY OF LIFE

Before we ask what it is about education that seems to have such long-lasting effects, it makes sense to consider not just length of life, but quality too. At younger ages we feel immortal. Young people can abuse their bodies in all kinds of interesting and exciting ways and appear to get away with it. Who knows, perhaps Maria in Brazil at nineteen was concerned at how many hours she could dance the night away and for how many days on end. At ninety, her life can be transformed if the bus stops closer to the kerb and the potholes are filled in. She can then enjoy the advantage of cut-price theatre tickets and the company of friends.

At older ages, we want to be alive but, more important, we want to be 'alive'. If the stereotype of older-age misery with which I began this chapter were true, a few more years of life would not be such a bargain. I said above that the difference between living to eighty-four and eighty-nine is highly significant if you are eighty-four. Possibly. If you are severely disabled another five years of life may seem a lot less attractive than another five years of golf, opera and luxury travel.

Golf at eighty? Really? It does appear so. In England, at age eighty-plus, more than 60 per cent of people describe their health as 'good', 'very good', or 'excellent'. These figures come from the English Longitudinal Study of Ageing (ELSA), which follows a representative sample of the English population. We look not only at how they feel but what they can do – their functioning. A good measure is walking speed – how fast is one's normal pace. Walking speed is highly correlated with reports of difficulty with the ordinary activities of daily life. At age eighty to eighty-four, nearly three-quarters of women and more than 80 per cent of men have no difficulty with walking speed.[5]

Golf is manageable by most people in England at eighty, except that it isn't, because only the more privileged play golf. Ditto opera and luxury travel. I choose them advisedly. If you have wealth not only will you have the money for golf, opera and travel, you are also more likely to have the health, physical and mental function needed to enjoy them. There is a sharp social gradient in health and functioning at older ages. In ELSA men and women of high status, measured by wealth or education, had the same level of reported good health as people of low status who were fifteen years younger. A seventy-five-year-old in the highest education group had the same likelihood of good health as a sixty-year-old in the lowest. In these years of mid- to later life, high status means not getting old so quickly.[6]

It may be that people of high status and those of low have similar rates of decline, but the high-status start from a higher level. I heard of a chess grand master who complained that he used to plan nine moves ahead. Now in his dotage he was reduced to five moves ahead. When he died, soon after, he was found to have the pathological picture of advanced Alzheimer's in his brain. He noted marked decline in his cognitive ability, yet he was still functioning at a level most of us could only dream of. The point is that if you start from a high level, even with the inevitable toll of age you can still function at a high enough level not only to lead an independent life, but to flourish.

I am not for a moment suggesting that nothing changes at older ages, but we should think of gains as well as losses.[7] Joints are stiffer, everything is slower – getting about, recovery from injury, remembering names – but some things get better. Knowledge, experience, reasoned solutions to problems, all improve with age. Wisdom is not a bad word for it. These, too, follow the social gradient.

At older ages, particularly then, reducing inequities in health means reducing inequities in physical and mental functioning as well as in mortality and length of life. In the first figure in this book, Figure 1.1, I showed that the social gradient in health was steeper for disability-free life expectancy than for life expectancy. The lower the position in the hierarchy the more years of life spent in disability – shorter lives with more pain and discomfort. Happily, there is good news to report on what can be done. Empowering older people and recognising their rights to a continued place in society is key.

ACHIEVING HEALTH EQUITY AT OLDER AGES

The great affairs of life are not performed by physical strength, or activity, or nimbleness of body, but by deliberation, character, expression of opinion. Of these, old age is not only not deprived but, as a rule, has them in greater degree . . .

Cicero on Old Age

We can wring our hands at the ageing of the world's population, subscribe to the miserable stereotype with which I began this chapter, and . . . then what? Then nothing. It is a counsel of despair. The world's population *is* ageing, and growing older will happen to all of us. Let's embrace it and recognise that, as I have just described, in many countries significant proportions of the older population are flourishing, but there are marked social inequities. The challenge is, as it is at earlier stages of life, to bring everyone up to the level of health and functioning of the most privileged – to reduce the social gradient in health by levelling up.

The best way to reduce social inequities in health at older ages is undoubtedly to start at the beginning of life. Arrive at age sixty or sixty-five with better cognitive function, better physical functioning and better health, and the future looks rosier than if you are lower on these measures – fifteen more years of rosiness for those in the top income, wealth or education group than for those in the bottom.

There is, though, much that can be done at later ages and for all social groups. Strong evidence comes from the United Nations. Some UN reports, by the time they have been through the political wringer of approval by member states, come out looking wrinkled and shrunken. Not all do. *Ageing in the Twenty-First Century: A Celebration and a Challenge* is a remarkably robust report from the UN Population Fund (UNFPA) and Help Age International, a charity.[8] At its heart it puts ageing with dignity and security and enjoying life through the full realisation of human rights or fundamental freedoms. The report appeals not only because it has good analyses of practical actions but because it has dignity and freedoms at its heart and makes the explicit link between dignity and economic security.

When I lecture to first-year medical students, I explain to them the concept of Minimum Income for Healthy Living.[9] A minimum income includes not only what is necessary for food and shelter, but what is required to live a life of dignity and to take one's place in society. An older person needs money for transport, to enable social engagement, and to buy presents for the grandchildren. I say to these brilliant young medical students who have performed extraordinarily well to get into medical school: you came to UCL to learn about genomics, and proteomics, and metabolomics, and here is a professor telling you that if your granny has too little money to buy you presents she is denied a life of dignity, which will be damaging to her health. The students love it!

This paragraph is a diversion. Indulge me, please. The concept of Minimum Income for Healthy Living was developed by Professor Jerry Morris. Jerry was a pioneer in what was then called Social Medicine in Britain. He was the one who put exercise and health on the map. He had showed that conductors on London's double-decker buses had lower rates of heart disease than drivers. Wiry, short, energetic, he would grab your elbow in an iron grip and order you to have lunch with him. Then would follow the rare privilege of ranging with him across his intellectual terrain from biochemistry to social welfare policies. After his ninetieth birthday, he was publishing papers on this 'new' concept he had developed: minimum income for healthy living. In 2008, after we published *Closing the Gap in a Generation*, the report of the WHO Commission on Social Determinants of Health, Jerry rang me at home one Saturday afternoon and said:

'Michael! Your report has transformed the debate.'
   Praise indeed. But, panic. Had I remembered to quote his work on minimum income? I had the report on my desk, thumbed quickly through it, and . . . Aha!
   'We quoted you on page ninety,' I said.
   'And on page seventy-nine,' said Jerry.

He was ninety-eight when that conversation took place. But still, he did what academics will: did they cite my work? That is healthy ageing. I have acknowledged one of my great teachers. Diversion over.

Ageing in the Twenty-First Century reports that, worldwide, the two most frequently mentioned concerns of older people are income security and health. They are closely linked.

I have stated already that the social gradient in health in older people has its origins in the life course. The time to start is before birth. Yet I am about to lay out evidence that there is much we can do at older ages to improve health and functioning and reduce social inequities. The evidence is of variable quality. Yet I reach conclusions. Suppose some of the evidence is not correct. Suppose empowering older people to lead lives of dignity and independence did not improve their health, and that being physically and socially active did not slow the rate of cognitive decline. Have we done damage by pursuing these ends? Is it a bad thing that older people should not have to choose between heating their home and eating, that they should be able to use public transport and make use of cut-price tickets to concerts and theatre, that the environment should make it easier for them to see friends and family? My own view is that these interventions *will* make a difference to health equity. But even if I am wrong, even if they won't improve health, they will make a significant contribution to the well-being of older people and their chance to lead lives of dignity. That, surely, is justification enough.

EMPOWERMENT: MATERIAL, PSYCHOSOCIAL AND POLITICAL

Hearken to Maria from Brazil. I described her needs as empowerment: material, psychosocial and political. They overlap. I think of social participation as psychosocial, but having enough money enables Maria to participate in a way that otherwise she could not. Fixing the potholes is 'material', but doing so enables her to get out more with confidence. Having rights is political, but may lead to action in the other domains.

Material empowerment . . . through wealth

You have reached retirement age, no more income from work. Now what do you live on? One aristocratic luminary in British public life described his parents as being members of the idle rich. Some fathers were richer, he said, but none was idler. The first possibility then is that some tiny percentage of the world's population can live on returns from their wealth. They are, in effect, members of the rentier class. Even in rich countries, though, most people have at most two assets, their dwelling and their pensions, and many do not have even that. Thus, even in high-income countries income from capital is not a route out of old-age poverty for most people.

. . . *and work*

A second possibility is to keep working beyond the formal retirement age, or for societies to change the retirement age. Here we
have the twin issues of gender discrimination and socio-economic
inequalities. In Chapter 6 I described the lot of Lalta, a human
scavenger in India. Even when she was retrained as a beautician
she was in informal employment – no job security, low pay. If a
younger woman comes along, she is easily dispensable. Even were
she fit enough to keep working beyond sixty or sixty-five, there
may simply be no work for her to do.

Globally, women are more likely than men to be in the informal
sector, to have less education, to be discriminated against when it
comes to work opportunities, and to have been paid less than men
doing the same job. They are also likely to outlive their husbands,
hence be single, and to be important in family caring. All of these
combine to make it more likely that older-age poverty is female
poverty. In the future this will change, as women's education
catches up on men's and, we hope, gender discrimination becomes
less widespread.

Suppose a country said that it would delay retirement age from
sixty-five to sixty-eight, so that people could work longer to keep
themselves out of poverty, or at least relative poverty. Step forward
employers and potential employees. What happens next? Employers
are likely to want people with skills and education. And potential
employees, if they are to seek work, have to be fit enough to do
it. Both of these mean that continuing in work to later ages is a
possibility that tracks the socio-economic gradient.

England serves as a modal example. As we saw in Figure 1.1
(p. 26), there is a striking social gradient in disability-free life
expectancy: the lower the socio-economic level the shorter is disability-free life expectancy. For people at the most deprived end of
the scale, disability-free life expectancy is about fifty-five; at the
upper end about seventy-two. The most affluent could do physical

work but probably wouldn't want to; the least affluent might want to, but couldn't do it. Not a good match.

Working longer is, and should be, a possibility, but why do we find it so hard to build in flexibility? For some, in privileged occupations, stopping work is anathema. A friend, a professor at a prestigious US university, tells me that half the full professors in his school are over seventy and some are in their eighties. It seems obvious that the old should step aside to make way for the young. There are only so many jobs to go around, and if the old won't move the young can't have them. Obvious, but wrong. The idea that older people are blocking jobs for younger people – the 'lump of labour' hypothesis – has been debunked as a myth.[10] The flaw is to assume that there is a fixed number of jobs. The evidence shows that, in general, the higher the participation of older people in the labour market the *higher* the employment rate of younger people – more jobs for the old and more jobs for the young. Yes, there may indeed be circumstances when the old should make way for the young – new brooms, fresh ideas, and so on – but not because if old people remain working young people cannot. Roles can and should change with age.

People whose work is their pleasure, such as many academics, are only too pleased to stay on working. More generally, the nature of work affects people's desire to want to keep doing it. In Chapter 6 I reported that jobs characterised by high effort and low reward were particularly stressful and increased risk of disease. My colleague Johannes Siegrist from Düsseldorf, who developed the effort/reward concept, has looked at how this relates to retirement across Europe. A study of fifteen European countries found that the more that jobs are characterised by imbalance between efforts and rewards, the more likely are people to declare that they intend to retire.[11] Attempts to raise retirement age in France led to mass strikes and Paris grinding to a halt. Keep the jobs lousy and it is hardly a surprise if people are not keen to keep doing them.

Anecdotal evidence from a large British retailer suggested that older staff see the advantage of staying in work not only in financial security, but in maintaining friendships and, being more experienced, having something special/extra to offer customers.[12]

The fact that the terrain is tricky does not mean that it can't be negotiated. One path out of older-age poverty is to work for longer. For those with education and skills in interesting jobs, surely what we need is some flexibility. The idea that people work to a certain age and then fall off a cliff into non-work seems bad for them personally, and a loss for others of the skills, experience and wisdom that some embody. Part-time work at older ages? Easing into retirement? These should be options. The ground is tricky because we then have to think about people in physically demanding jobs that are boring or worse. Would it be such a boon to Alan or Lalta to keep working longer? They may need the money but they do not need the indignity and stress. If the adverse impact on health is a reason for addressing the nature of work at younger ages, all the more is it a reason for improving working conditions at older ages – to provide the conditions and flexibility to enable older people to continue at work.

Academics, orchestra conductors and novelists may want to keep working for ever, but most people do not. Even Philip Roth, novelist, who wrote some of his greatest novels to great acclaim in his sixties and seventies, declared at eighty that it was time to stop. After work finishes, and if there is little private wealth, pensions or some form of social security and family support become vital.

. . . and pensions

'*Annual income twenty pounds, annual expenditure nineteen [pounds] nineteen [shillings] and six [pence], result happiness. Annual income twenty pounds, annual expenditure twenty pounds ought and six, result misery.*'

Mr Micawber in Charles Dickens, *David Copperfield*

A few years ago in Finland, I was told that they had designed their social security system on the assumption that people would work for forty years and die soon after they stopped. With longer spent in education, the mean age at entry to the workforce was then twenty-six, and the mean age at exit was then fifty-two – time in the work force twenty-six years. Life expectancy at sixty continued to rise. Finland was heading for Mr Micawber's unhappiness.

An ageing of populations entails political choices. Pensions are complicated. Some combination of workers themselves, their employers and the government put money into a scheme. It may be you notionally putting money aside for your own non-working future, or today's workers supporting today's older people. If the money is invested, the performance of the market will of course be important.

If there seems to be too little money for today's retirees, society has three choices: people can work longer, pensioners be poorer, or workers be poorer as they put more money aside for their own or others' old age. There may be some other more complicated choices to do with manipulation of money, but those three will do to demonstrate that societies can choose how they want to manage things.

Indeed societies do make different choices. Figure 6.1 (p. 184) in the previous chapter showed that in Britain the number of workless households in poverty has been declining while the number of working households in poverty has been on the increase. Figure 7.4 shows more generally for the rich country club, the OECD, the choices countries make.

Compare Ireland and Poland, for example. Both have a poverty rate in the general population of about 15 per cent, but in Ireland the poverty rate for older people is around 30 per cent, in Poland it is about 5 per cent. Poland has organised its affairs, or been subject to historical accident, so that older people are better off than the general population. In Ireland the opposite is true. In Sweden and Austria the poverty rate is low both generally and in the elderly. Clearly the best is to have low poverty rates, but if poverty is defined *relative to some standard*, 60 per cent of median income for example, someone has to be poor. Society has a good deal of discretion as to where the hardship should fall.

Figure 7.4 covers rich countries, most of which have well-developed social security or pension systems of one sort or another. It is worth asking if such a thing is even conceivable in a middle- or low-income country. The answer is yes.

Bolivia is one of the poorest countries in Latin America. Nilda at sixty-eight had no source of income. She heard that there was a state pension: older people could receive an annual payment of about $217. She lived in a rural area and the pension was available from a bank in an urban area. About to make the trek to collect it, she was told she needed an identification document to register for the pension, but she didn't have one. About one-sixth of older

FIGURE 7.4: ARE OLDER PEOPLE MORE LIKELY TO BE POOR THAN
THE REST OF THE POPULATION? NOT NECESSARILY...

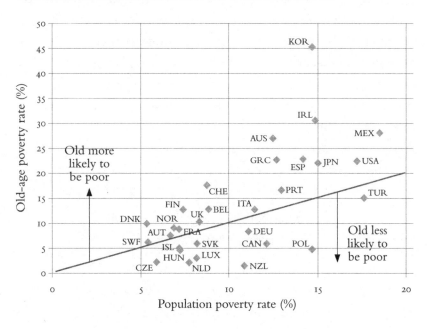

Source: *OECD Income-Distribution Database*; see OECD (2008), *Growing Unequal?*, Tables 5.1 and 5.3.

Bolivians, almost all rural-born indigenous people, had no birth certificate or identity document. Without it they did not exist in the system. HelpAge International, an NGO, supports legal centres in Bolivia that help people obtain birth certificates. For Nilda the steps were, first – birth certificate, second – pension, and then transformation of her life. The pension was way below average income for the country, but it was enough for household expenses and basic medications. For some of Nilda's neighbours the pension was a lifeline of another sort. It provided a small amount of capital for income-generating activities or to help their children do the same.[13]

Bolivia is not alone among poorer countries. When we were conducting the Commission on Social Determinants of Health we were given evidence of pension schemes in low- and middle-income countries from A to V, Argentina to Vietnam, including among others Bangladesh, Botswana, Nepal and Uruguay. That said, only about 65 per cent of people in Latin America are covered by pension schemes, 20 per cent in South Asia, and less than 10 per cent in Sub-Saharan Africa. Where contributory pension schemes, to which the employee and employer contribute, fall short, some form of social scheme, provided by the state, is necessary. Now, more than 100 countries have social pension schemes.[14]

If a country is poor the prevalence of poverty among the elderly will be high. But even for a low-income country there is ample precedent for schemes that make a qualitative difference to the lives that the elderly are able to lead, to their empowerment.

Psychosocial – empowerment as control and participation with dignity

I have two approaches to empowerment at older age of the psychosocial variety. The first is impact on health behaviours, or lifestyle. The second is social participation. Starting with health behavior, a friend put it to me: I have devoted my life, studiously and conscientiously, to avoiding physical activity of any kind. Why in my sixties should I change? It is true that when standing upright he has some difficulty seeing his toes, let alone stooping to touch them, because of a generous midriff. But he takes that as a modern equivalent of Shakespeare's fifth age of man: 'In fair round belly with good capon lined'. It goes along with being 'Full of wise saws and modern instances'.[15] My friend has a poetic, indeed Shakespearean, turn of phrase, and can bring a tear to the eye with descriptions of his Falstaffian enjoyment of a roast running with fatty juices, and roast potatoes glistening with their oily covering. Saturated fat? Bring it on. He tried green vegetables once, but couldn't see the point. His description of his enjoyment of rich puddings would make 'Shall I compare thee to a summer's day?' read like a legal letter.[16]

At least my friend has his high socio-economic position going for him in the survival stakes. Given that position, I argue that he should take control of his life and enjoy healthy food and physical fitness, and moderate alcohol consumption, in addition to continuing not to smoke. Echoing Woody Allen, my friend wants to know what the point is of living to a hundred if, to do it, you have to give up all the things that make you want to live to a hundred. He has a prior question, though. He wants to know, given that he has been deliciously wicked as far as diet and exercise go from childhood into the latter part of his seventh decade, whether it would make any difference to change now.

His question is a good one. It underlies the premise of this whole chapter. If health and health inequities at older ages are determined by what happened through the whole of the life course before people were elderly, it may not matter what the elderly do, or what they have to endure. I have just been arguing that it does matter if the elderly are in poverty. It may matter, too, how they behave.

One powerful piece of evidence comes from a European study of people aged seventy to ninety in eleven European countries.[17] People who consumed a Mediterranean diet – lots of olive oil, legumes, nuts and seeds, grains, fruit and vegetables, fish, relatively little meat and dairy, alcohol in moderation – were physically active, and had not smoked for fifteen years appeared to derive great health benefits. Over ten years of follow-up they had less than half the mortality rate of the people who, like my friend, were doing the 'wrong' things. But they had presumably been doing, or not doing, these things for most of their lives before they reached seventy. The study does not quite tell us if contemporary behaviour matters. It almost certainly does for smoking. People who give up smoking gain health benefits after a lag period. There are also probably contemporary benefits in physical activity, not only for mortality but, as we shall see in a moment, for cognitive function.

If all it took was evidence of benefit then everyone could be healthy. As I laid out in Chapter 2, there are constraints on healthy behaviours, which apply in the elderly as they do at earlier ages. In the elderly, as at other ages, two of these four behaviours, physical activity and smoking, follow the social gradient as, in some countries, does healthy diet.[18] It is likely that they are contributing to the social gradient in health. One form of psychosocial empowerment, then, is taking control over behaviours.

There is significant evidence relating to cognitive function and dementia. Researchers are divided into two camps: those who subscribe to 'use it or lose it' and those who do not. Both camps have evidence to support their view. The question is: if you stop doing the sudoku, will your cognitive powers decline; or do your cognitive powers decline, which is why you stop doing the sudoku?

Several studies have looked at this question.[19] One in the Bronx in New York interviewed and examined generally healthy people aged seventy-five to eighty-five.[20] These people were asked about their physical activity patterns and how often they participated in six 'cognitive' activities: reading books or newspapers, writing for pleasure, doing crossword puzzles, playing board games or cards, participating in organised group discussions, and playing musical instruments. In this study physical activity was not protective of cognitive decline or dementia, but cognitive activities were. The question was, which came first – the dementia or the lack of cognitive activities? The researchers' way of answering it was to use a cognitive test at baseline that satisfied them that they were ruling out the possibility that pre-clinical dementia was leading to lack of activities. Participation in cognitive activities was protective – it linked to less cognitive decline.

Other studies have found moderate physical activity to be protective against cognitive decline, again taking into account the possibility that cognitive decline precedes lack of interest in physical activity.[21] A study of former US nurses aged seventy and above assessed habitual physical activity nine years before looking at the rate of cognitive decline, and still they found that physical activity, even just walking, was protective.[22]

I have shown my bias by not giving the other side of the story of which comes first: whether decrease of activity or cognitive decline. One longitudinal study of the elderly, the Victoria Longitudinal Study, shows evidence that the relation between activity and cognitive performance goes both ways.[23] Certainly, people who were active socially, cognitively and physically had less subsequent decline in cognitive performance, but there was also clear evidence that it goes the other way too. Decline in cognitive performance can lead to reduced participation in activities. Hardly surprising, really.

This controversy of which comes first, use it or lose it, is not over. That said, it seems likely that there is *some* protective effect on physical and mental functioning of cognitive, social and physical activities. Given that such activities follow the social gradient, they will contribute to a social gradient in healthy ageing.

After health behaviours, the second approach to empowerment is social participation. As we have just seen, lack of activity can be bad both for the brain and for the body. Loneliness makes things worse, but can be 'cured'.

Mr. O, a 68-year-old amputee (due to diabetes), was wheel chair bound; a longtime smoker; lived in – and hadn't left – his senior high rise apartment building in 5 years. A new project, Experience Corps, enrolled elderly volunteers to spend time with young children in school. Mr. O volunteered and came to school three or more days per week for 15 hours a week. The School Principal saw him in his wheel chair, and told me she went back to her office and wept because she was afraid she had agreed to having to baby sit old people as well as lead a challenging school. One month later, she described to me the following scene: three children were arguing in front of the elevator and around Mr. O and his wheelchair. She listened and found that they were arguing about who would get to push Mr. O onto the elevator. They resolved it: one pushed, one pressed the elevator button, one sat on Mr. O's lap. Two months later, the Principal asked for sixty volunteers – an addition of 45 over what she had.

> Linda Fried, geriatrician, gerontologist, epidemiologist

Lack of social integration can be fatal. If Mr O. had the choice of giving up smoking or being more enmeshed socially, it is a close thing: both are potentially life-saving, but social integration is marginally better for his health.

A 'meta-analysis' combined results from 148 studies of men and women with an average age of sixty-four at the start of the study. It found that over an average 7.5 years of follow-up, people who were socially engaged had a 50 per cent lower chance of dying. Being socially integrated in a variety of ways was more protective than simply being married or not living alone.[24]

The protective effect was similar in men and women. This lack of gender difference is interesting. It has long been known that married people have lower mortality than those who are single, widowed or divorced. It never failed to raise a chuckle when someone would report that marriage was good for men and not for women. Not difficult to think of an explanation for that one. What this study shows, however, is that when men and women are involved with society and organisations in a variety of ways, it is equally protective for both genders.

You do not have to be an African-American in Baltimore, like Mr O. to be socially isolated in your older age. In the English Longitudinal Study of Ageing, the evidence shows clearly that it is not lonely at the top, but at the bottom.[25] As usual it is socially graded. People in the study were classified according to their wealth: the lower their wealth, the more likely not to belong to clubs or organisations, to be socially disengaged, to have less contact with friends, and to feel lonely.

Social isolation is not just a matter of personal choice, but is influenced by the environment broadly conceived. For older people, working, caring, subsidised transport, age-friendly cities that remove the physical barriers against the elderly, crime-free neighbourhoods, having enough money to engage, are all ways of reducing the problem of social isolation. Chapter 8 will look at the question of building healthy communities.

A particularly exciting way of involving older people in society, Experience Corps, was devised by Linda Fried, quoted above, who was a professor in Baltimore and is now Dean of the School of Public Health at Columbia University.[26] Her concern was with the Mr O.s of Baltimore – elderly people, socially isolated, with no useful role in society. Could she and her colleagues solve the social isolation, give people a useful role, and improve their health and well-being all at the same time? The useful role they chose was working with young children in schools in deprived areas. It was a strategic choice. Older people could satisfy their need to give something back to society, and young children would benefit.

Conventional wisdom in US cities was that upper-income white women are the volunteers for good causes. Experience Corps tapped into wells of enthusiasm among men, as well as women, who were of low income, and African-American. Preliminary evidence from controlled trials of Experience Corps point in a good direction: children have improved reading scores and fewer referrals for behaviour problems. The elderly volunteers have higher levels of social integration and sense of generative achievement; have modest increases in intellectual and physical activity; and feel, in the words of participants, like they had 'dusted off the cobwebs in their brains'.

Political empowerment

What if you are old and don't feel it? More than 60 per cent of people in England over the age of seventy-five said they did not feel 'old'.[27] Interesting. My first reaction to these figures was: that's good. In fact, that's great that seventy-five does not mean feeling old. My second reaction: oh dear! I am trapped in the negative stereotype of what 'old' means. That is not great at all.

Here's an alternative thought. What if the word 'old' conjured up images not of frailty, decrepitude and dependence but the wisdom of Cicero, the wit of Woody Allen, the sparkle of a mischievous grandparent, the love that only grandparents can have for their grandchildren and vice versa? With this in mind, we would lament that only 40 per cent of seventy-five-year-olds felt old – sparkling, witty, wise, mischievous and loving to their grandchildren – rather than rejoice that 60 per cent do not feel old.

Changing the cultural meaning of 'old' is not to deny the inevitable physical and mental declines. But as I showed above, society is defining old as sixty or sixty-five, and many people's minds and bodies are not behaving 'old' until fifteen or twenty years later – earlier if you are relatively socially disadvantaged, later if your life has been more privileged.

I am not sure which comes first, change of culture or change of laws and regulations. Clearly we need both when it comes to ageing populations. I began the chapter with Maria from Brazil saying that her life had been changed by a law guaranteeing her rights, her entitlements. Certainly, in democracies, governments can no longer ignore the rights and other claims of older people. There are so many voters who are older. In the US, the AARP (it used to be the American Association of Retired Persons) has 37 million members – a force that cannot be ignored.

As each stage of the life course has come to prominence I have argued that now *this* is the really important stage. Early child development sets the stage for the rest of life. Education determines whether a promising beginning will translate into better life chances all the way, right into the oldest age. Working age is of vital importance. We spend so long in work that it matters what work does to our health and well-being and whether work gives the economic security to guarantee good life chances for the next generation. And now, I have argued that older age is where we really see the effects of the whole of life. As childhood mortality declines, as the world ages, and as non-communicable diseases come to dominate the global health picture, then health inequities at older ages become increasingly important. The evidence is clear that what happens through the whole of the life course impacts on the health and well-being of older people. So too do the conditions in which older people live out the remaining ten, twenty or thirty years of their lives. What happens in the wider society affects older people as it does people at earlier ages. The aspect of the wider society that we turn to next is the communities where people are born, grow, live, work and age.

8

Building Resilient Communities

There's nothing ill can dwell in such a temple.
If the ill spirit have so fair a house,
Good things will strive to dwell with 't.

William Shakespeare, *The Tempest* (Act I, Scene ii)

In May 2011 Mary hanged herself.* She was found in the yard of her grandparents' house on a First Nations Reserve in the province of British Columbia in Canada. She was fourteen. She was a First Nations, aboriginal, Canadian.[1]

Her story has particulars. All suicides do. She had been physically and emotionally abused at home and in her community, and possibly sexually abused. Her mother was mentally unstable and heard voices telling her to 'snap' her child's head. Officials attributed the suicide to a dysfunctional child welfare system, and to the fact that no one took her complaints of abuse seriously or acted on them.

There is another way to look at Mary's sadly foreshortened life, and that is to realise that though her personal tragedy was unique, there are many young aboriginal Canadians who experience similar tragedies. In fact, the aboriginal youth suicide rate in British Columbia is five times the average for all young Canadians.[2] One

---

* Mary is not her real name. Her name is withheld for legal reasons.

cannot understand fully why Mary saw no way out without also asking why so many other young aboriginal people in British Columbia reached the same desperate point.

Christopher Lalonde, a professor of psychology at the University of Victoria in British Columbia, says: 'There are media reports of an epidemic of youth suicides among First Nation communities, but half the communities we studied had not had a youth suicide in twenty-one years.' Lalonde and Michael Chandler, now an emeritus professor at the University of British Columbia, studied aboriginal youth suicide from 1987 to 2000 in British Columbia. They found that although the Province had about 200 aboriginal 'bands', in the first six years of their study more than 90 per cent of the suicides occurred in 12 per cent of the bands.

What features distinguished communities where suicides occurred from others that were not so scarred? The starting point for Chandler and Lalonde was poverty, what they call bone-grinding poverty. They say: 'The aboriginal population of North America is known to be the most poverty-stricken group on the continent, to have the highest unemployment rates, to be the most undereducated, to be the shortest lived, and to suffer the poorest health.'[3] Poverty had to be part of the explanation, but only part. All the aboriginal communities were poor, almost without exception. There had to be something that put some poor communities at higher risk than others.

According to Lalonde, 'communities that were able to hold on to their cultural history and promote their own collective future' were the ones with low rates of suicide. To measure this they collected six markers from each community that assessed cultural continuity. These included participation in land claims; aspects of self-government; community control over education, police, fire and health services; and establishment of 'cultural' facilities. The results were clear: the greater the cultural continuity and community control over their destiny, the lower was the youth suicide rate. Poverty is bad but, to echo the schoolteacher from Tower Hamlets, poverty is not destiny.

The officials' account is that the provincial child welfare system failed to prevent Mary's suicide. Lalonde puts it differently: 'Don't target suicide; what you should target is making the community a healthier place for youth to live.' And the way to do that is to empower the community, to use my language. In Lalonde's language: communities should be able to hold on to their culture and promote their collective future.

The grim picture played out to deadly consequences in Canadian aboriginal populations is also present in Native American,[4] Australian aborigine[5] and New Zealand Maori communities.[6] Social exclusion and disempowerment can kill.

Social exclusion is not an all-or-nothing phenomenon. Degree of social exclusion and disempowerment can contribute to the social gradient in health – not just in aboriginals but in all our communities. The environments where people are born, grow, live, work and age pose material and social hazards to health. At the same time, communities can be resilient in the face of hazards, and can be health-enhancing.

What happens at the local level can contribute to crime, alcohol-related deaths, obesity, road traffic injuries, depression, health problems linked to pollution of air and water, problems with housing. On the plus side, the local level can improve health through a high level of social cohesion and social participation, security and low fear of crime, active transport, provision of green space, walkability, availability of healthy food, good services.

The best is not to have bone-grinding poverty. But even in the face of such poverty communities can flourish to a greater or lesser extent with profound consequences for health equity. There are encouraging stories of community developments in the face of grinding poverty. Local influences are important all the way up the social gradient and at all ages. I want to begin with social hazards and resilience, then move on to material hazards.

MAKING COMMUNITIES SOCIALLY HABITABLE

The distinction between social and physical that I am making is somewhat arbitrary. Good urban design allows social interaction. Affordable public transport enables people old and young to be socially active. That said, the more obviously social is a good place to start.

Crime is a public health issue . . . fear of crime

'De folks wid plenty o' plenty got a lock on de door,' sang Porgy in George Gershwin's *Porgy and Bess*. Someone with 'plenty of nuttin' needed no lock on the door. The implication was that crime happened to the rich. But thinking you need no lock because if you haven't got much would-be robbers will look elsewhere suggests that Porgy had not been reading the figures from the Department of Justice in the US.[7] These show that the lower the household income the higher the risk of property crime. We have a similar situation in the UK: the more deprived the area the higher the crime rate. One civil servant said, sardonically: that's joined-up government. The public transport is so bad, the poor have to rob where they live.

Bank robber Willie Sutton may have explained his penchant for robbing banks as because 'that's where the money is', but more property crime takes place in the US and the UK where the money isn't.[8] The same is largely true for violent crime: higher rates in low-income areas. Both theft and violence lead to fear of crime.

As we saw at the start of the chapter, suicide is an individual act, but the suicide *rate* is a property of the community. So it is with crime. An individual gets attacked or robbed. But the crime rate becomes a community characteristic. One way we see this is fear of crime, which is influenced by the actual crime rate, but may not change as fast as the rate of crime changes.[9]

With my colleagues Mai Stafford and Tarani Chandola we demonstrated the link between fear of crime and ill health in the Whitehall II study of British Civil Servants, aged fifty to seventy at the time of this particular study.[10] As I have reported in earlier chapters, we used the employment grade of civil servants to mark out their position in the social hierarchy. The results were astonishing. There was a steep social gradient – lower grade more fear – in fear of mugging, burglary, car crime and rape. A third of the lower grades were worried about mugging, 7 per cent of the high grades; a third of the lower grades were worried about robbery, a sixth of the higher grades were.

The greater the fear of crime the worse was the mental health and the worse the general level of physical functioning. Fear of crime, as well as directly influencing anxiety and stress, seemed to be isolating people – they spent less time visiting friends, participating in social activities, walking outside or exercising. This reduction in activities was a clear part of the link between fear of crime and ill health.[11] The social gradient in fear of crime was part of the explanation for the social gradient in health. If fear of crime leads to social isolation of older people they become indirect victims of fear of crime as a community characteristic.

. . . dealing with grievous bodily harm

Saturday nights are busy in Cardiff, capital of Wales, not least in the accident and emergency rooms. Youngsters, usually men, get to hospital in various states of disrepair. A typical case would be a brawl in a pub, smashed beer glasses used as weapons, jagged gashes to the face and body of a drunken young man.

Jonathan Shepherd, an oral and maxillofacial surgeon, spent his Saturday nights stitching up these torn young and sometimes not so young men, and wondering. He wondered, in the words of the standard public health metaphor, why no one was looking upstream at the causes of these violent injuries. Surgeons are supposed to stitch people up, not 'do' prevention and public health. I'll display my prejudice if I say that the best do public health alongside their clinical duties. Jonathan Shepherd in Wales is a shining example.

Professor Shepherd was not surprised to note that violence was not randomly distributed through the city, but there were violent hotspots. The problem was that the police did not know about the majority of violent incidents, so had not identified the hotspots. Only a quarter to one-third of the violent incidents that are treated in accident and emergency departments in the UK are reported to the police. There is similar low reporting in the US and other countries. The victims of violence are reluctant to report the crime because they fear reprisals, they may not know the identity of the assailant – 'a drunk bloke in a pub' hardly narrows it down – and are concerned over having their own circumstances closely scrutinised.

In order to prevent violent harm, Shepherd set up and led a partnership of health practitioners, police, city alcohol-licensing authorities, education, transport and ambulance services. A key element was the accident and emergency departments' reporting of violent incidents to the police, anonymised – that is, the identity of the victim was withheld but the location was reported so that the police could identify hotspots.

One issue is displacement. If the police actively target a high-risk area, will the violence simply move somewhere else? The answer appears to be a clear no, which is interesting – a 'yes' answer, it does move, would not have surprised. One might speculate that if violence is a property of society, then young people unable to create mayhem in one place would do it somewhere else. Apparently not. Perhaps the people who get into drunken, broken-glass-wielding brawls are not thinking quite so rationally. They are hardly evaluating their options, the risks and benefits of slashing someone round the face with a makeshift weapon, and maximising their utility.

The prongs of the prevention strategy, in addition to targeted, high-visibility policing in hotspots, included pedestrianising streets

in high-risk areas, providing late-night public transport, and working with staff in the taverns and pubs where violence was frequent.
It seems to have worked. Over a four-year period, Cardiff had a
42 per cent reduction in hospital admissions related to violence
compared to similar cities without such intervention.[12]

Broadening his approach to the whole of England and Wales,
Shepherd and colleagues sought to explain the greater than threefold difference in rates of violence-related injuries across regions.
They found higher rates of violence in areas that were both poorer
and had higher rates of youth unemployment; rates were higher
in the summer, and when major national sporting events took
place. In addition to all of that was the price of beer: higher beer
price, lower violence-related injury.[13] Simple, really. As we saw in
Chapter 2: raise the price of alcohol and consumption goes down.
I have been a bit critical of overly simple, not to say simplistic,
applications of rational choice theories of economic behaviour, but
if raising the beer price reduces violent behaviour it can make a
contribution to communities becoming more liveable.

. . . combating gangs

It is likely that most violence-related injury involving gangs comes
from them fighting each other. It is unlikely, but just possible,
that someone might argue: let them do each other in. I have two
objections, practical and moral. Practical, in that the rest of us can
get caught in the cross-fire, literally or figuratively. Crime-ridden
neighbourhoods engender fear of crime, see above, and they may
sweep innocent people up in the net of violence.

Second, on the moral objection, it is core to the beliefs and
practice of doctors to help the sick and injured. Doctors do not,
nor should they, make moral judgements about people and treat or
not depending on those judgements. Just as I argued in Chapter 3
that we would treat people even though they were 'responsible' for

their own illness, we do the same if people are harmed by violence in which they were willing participants.

Gang-related violence is widespread. On the US–Mexican border there have been thousands killed in warfare between drug cartels in the last seven years or so. There are approximately 6,700 licensed firearms dealers in the US along the border with Mexico, and only one legal firearms retailer in Mexico itself. Approximately 70 per cent of guns recovered from Mexican criminal activity come from the USA.[14] Tackling that might be a way to reduce gang violence.

Organised violence in favelas in Brazil plagues these informal settlements with some of the worst murder rates in the world. Colombia's drug-related violence is legendary.

The US has been in the lead in developing approaches to combatting gang violence.[15] The US approach has been adapted in Glasgow. Police officers bring gang members who have offended to a meeting. They treat the gang as a unit rather than as individuals and they say that if any of the members of the gang – including those not present in the meeting – commit a crime after the meeting, the police will pursue the whole group rather than the individual. The police make the message clear: we know who you are and if you continue offending, we will come down on you, hard! Imagine that line delivered in a tough Glaswegian accent. The threat to punish the whole group also encourages gangs to police their own behaviour.

A mother of a victim comes to the meeting and talks movingly of what it is like to have a son knifed in gang violence, what it means to a mother. An A&E consultant describes having to treat injured gang members, and community members describe the damage that the gang is doing to their local communities. There follow group discussions. At one of these, one young man spoke up angrily and said: I've been fighting them for years (pointing at members of a rival gang), and I want to know why!

The warning is the stick. The carrot is crucial. The opportunity to develop skills and be trained for employment offers visions of an alternative future. Here, the cooperation of potential employers in both the public and private sectors is vital. Gang members are given the phone number of a 'one-stop shop' where they are able to access education, health services, careers advice and social services, and once they have signed up to the programme, their needs are assessed and they are put on relevant programmes, such as anger management and conflict resolution, or training in employment skills. The violence reduction unit (Community Initiative to Reduce Violence: CIRV) of the police that runs this programme reports a near-50 per cent reduction in violence among the 400 or so gang members who have been through it.[16] These programmes cost money, but the benefit is not only in the short-term reduction in violence: the potential long-term gains are large.

Building socially sustainable communities and resilience

. . . with community groups

While conducting my English Review of Health Inequalities, I talked to community groups in the English city of Liverpool.[17] They listened, went away and discussed what they heard, and came back with the following challenges – my summary:

- We do not want an outside expert telling us what to do. *Our* values should determine our goals.
- Nor do we want an expert telling us what to measure. Our value-driven goals should determine how we measure success.
- The journey is important as well as the destination. How we get there is important, as is where we want to get.
- We thought that the problem was poor-quality programmes. Now we recognise that the problem is the nature of society. But there is still much that we can do.

I felt a bit confronted by 'We do not want an outside expert tell-
ing us what to do.' Having just caught the early train from London,
I was the only outside expert in the room. They must mean me.
Good Liverpudlian stuff. They folded their arms, metaphorically.

I folded mine and came back: 'So, it is more important that an
intervention be designed locally than it be effective? After all, I would
only recommend what the evidence shows is likely to work.'

Now we had a standoff.

'OK,' they said, 'tell us what has been shown to work, but we
will do it in our own way.'

Sounds to me like a good principle. The community should
take control, but it will be helpful to know what has worked
elsewhere to build socially sustainable communities. There are
two issues here: preventing bad things happening, and building
the capacity to bounce back from adversity. We could call this
latter 'community resilience' – a property of socially sustainable
communities.

These community groups in Liverpool eloquently described
empowerment, the community taking control in its efforts to build
resilience. They also pointed to the fact that although the problems
they faced, specifically health inequities, were attributable to the
wider society, there was much that could happen to reduce these
inequalities at community level.

A good example of a well-evaluated community intervention
comes from Seattle: Communities that Care. They make the entirely
reasonable assumption that the time to get the community mobi-
lised is while children are in school, and suggest a menu of proven
interventions that a community can adopt. Central to the approach
is assembling a coalition of community people to work with families and schools. The interventions can take place right through
the school years. A recent evaluation in seven US states focused on
ten- to fourteen-year-olds and showed that youths who had been
through the programme were significantly less likely to be using

drugs, tobacco, or alcohol by grade 12, and were less likely to have been involved in delinquent behaviour and violence.[18]

An earlier study from Seattle has followed young people until age thirty-three and shown that the 'Seattle Social Development Project' involving the community helps young people to develop bonds to their school and community. Over the long term, in addition to less use of drugs, alcohol and tobacco, there was less history of multiple sexual partners, greater use of contraception, less involvement in crime, and lower incidence of mental illness.[19]

It may be objected that Seattle is not the nastiest place in the US, and that the Communities that Care project was in medium-size cities rather than in the most deprived and crime-ridden of places. However, these programmes still show that involving communities in developing more socially appropriate behaviours in young people can work. There is proof of concept. Indeed, it could be harder to apply in large cities, but it is worth working to make it succeed.

There is a different aspect that worries me. If gross inequalities in income and associated social conditions are driving inequalities in outcomes, as in Baltimore, is it really sensible to be struggling to make communities more resilient? It is analogous to my argument in Chapter 4 that there are two ways to reduce inequities in early child development: reduce the level of economic and social deprivation; and implement proven programmes that have been shown to work. We need to do both: reduce hazards associated with poverty and exclusion *and* promote resilience.

. . . and surprising bedfellows

On a visit to Liverpool I found myself in a fire station. A fire chief from the Merseyside Fire and Rescue Service explained:

> We are all macho men. We would come back from fighting a fire in which someone had died and say to ourselves: that is so unnecessary;

they should have done something to prevent that death. Then we said: why 'they'? Perhaps 'we' should do something about preventing deaths by fire. We spend six per cent of our time fighting fires, the rest is preparing, and so on.

So, we went into people's homes – everyone likes fire fighters and we were welcome – to talk to them about fitting smoke alarms. But people said to us: smoke alarms! What about my leaky roof? We told them how they could get help from the council in fixing their roof. In effect, we became social workers, we burly macho men.

We counselled people not to smoke in bed. Then we thought: while we're up why don't we counsel people on giving up smoking.

We worked with Liverpool Football Club to get the kids off the streets and playing sport. We gave pensioners cards to get free access to our gym. We brought the kids into the fire station and got them growing vegetables. Better than creating mayhem on the streets.

I now get asked to talk to fire officers in various parts of the country. It is fun being met at the railway station by a fire service vehicle – regrettably not a real-life red fire engine. That ambition is yet to be realised. I can now say to general practitioners and other health professionals: 'This is what the fire-fighters are doing to improve health in deprived communities. What are you doing?'

The more general point is that improving the lives of members of communities is likely to have positive effects on health equity. It is not only those whose statutory duty includes health that can be active players. In our English Review, *Fair Society, Healthy Lives*, we emphasised proportionate universalism: universal solutions with effort proportional to need. It is not only 'middle-class' communities that can benefit from community action, but the more effort

put into developing communities that are more disadvantaged, the
more they too are likely to benefit.

. . . including everyone in Australia

*If you have come to help me, you are wasting your time. But if you have
come because your liberation is bound up with mine, then let us work
together.*

Aboriginal activists group, Queensland, 1970s

I was sitting at lunch in Darwin, capital of Australia's Northern
Territory, with two aboriginal men, leaders of the Aboriginal
Medical Service. They said: we use your reports all the time.

Now *that* is success. It is unseemly to boast, I know, but I could
not have been more pleased.

To put Darwin in context, think Australia. Sydney, with its iconic
Opera House and Harbour Bridge, played host to a universally
acclaimed Olympic Games. Australia ranks second, after Norway,
on the UNDP (United Nations Development Programme) Human
Development Index, which combines life expectancy, education
and literacy, and national income.[20]

Now travel more than 3,000 km from Sydney to Darwin, in the
Northern Territory at Australia's top end – a frontier town that
has got richer with nearby mining, and some tourism, but otherwise a world away from the boulevards of Sydney and Melbourne.
Not so much in Darwin, itself, but in scattered communities all
around, are aboriginal settlements. I visited Gunbalanya, a 'large'
aboriginal town of about 1,200 people in West Arnhem Land.
The local languages are Kunwinkju and English. You have to cross
the East Alligator River – mistakenly named after the crocodiles
that are so numerous, and impressive – and the town is inacces-
sible by road from Darwin in the wet season. Two first impres-
sions: the awesome beauty of the landscape, and the put-together
third-world-style convenience store, made this feel more like

New Guinea than the Australia of opera houses and Melbourne Cricket Ground.

Australia may rank second on the human development index, but ... if Australian aborigines were considered as a separate country, they would rank 122 (out of 187 countries).[21] A few years ago, the figures were Australia 4, Australian aborigines 104.[22] Getting more unequal? I would not jump to that conclusion before being sure about changes in methodology.

The health problems are considerable. In 2010–12, life expectancy for aboriginals in the Northern Territory was 63.4 for men and 68.7 for women – 14.4 years shorter than for non-indigenous men and women.[23] The life-expectancy gap signals that there is a substantial difference in the conditions in which people are born, grow, live, work and age – the social determinants of health – between indigenous and other Australians.

No one is in any doubt that most Australian aborigines live in bone-grinding poverty. Their health problems, though, are not those we associate with countries in the lower half of the human development index ranking. We know what third world poverty does to health: babies die. Infant mortality in Sierra Leone is 117 per 1,000 live births. In Iceland, the lowest in the world, it is 2. On a global scale, from 117 to 2, Australian aborigines, at 9.6 per 1,000, look a great deal more like Iceland than like Sierra Leone. True, for non-indigenous Australians it is 4.3.[24] But the illnesses leading to a bigger than fourteen-year gap in life expectancy are occurring mainly at ages twenty-five to sixty-four. They are precisely those diseases that, as we have seen earlier, follow the social gradient: heart disease, diabetes, respiratory disease, cancer, as well as accidents and violence.

The differences are huge. Australian aboriginal men are six times more likely, and aboriginal women eleven times more likely, to die of ischaemic heart disease than non-indigenous men and women.[25] For diabetes, the differences are more alarming. The diabetes death rate is nineteen times higher in aboriginal men, and twenty-seven times higher in aboriginal women, than in the non-indigenous population.

We need to be thinking, then, not of aboriginal poverty as third-world-style destitution but as disempowerment, community disruption, the kind of conditions that lead to aboriginal youth suicide in British Columbia. Diagnosing the problem is relatively straightforward, dealing with it less so.

Starting with the diagnosis. More typical than Gunbalanya, to which we will return in a moment, is a rural town described by one aboriginal leader as:

> Screams of pain and fear piercing the night. Children roaming dark streets afraid of home where sexual assault awaits. Parents taking money to let their children be abused.
>
> A snapshot of Aboriginal life in several small towns in north western New South Wales overwhelmed by hopelessness, alcoholism, drug abuse, domestic violence, child crime – you name it, we've got it.[26]

In Australia, the indigenous population is 2.5 per cent of the whole but 30 per cent of the prison population. In the Northern Territory, the indigenous population is 30 per cent of the whole but 83 per cent of the prison population.[27] Some of that shockingly high prison population represents high crime rates and some comes from discrimination in the justice system.

It is a long way from Gunbalanya or a benighted country town in New South Wales to Liverpool or Baltimore, but remember that the diseases, and accidents and violence, that carry you off in a deprived English or American community are the same that are killing Australian aborigines. Diseases and violence are likely to have the same causes wherever we find them. It follows that the remedies should, in principle, be similar. In *Fair Society, Healthy Lives*, the report of my English Review of Health Inequalities, we emphasised six areas both as explanations of the social gradient in health and as solutions.[28] They are:

- Early child development
- Education and lifelong learning
- Employment and working conditions
- Minimum income for healthy living
- Healthy and sustainable communities
- A social determinants approach to prevention

Basic are inequities in power, money and resources.

The causes of the extreme health disadvantage of Australian aborigines are not different in kind from the causes of the social gradient in health in Liverpool, London or Baltimore, but in degree. If you have a social gradient, someone or some groups will be at the bottom. That is what we have with Australian aborigines: high levels of child neglect and domestic violence, low levels of education, unemployment and poor working conditions, little money, lack of adequate housing, high levels of smoking and drinking, and poor diet. All are causes of the gradient that we highlighted in the English Review, building on the Commission on Social Determinants of Health (CSDH). They are seen to a chilling level in indigenous populations that are socially excluded.

The problems are so entrenched, have been there for so long, one can be forgiven for wondering if things can change. You will know by now that I am not given to counsels of despair. Education illustrates.

Whatever pleasure I feel at my reports being taken up by aboriginals in Darwin does not make up for my feeling ashamed, doubly so, at prior history. Charlie Perkins graduated from the University of Sydney in 1966.[29] He was the first Australian aborigine to graduate from university. The university was founded in 1850. It took

116 years for the first original Australian to graduate. I feel ashamed, because I spent twenty years of my young life going to school and medical school in Sydney and, though my passport is British, I feel implicated.

Doubly ashamed, because at the time, 1966, I was a medical student at Sydney University and I am ashamed, now, at my own lack of outrage then. What was I thinking? Or, more to the point, not thinking. But whatever people, including me, were thinking then, things have changed, rapidly. Twenty-five years later, in 1991, it was estimated that there were more than 3,600 Indigenous Australian graduates, and this number had risen to over 20,000 in 2006.[30]

In 1998 there were twenty aboriginal medical graduates. At last count there are 150, and every year now in the Northern Territory another dozen or so aboriginals enrol in medical training. The problems are huge but progress can be rapid. If, despite the odds against them, aboriginals can be doctors, teachers and administrators they can be role models. It is not straightforward. I travelled with one aboriginal doctor who told me that angry young people thought that he had sold out, because he talks to the white man and sits on their committees.

The young men's anger does, though, illustrate a problem. Improving social conditions takes national action, but solutions to such problems that have been devised in Canberra, Melbourne or Sydney have most certainly failed. The question is what would success look like for aborigines: to abandon traditional culture and become carpenters, nurses, bank clerks and teachers, or to live as hunter-gatherers in traditional fashion? What is clear is that no one thinks alcoholism, unemployment and child abuse, diabetes, renal disease and dying early, count as success.

The lesson from Canadian British Columbia with which I began the chapter is that there is another way. Cultural continuity and communities taking control over their futures is vital. It is possible to be a teacher or nurse and maintain important elements of the cultural heritage.

Back across the East Alligator River in Gunbalanya there is an experiment going on that involves a good attempt to put these insights into action. It is too early to tell if it is working, but there are some good signs. Gunbalanya is one of twenty-nine remote indigenous communities across Australia where there is a local development plan in which the local indigenous community is heavily involved.[31]

The school in Gunbalanya is impressive. It has now become part of West Arnhem College – combining schools in Gunbalanya and Jabiru. West Arnhem College has a programme called Strong Start Bright Future. It certainly sounds right. I met John, the director, Esther, the long-standing aboriginal head teacher of Gunbalanya school, and Sue, the (white) co-principal of the school. The picture Esther painted before the advent of West Arnhem College in 2010 was of high levels of non-attendance, poor completion rates, and no jobs for those who did complete school. A depressing account.

Now comes the new regime. Esther has a whole new programme of work in the school. The transition cannot have been easy. There is likely to have been some blood on the carpet, but the stains had been removed by the time I visited, and all appeared harmonious. Significantly, the government says it will guarantee a job for any student who completes year 12.

One example of the attempts to resolve the conflict between traditional culture and training for a place in modern society is seen in the flexible school year. Students were being taken out of school at the time when it was traditional to go hunting and fishing with family members. Instead of scolding parents, an exercise in futility, the school adapted and changed the term timetable to allow for these excursions to happen.

Does the new school regime work? Too early to tell. But there is a spirit of optimism in and around the college. This time things are going to get better. Let's hope so.

... and in New Zealand

The Marae is a Maori communal centre. I visited the Kokiri Marae Health and Social Services Centre in Lower Hutt, a down-at-heel area outside the main city of Wellington. The story we were told was one of Maoris being encouraged off the land into the cities to find work and finding not so much work but marginality and social exclusion – a regrettably familiar tale of gangs of young males getting into trouble, alcohol and physical abuse of women and children.

Kokiri Marae was started by and is run by women. They get a variety of government grants to run services. The one man that we met, and it was he who did the traditional Maori greeting, told us the story of how the Marae was founded by his grandmother.

The story of Grandma and the gangs is the stuff of movies. In short, Grandma was in Lower Hutt in the same poverty as all the other Maoris, but wanted to provide a community centre for the young men who were getting into all sorts of trouble in gangs. Every day, with whatever ingredients she could find, Grandma made a tureen of soup. She invited the gang members to come and eat, but it had to be on her terms: shoes off, respect, no violence. No respect, no soup. For two months the standoff between Grandma and the gangs continued. They wouldn't meet her terms and she threw the soup out at the end of the day. At last they took their shoes off and came and ate.

'Hollywood ending?' I asked. 'The gang members all became lawyers and members of parliament?' Not quite. There was still a lot of mayhem and family violence, but Grandma's vision flourished.

Among the programmes of the Kokiri Marae is one called 'Whanau Ora'. The CSDH and the Marmot Review highlighted empowerment, dignity, participation in society, and the Amartya Sen concept of freedom to lead a life one has reason to value. I was therefore entranced to read the following description of enhancing whanau (extended family) capabilities:

- To become self-managing
- To be living healthy lifestyles
- To be participating fully in society
- To be confidently participating in Te Ao Maori (the Maori world)
- To be economically secure and successfully involved in wealth creation
- To be cohesive, resilient and nurturing

Terrific. This is putting into practice the kind of principles espoused by the CSDH and *Fair Society, Healthy Lives*. Does it work? We had a highly nuanced discussion about the need for evidence of what works, but also about the difficulties of doing the right kind of evaluation and their miserable experience in the past at the hands of researchers whose interest was much more in research than it was in the welfare of the community.

They painted a realistic picture of continuing processes of exclusion, of family violence and young men getting into trouble. But they have hope and commitment and it gives grounds for optimism.

It is tempting to believe that the kinds of initiative that I saw in the Marae outside Wellington, bringing together Maori traditions, social programmes and adaptations to the wider society, will bear fruit. Certainly, the gap in life expectancy between Maori and non-Maori is narrowing, but there could be other reasons for that.

IMPROVING THE MATERIAL ENVIRONMENT

Environmental quality . . . indoors

It cannot be that everyone in the New Guinea Highlands has a cough, but it seems like it, particularly the women and children. There is a lot of it about.[32] Some of the lung disease that the cough represented is linked to infection but a great deal can be traced to indoor fires. Highland huts have a distinctive odour. For warmth in the cold highlands night, and for cooking, indoor fires are common. As a result, so is indoor smoke.

It is estimated that 3 billion people in the world cook on open fires or rudimentary cooking stoves that burn coal or solid biomass such as wood.[33] Such cooking methods are not good, in almost any way you look at it. They are bad for the planet and inefficient. For a given amount of heat you need to burn more fuel than a simply designed alternative cooker, hence increase output of greenhouse gases.

There is a shortage of fuel in great swathes of the world, particularly in South and East Asia. Picture Indian women going further and further from home to gather what fuel they can. In addition to the physical burden of carrying wood or manure, they are at increased risk of sexual violence.

Cooking over open fires, and indoors in smoky badly ventilated dwellings, is also bad for health. The World Health Organisation estimates that in 2012, globally, 4.3 million deaths were attributable to indoor air pollution, almost all of them in low- and middle-income countries. We have, then, a significant contributor to health inequities between countries.

The pity of this problem is that it is soluble, and quickly. Global poverty is soluble too, but will take a little longer. The Global Alliance for Clean Cookstoves is one among many organisations that are committed to helping hundreds of millions of families escape the unnecessary toil of having no cooking stove or only a rudimentary one. The strategy involves technology of both fuel and efficient stoves, and innovative approaches to delivery.

. . . and outdoors

There are pleasures to be had in Beijing. Going for a walk in the early morning sunshine is not among them. Peering through the gloom I can make out that the elderly people doing t'ai chi are wearing face masks. Same the next day. Beijing has a smog problem.

Concern over air pollution has a long history. In 1661 the diarist John Evelyn, determined to draw attention to the foul air in London, wrote a pamphlet called *Fumifugium: or, The Inconveniencie of the Aer and Smoak of London Dissipated.* Two years later an anonymous satirist reported that Evelyn:

> Shows that 'tis the sea-coal smoke
> That always London does environ,
> Which does our lungs and spirits choke,
> Our hanging spoil, and rust our iron.
> Let none at Fumifuge be scoffing
> Who heard at Church our Sunday's coughing.

We can say that Evelyn's activism was successful . . . if you take the long view. Britain passed the Clean Air Act in 1956. It took less than 300 years to take John Evelyn seriously. It would help if we could act a little faster this time, given the scale of the problem. The World Health Organization estimates that in 2012, globally 3.7 million deaths were attributable to outdoor air pollution. As with indoor air pollution, the big problem is in middle- and low-income countries, thus contributing to global health inequity.

Richer countries have done much to reduce the burden of air-pollution-related deaths, suggesting that it is entirely feasible to have cleaner cars, cleaner factories, restrictions on urban pollution. In high-income countries, not surprisingly, the issue is who is exposed. Mostly, if there is something bad going, society tries to organise so that those lower down the hierarchy get more of it. So it seems to be with environmental quality generally, and air pollution specifically.[34]

Nitrogen dioxide, NO_2, is mainly emitted by combustion in vehicles and power plants.[35] A US study looked at variation in air concentrations and found that average NO_2 concentrations were 38 per cent higher among non-whites than among whites; 10 per cent higher for people in poverty than among those above the poverty line. In contradiction to my general theme, there was no clear gradient – in this case non-whites and people in poverty were particularly exposed. The authors of this study asked themselves if 38 per cent higher matters, whether it is a lot or a little. Their answer was that 38 per cent matters a great deal. They calculate that if the non-white exposure to NO_2 were reduced to the exposure levels of whites, there would be 7,000 fewer deaths each year from ischaemic heart disease. A different way of achieving a reduction of 7,000 deaths would be to get 16 million people to increase their physical activity from inactive to 2.5 hours a week.

. . . and by going green

I read that green 'is the color of balance and harmony. From a color psychology perspective, it is the great balancer of the heart and the emotions, creating equilibrium between the head and the heart.' I can't quite put my finger on it, but given that I read it on a website called 'empower-yourself-with-color-psychology.com' I want a little more evidence. It turns out that there is evidence in abundance that living near and using green space is good for mental health. The key issue is urban green space, as a majority of us, worldwide, now live in cities.

One study, among many, examined the population of England and showed that people living near green space had better mental health and greater well-being than those with poorer access.[36] The effect was not enormous, about a tenth of the positive effect from being employed compared with unemployed, but it was worth having.

In later research these same investigators showed that moving to a greener area enhanced mental health, whereas the very thought of going the other way seemed to suffice to lessen mental health – it got worse before those destined to go to more built-up areas made the move.[37]

If the thought occurred that 'I'm just dying for a bit of green space', it may well be true. Lack of access to urban green space may make a contribution to the social gradient in deaths from heart disease.[38] Richard Mitchell in Glasgow and Frank Popham at St Andrews in Scotland have conducted research that addresses whether access to green space might be protective against the negative impact on health of low income. Indeed, that is what they found. For people with the least access to green space, the lowest income group had 2.2 times the mortality from circulatory disease compared with the highest income group. For those in the greenest areas, the lowest income group had 1.5 times the risk. It seems as though living near green space can diminish the negative effect of poverty on health. Green space did not abolish the social gradient in mortality, but it appeared to have a big impact. Why?

Mitchell and Popham found no difference in lung cancer mortality between areas ranked on green space. That ruled out smoking. The two most plausible pathways for the green-space effect on reducing the social gradient in mortality were reduction of stress and promotion of physical activity. Both are plausible and both may be playing a role.

Either way, making access to green space a priority for urban environments should be a priority. In Britain the Commission for Architecture and the Built Environment estimates that if the budget for new road building were diverted, it could provide for 1,000 new urban parks at an initial capital cost of £10 million each. Creating 1,000 new parks would save around 74,000 tons of carbon from being emitted.[39] Options are available that would create a greener and more health-equitable urban environment.

Active transport, usually travelling by bike or foot, but also including any form of transport that involves exercise, should be the complement to spending more on parks and less on roads.

In the US, the love affair with the automobile is responsible for much of the urban pollution that I described above when discussing NO_2 concentrations. It may also be contributing to obesity. Active transport is not only good for the planet, it may be good for health and for the social gradient.

In Britain, the nation was diverted for a while by an altercation between a rather posh Conservative government minister with a bicycle, and the police guarding No. 10 Downing Street. The image of a toff on a bicycle is not far from what the evidence shows: the higher the social position, the more likely are people to have used a bicycle in the previous week. People at the top make more trips of all types than those at the bottom *and* more by walking and cycling.[40]

Happily, some in urban planning are putting their talents to designing cities with a view to walkability and active transport. I want to highlight two issues. First is the safe journey to school – taking steps to encourage children to walk or cycle to school. To achieve this will take concentration on the second issue: making cycling and walking safe. In Copenhagen, 36 per cent of the journeys to work or education are by bicycle.[41] Cycle travel is relatively safe because of the separation of cars, pedestrians and cycles.

Even were there the political will to change, it would take a long time to change the design of cities to encourage active transport. That said, some changes can happen quickly. Introducing 20 mph speed limits in areas of cities has been shown to reduce traffic-related injuries and death.[42] Traffic calming has been shown to reduce the social gradient in traffic-related deaths of children.

AGE-FRIENDLY CITIES

If I challenged you, the reader, to come up with a set of criteria for the age-friendly city, you would not feel baffled. Conceptually, it is not hard to do. Practically, it is not too hard to do. We just have to do it.

Alex Kalache, a Brazilian who I have mentioned earlier, has devoted his career to improving the lot of older people globally. While at the World Health Organization he developed a guide to the Age-Friendly City.[43] It is so sensible, so right, that one wonders why all cities are not doing it. There are two major reasons why it is so sensible. First, it is based on the principle of active ageing, the same principle that animated my discussions in Chapter 7: older age is not a time to be put out to pasture. Second, the practical recommendations were developed bottom up: by listening to the voices of older people round the world who said what they needed, and to service-providers who have experience from the coal face.

The guide has eight topics: outdoor spaces and buildings, transport, housing, social participation, respect and social inclusion, civic participation and employment, communication and information, community support and health services. Seventy-six pages of common-sense advice as to how to make cities more habitable for older people should be on the reading list of every urban planner and local politician.

HOUSING

Closing the Gap in a Generation is the title we gave the report of the Commission on Social Determinants of Health. We referred to a forty-year gap in life expectancy between countries, and as much as twenty-eight years within countries, and we want to close those gaps in a generation. What are we thinking? I claim that we have both the knowledge and the money to close the gap in a generation. The question is whether we have the will.

I admit it is a bold claim, particularly with respect to the money. We said in *Closing the Gap* that a billion people live in slums. Further, we said that it would take $100 billion to upgrade the slums, to make them decent housing. One hundred billion dollars sounds enormous. No one will take us seriously, I thought; who would find $100 billion for anything? Last time I looked, 'we' had found $11 trillion to bail out the banks. For less than one-hundredth of the money we found for the banks, every urban dweller could have clean running water. We have the knowledge, we have the money. Do we have the will?

Of course, I am oversimplifying, but not by much. A key part of having the will is getting the players aligned: governments, funders and people. There are many ways to do it wrong. An academic in Kenya, for example, wanted to raze to the ground the slum of Kibera, close to the centre of Nairobi, and transfer to new-build housing, out of town, the half-million people who currently live in Kibera. He had no idea if that was what the people of Kibera wanted, but he knew that the land thus liberated was potentially valuable real estate that, in his view, could be put to 'better' use than housing poor people. And the poor people? They should be grateful for what they ended up with. I wish I were caricaturing.

To put it in context, Kibera, reportedly the biggest urban slum in Africa, has a lot wrong with it. It is a makeshift settlement, with makeshift housing and substandard or no services. People pay more for a litre of water, collected in a jerrycan, than a litre of water would cost in London. That said, 'high streets' have developed. Shops with advertisements for mobile phones are next to food shops and convenience stores, medical clinics and pharmacies. Kibera is a hotbed of crime, to be sure, but it has aspects of community, too, that would take great effort to reproduce elsewhere, in rows of breeze-block new housing, for example.

One way to do it better is shown by what the Self-Employed Women's Association (SEWA – we met it earlier) has done in Ahmedabad in Gujarat. SEWA members, living in shanties, gathered together and said what they wanted to improve their housing. The first thing they said was: we do not want to be moved! We want to stay right where we are, but we would like a place to cook, a bathroom and running water. SEWA negotiated loans equivalent to $500 for each household. The women themselves had to contribute $50, a great amount if you are living on $2 a day.[44]

The results are impressive: same streets, same modest houses, but spruced up, made pukka, and the required additions made. It feels cared for. I don't know whether it would lead to less crime. It feels like it might, if there is anything to the broken windows theory.[45] What is clear, though, is that women no longer have to stand in long queues to collect water, there is less water-borne disease, and as a result children lose fewer days of school.

In *Bonfire of the Vanities*, the novelist Tom Wolfe talks of his obscenely rich banker achieving 'isolation' from the chaos of New York. He could have been living in New York, London or Frankfurt for all the contact he had with people who were not in his rarefied stratum. For people with less money and privilege, and particularly for families, community is where life happens, death too. Communities can be a place of social, physical and biological hazards, but the social and physical attributes of the places where people are born, grow, live, work and age can have a profoundly positive effect on the lives they are able to lead and hence on health equity.

Local government, in partnership with civil society and with community residents, has a key role to play in promoting health equity. That said, central government sets the context and determines the power, money and resources that are available to communities, individuals and families. It is that broader sphere, social influences, to which we turn in Chapter 9, and global influences on health equity in Chapter 10.

9

Fair Societies

Many Americans are well aware that something is seriously amiss. They do not live as well as they once did. Everyone would like their child to have improved life chances at birth: better education and better job prospects. They would prefer it if their wife or daughter had the same odds of surviving maternity as women in other advanced countries. They would appreciate full medical coverage at lower cost, longer life expectancy, better public services, and less crime. However, when advised that such benefits are available in Western Europe, many Americans respond: 'But they have socialism! We don't want the state interfering in our affairs.'

Tony Judt, *Ill Fares the Land*[1]

In January 2010, Haiti's earthquake wreaked havoc and 200,000 people died. Less than two months later a quake 500 times stronger hit Chile and the death toll was in the hundreds. Haiti was underprepared in every way imaginable; Chile was well prepared, with strict building codes, well-organised emergency responses and a long history of dealing with earthquakes. True, the epicentre of the Haitian earthquake was closer to population centres than that of the Chilean quake, but that was only part of the explanation for the different scale of devastation.[2] Here is one indication of the differences in response: in Chile, President Bachelet was out within hours giving minute-by-minute reports in the middle of the night. People were reassured by the well-organised emergency response, as well as by the secure buildings. In Haiti, most people did not know if the president was alive for at least a day after the quake. The National Palace and the president's residence – like most government buildings – had collapsed.[3] What turns a natural phenomenon into a disaster is the nature of society. The number of people who died had more to do with Haiti's societal readiness and response than with the strength of the quake.

Here is another societal contrast. I received an email from an American colleague: 'I woke up this morning to learn that my country had lost the health wars to England.' This was his response to the news coverage of the paper I discussed in Chapter 2 which showed that middle-aged Americans are sicker than their English equivalents.[4] One of the two themes with which I began this book was the surprisingly poor health of Americans at younger ages, from ages fifteen to sixty. The health wars were lost at ages fifty-five to sixty-four, too.

The National Academy of Science (NAS) pursued the issue.[5] Its report compared health in the US with that of sixteen other high-income 'peer' countries. The US comes out of this badly. Compared with the average of its peers it ranks near or at the bottom of the league for nine health domains: adverse birth outcomes, injuries and homicide, adolescent pregnancy and sexually transmitted infections, HIV and AIDS, drug-related mortality, obesity and diabetes, heart disease, chronic lung disease, disability. Given that the US spends more on health care than each of the peer countries in the study, and given the nature of the health problems, the authors of the report did not look to health care for explanations. They say that there is no single cause of the US health disadvantage, but they do attribute it in part to the nature of US society.

A third societal contrast comes from South Asia. India is richer than Bangladesh, yet Bangladesh has had more rapid improvement in infant and child mortality. The Indian state of Kerala runs its affairs rather differently from most other Indian states, with higher status for women and a more communal orientation. The fabled good health of Kerala, compared with other Indian states, again points to the importance of society.[6]

A fourth striking contrast is that between eastern and western Europe.[7] During the communist period there was marked divergence in health as measured by life expectancy. In the Soviet Union and the other communist countries of Central and Eastern Europe, life expectancy stagnated. In western Europe, life expectancy improved year on year. Life was bleak in the communist countries, but was improving yearly for people in western Europe. After communism collapsed, countries such as the Czech Republic and Poland saw marked improvements in life expectancy. Russia has been on a roller-coaster ride, with dramatic increases in mortality, fall, rise and now fall again. But life expectancy for men in Russia is still a massive eighteen years shorter than the best in Europe: Iceland. The nature of society is crucial.

I could go on. Cuba, Costa Rica and Chile have better health than other countries in Central and South America. Japan beats us all – good health and relatively narrow health inequalities.[8]

Looking at these health contrasts between societies leads us to consider what constitutes the good society. When discussing theories of social justice in Chapter 3, I quoted Stuart Hampshire saying that there was no answer to that question. Philosophers disagree. I made the bold claim that health equity could decide the question. The good society is one where health and health equity are high and improve over time.

Some of the ways countries achieve better health than others will come from the specific things they do – provide universal access to high-quality medical care, for example, regardless of ability to pay. Each of the preceding five chapters dealt with specific changes that would improve health and reduce health inequity:

early child development, education, employment and working conditions, conditions for older people, and development of resilient communities. A society that ensures that all of these are well supported is likely to have good health and health equity.

There is more. Societies have cultures, values and economic arrangements that set the context for conditions through the life course that influence health. We talk of community resilience, but the nature of society will influence the hazards to which individuals and communities are exposed. This chapter, then, is about our social arrangements in society, and how they influence health equity. To repeat, my general theme is that inequities in power, money and resources give rise to inequities in the conditions of daily life, which in turn lead to inequities in health.

SOCIETY: RIGHT AND LEFT

In Britain, the standard view has been that Conservatives come to power and improve the economy while reducing social spending. After a while, the population tires of shoddy public services and miserly support for the needy, and votes Labour in. Labour proceeds to raise social spending and improve the public realm while messing up the economy. The population tires of the economic problems and votes Conservative ... who reverse things ... and so on. It is something of a caricature, especially now with multiple political parties, and some of our leaders seem able to mess up both the public realm and the economy at the same time. That said, there is continued debate between the public realm and individual freedom, the latter perceived as the route to economic success. The US is slightly more complicated because there may be a Democratic president with a Republican Congress, which ensures that not too much happens to the right or the left, or at all. At least in the US and Britain we play out these tensions through the ballot box. For a long time in Argentina, for example, the same kinds of tension between populism and the 'needs' of the wealthy for a robust economy led to periodic military coups alternating with episodes of democracy.

I asked a Chilean colleague, on the left politically, who was a refugee from Pinochet's junta and only returned to Chile when democracy was restored: 'Quite apart from Pinochet being a right-wing dictator who trampled on human rights, the political right would say that Pinochet was good for the economy. What do you say to that?'

'Unfortunately, the right are correct,' said my colleague.

'Why did Pinochet submit himself to an election [which he lost] after all those years of military rule?' I asked.

'To lie about the society you have created is very bad,' said my colleague. 'But to believe your own lies is really stupid.'

There, in extreme form, we have the same debate I described in Britain: the idea that the far 'right' are good for the economy but terrible for other things that people care about, such as human rights, social cohesion, and tolerance of diversity of views.

One thing is fairly certain. You have your own set of views, prejudices even, about this political terrain of the state versus the individual. If of one persuasion, you are on the alert in case I trot out old leftie solutions that rely on the state to do this, that and the other, all at great expense to the taxpayer. Am I not aware that bureaucracies are inefficient, ineffective, and create dependencies? If I am in favour of empowerment, do I not realise that people need to be set free from a controlling state? Do I want to create European socialism, which terrifies the Americans described by Tony Judt?

If of a different persuasion, your antennae may be waving in case I seem too soft on capitalism. When we published *Closing the Gap in a Generation*, historians at UCL convened a conference to discuss the Commission's report in light of the history of social determinants of health.[9] One critic, from the political left, said he had gone through the whole of *Closing the Gap* and found only one mention of neoliberalism. I apologised. I thought I had removed them all. One must have slipped through my net.

'Does that mean you support neoliberalism?' he asked, aghast.

'No, of course not. If you read the report, you would see that we are highly critical of unbridled markets in education and health care, and the kind of inequality that neoliberalism brings in its train. We called for sound institutions and market responsibility and saw a vital role for the state.'

'If you are against neoliberalism, why didn't you say so?' he and others wanted to know.

Once you start to sign up for or against 'isms' there is the danger of joining clans and stopping the analysis. Communism in Central and Eastern Europe did not deliver continued good health. By contrast, health did improve under communism in China, and continued to improve under whatever we call the current mix of Chinese communism and capitalism. Capitalism brings with it great problems of inequality which, in their own turn, can damage health and well-being. Rather than ride to the barricades waving 'ism' banners, we need to examine the evidence of how the rights of the individual and the requirements of the public realm can be balanced.

Jean Drèze, a Belgian/Indian economist, and Amartya Sen have collaborated on important books on India. In their most recent, *An Uncertain Glory*, they write that when India began its economic reforms in the early 1990s it faced 'two gigantic failures of economic governance. The first was a failure to tap the constructive role of the market.' The second was a 'resounding failure to harness the constructive role of the state for growth and development'.[10] It could not be clearer: both markets and state institutions are vital.

The critique of neoliberalism is correct. The idea that unbridled free markets in everything (the so-called Washington Consensus) is the way for countries to grow, develop and ensure better health and greater health equity is contradicted by the evidence. Equally, market dynamism is a route to greater productivity and economic growth. The question should no longer be capitalism or not, but what kind of capitalistic society do we want to have.

LEARNING

. . . from what is working

Suspending ideological predispositions, as far as is possible, where could we find societies that combine economic success, a profitable private sector, a constructive role for the state, and a record of good health? Picking up data from earlier in the book, Norway ranks top in the Human Development Index, Sweden is near the top in life expectancy, Finland has the best education scores on the PISA index in Europe, Denmark the best social mobility – but not, interestingly, the best health. The Nordic countries seem to be a good place to look.

First, though, it is necessary to scotch a rumour. In 1960 President Eisenhower made a speech in which he claimed that Sweden's socialist policies lead to 'sin, nudity, drunkenness, and suicide'. I've been a bit too preoccupied to investigate sin or nudity – although the teenage pregnancy rates are low in Sweden – but the latter two are wrong. Despite that, the rumour has persisted: people are so unhappy with their socialist 'paradise' that they kill themselves. It is a pity to spoil a good story, but it is simply untrue. Sweden's suicide rate per 100,000 is lower than the OECD average and marginally lower than in the US.[11] Norway's is about the same as Sweden's, Finland's is higher, and Denmark's is lower. There is no consistent story of social democracy and high suicide here.

When I was chairing the Commission on Social Determinants of Health, with my Swedish colleague and fellow commissioner Denny Vågerö, we approached the Swedish government to ask if they would fund a Nordic network of scholars to ask what we could learn from the Nordic Experience of the Welfare State – they called themselves the NEWS group.[12] Meeting with the group, I said that the rest of the world thinks that the Nordic countries are on another planet: good health, low crime, high degrees of gender equity, thriving social welfare. Are there some general lessons we can learn that could be applied elsewhere?

The NEWS group's review of the evidence suggested that the following were important in producing good health in the Nordic countries:

- Universal social policies rather than reliance on targeted, means-tested selective policies
- Reducing poverty through welfare state redistribution policies
- Relatively narrow income inequalities
- Emphasis on equality of opportunity *and* outcomes according to class and gender, and for socially excluded groups
- A broad scope of public services with provision of services mainly by the public sector at local level
- Social spending and social protection are important
- No one single policy solution but an accumulation of policies across the life course, each with its specific effects

. . . and from what is not working

If that is what the Nordic countries are doing right to gain good health, what is the US doing wrong? Above, I quoted the US National Academy of Science Report that showed that the US did particularly badly on health as compared with sixteen other 'peer' countries. The US health disadvantage was particularly strong among socially disadvantaged groups, but the better off were not doing wonderfully. In contradiction of President Eisenhower's concern about 'sin' in Sweden, the NAS notes that US adolescents are more likely to become sexually active at a young age, to have more sexual partners, and are less likely to practise safe sex than adolescents in other high-income countries.

The US had poor health compared with other rich countries in every age group under seventy-five – it ranked 16 or 17 out of 17 for most age groups (1 out of 17 is the healthiest), until it 'soared' to 16th or even 14th at age groups after fifty. One way of expressing health disadvantage is to examine the years of life lost from birth to age fifty. Around 1900, in the US and Europe, a newborn could expect to live about thirty-four years. This can be expressed as 'losing' sixteen years before age fifty. Today, not many people die before the age of fifty. Nevertheless the US ranks bottom on this measure as shown in Figure 9.1. In addition to this difference in years of life lost there is a great deal of non-fatal illness and suffering.

The National Academy of Science authors describe the reasons for the poor health of Americans as follows:

Adverse social and economic conditions also matter greatly to health and affect a large segment of the U.S. population. Despite its large and powerful economy, the United States has higher rates of poverty and income inequality than most high-income countries. U.S. children are more likely than children in peer countries to grow up in poverty, and the proportion of today's children who will improve their socioeconomic position and earn more than their parents is smaller than in many other high-income countries. In addition, although the United States was once the world leader in education, students in many countries now outperform U.S. students. Finally, Americans have less access to the kinds of 'safety net' programs that help buffer the effects of adverse economic and social conditions in other countries.[13]

It is almost a mirror image of the report of the NEWS group: poverty, inequality, and less access to social safety nets – in particular income support in times of need.

FIGURE 9.1: A CANDIDATE FOR RELEGATION FROM THE TOP LEAGUE

Years of life lost before age 50 by males and females in 17 peer countries, 2006–2008

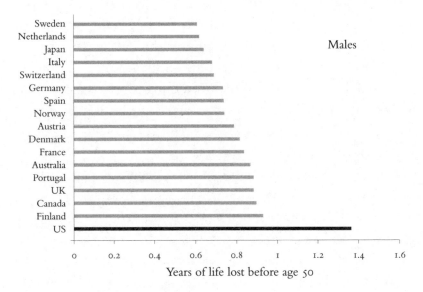

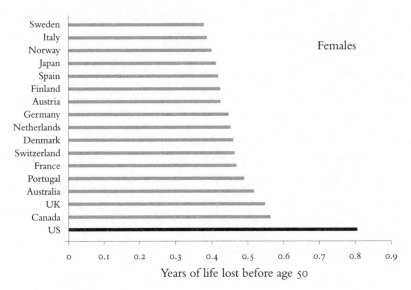

Source: Woolf SH, Aron L, editors. *U.S. Health in International Perspective: Shorter Lives, Poorer Health.* National Research Council; Institute of Medicine. Washington, D.C.: The National Academies Press, 2013.

MONEY AND OTHER THINGS THAT MATTER

The Nordic and US reports highlight income inequality and poverty as major causes of ill health. Through the book so far I have flirted with money. I condemned countries for not being more active in reducing child poverty, but then veered away and talked about parenting and the quality of the environment in which children are raised. I said that one of the main things we look for in work is monetary reward, but then talked about the quality of working life. I worried about poverty in retirement but then discussed social relationships and age-friendly cities.

At a more fundamental level I said that inequity in power, money and resources drives the inequities in daily life that cause health inequity. One key dimension of empowerment is 'material' – having the resources to lead a decent life. Which led me to quote, approvingly, Jerry Morris's pioneering work on minimum income for healthy living. Being able to afford the basics and lead a life of dignity and participate in society will take money, but much more than money.

If money is important, even if only part of the story when it comes to health inequity, we need to consider inequalities in income and wealth. We will also need to consider inequities in features of society, other than money, that are important for generating health inequities, but let's start with money.

Two of the most important recent contributions to the analysis of economic inequality come from the economists Joseph Stiglitz[14] and Thomas Piketty.[15] Neither is centrally concerned with health, but their analyses have much to say on the kind of society we are creating, and provide a context to Tony Judt's cry of anguish with which I began this chapter.

PATRIMONIAL CAPITALISM – PIKETTY STYLE

'It is illusory to think that social success can be achieved through study, talent and effort' is the essence of a lecture given by Vautrin to an impoverished nobleman, Rastignac, in Balzac's novel *Père Goriot*, published in 1835. Vautrin says (I am paraphrasing): there is no point pursuing your law studies. If by dint of great success and a deal of political scheming you become one of only twenty prosecutor-generals in France you could earn 5,000 francs a year. By contrast, marry the rich heiress Mademoiselle Victorine, who has eyes for you, and you will immediately have an income ten times that, of 50,000 a year.

For Vautrin's advice to be correct, the financial return from capital had to be greater than earnings from work (labour), the inequality had to be large, and a major source of capital had to be inherited, as distinct from what could be saved from earnings. Those conditions undoubtedly applied in nineteenth-century France, as they did in Britain of the time. Try to think of a Jane Austen hero or heroine who worked for a living – difficult. The income from inherited wealth had to be substantial. For a Jane Austen character to lead a dignified life, the material and psychological threshold was about thirty times the average income of the day. The unfortunate young Dashwood women in *Sense and Sensibility*, reduced to an unearned income of barely four times average income per head, have their marriage chances drastically reduced. Perish the thought that they should work.

(Jane Austen writes about the rich and scarcely notices anyone else. I have long harboured a wish to adapt her most famous opening line, and write: 'It is a truth universally acknowledged that a single man *not* in possession of a good fortune must be in want of a life.' Single, poor, his prospects for life expectancy are not good.)

Large inequalities of wealth and income and a preponderance of inherited wealth characterised nineteenth-century Britain and France. These insights and the concern that we may be heading that way again are the message of Thomas Piketty's *Capital in the Twenty-First Century*. For a 685-page economics book, published by a university press, to become a best-seller – it sold out within days, and was likely to have sold 200,000 copies within three months – and for its author, a serious French economics professor, to become a superstar, *Capital* must be tapping in to something important. It is.

There are two issues that Piketty highlights: growing inequalities of wealth and income and the fact that, in the future, much of the wealth will be inherited rather than earned. The first issue, growing inequalities, is of particular concern for health inequalities; the second, a preponderance of inherited wealth, is of concern for society as a whole, not only for health. I want to start with Piketty's concern over the way wealth is being accumulated. The bulk of the chapter will then deal with health inequalities.

Piketty's central point is that the return on capital is higher than the growth of income. Therefore capital accumulates. Prior to Piketty's painstaking collection and analysis of data, economists were not so concerned with distribution. Simon Kuznets, a distinguished US economist, observed that in the US and some other countries, as their economies developed and grew, up to the mid-twentieth century, inequality diminished. Inequality was just a stage of development, no need to worry about it, no politics involved.

Piketty, drawing on detailed study of the data over a longer period of time, points out that the period Kuznets was observing, roughly 1914–70, was an aberration. The shock of two world wars with an intervening depression did indeed lead to a marked reduction in inequalities of both income and capital. During that time, the return to capital was *less* than the growth of incomes. From about 1970 on, and continuing into the twenty-first century, we seem to be returning to the Belle Époque inequalities of the nineteenth century. Piketty's simple measure is capital as a ratio of national income. In Britain, for example, in 1870 the capital:income ratio was about 7. It went as low as 3 in 1950, and began to climb from about 1970, rising to above 5 by 2010. The US did not have such concentration of capital in the nineteenth century, but its capital: income ratio is now at the 5 level and, Piketty fears, is rising.

In the US, and to a lesser extent in other Anglophone economies, the growth in inequality is fuelled not only by increasing capital: income ratios but by the growth of top incomes. In 1928, the top 1 per cent of US income earners had 23 per cent of total household income. This lion's share tumbled if not to a kitten's, at least to a cat's share, of less than 10 per cent, after the 1929 crash. It had a rapid increase again, starting in the 1970s, so by 2007 the top 1 per cent had again 23 per cent of total household income. After the 1928 peak came a crash; similarly after the 2007 peak. Correlation or causation? Piketty is in no doubt that the concentration of income led to instability in the US economy, not least because the bottom 90 per cent had income growth of less than 0.5 per cent a year in the thirty years up to 2007. They had to either stop consuming or borrow. Increased inequality, then, can damage the economy in addition to other ills.

What are the top 1 per cent of earners going to do with all that money? How many yachts and houses can one family own? What they will do is save it and pass it on to the next generation. Says Piketty: 'It is all but inevitable that inheritance (of fortunes accumulating in the past) predominates over saving (wealth accumulated in the present) . . . the past tends to devour the future.' We will reproduce the kind of inherited wealth that we saw in the nineteenth century – the patrimonial society of Balzac and Austen. As we shall see, accumulating so much income and wealth at the top will not make the rich healthier, but it may slow the health improvement of those lower down.

Piketty's concern is not only with the size of the inequalities in wealth and income, but how they come about – the shift to inheritance. As Piketty says: 'Our democratic societies rest on a meritocratic worldview, or at any rate a meritocratic hope, by which I mean a belief in a society in which inequality is based more on merit and effort than on kinship and rents.' He continues: 'In a democracy, the professed equality of rights of all citizens contrasts sharply with the very real inequality of living conditions, and in order to overcome this contradiction it is vital to make sure that social inequalities derive from rational and universal principles rather than arbitrary contingencies' such as inheritance and 'rent' (shorthand for income received from capital, which equals wealth in the Piketty schema).

To summarise, then, Piketty thinks the rise of income and wealth inequalities, and the return of patrimonial capitalism, are bad for the economy, contravene our sense of what is just in the world, and have the potential for social unrest.

As I read Piketty, it is clear that societies do have political choices. If they want to *increase* inequalities of wealth and income they should do the following: transfer publicly owned assets into private hands; be complicit in low general rates of income growth, but engineer the economy so there are runaway salaries at the top; make taxes on income and spending less progressive; reduce taxes on capital, including corporation tax, capital gains and inheritance tax. Sounds rather familiar. It is what we have been doing in the US and the UK. It is hardly surprising that we are having trouble reducing health inequalities.

Bringing his vast knowledge and penetrating mind to the rise of inequalities in the US, Joseph Stiglitz similarly makes the point that moving money from the bottom to the top of the income distribution, as has been happening, lowers consumption. Those at the top save 15–25 per cent of their income, those at the bottom spend all of theirs. The resultant dampening of aggregate demand leads to unemployment. I would add: and unemployment leads to ill-health and worsens health equity.

Stiglitz says we know what extremes of inequality can do, we have seen it in Latin America: threats to social cohesion, crime, social instability, civil conflict. Stiglitz writes: 'Of all the costs imposed on our society by the top 1 per cent, perhaps the greatest is this: erosion of our sense of identity in which fair play, equality of opportunity, and a sense of community are so important.' I would add that the ills that Piketty and Stiglitz have so clearly identified bring in their train another concern.

INEQUALITIES IN SOCIETY LEAD TO INEQUALITIES IN HEALTH; MONEY MATTERS

. . . because money makes the poor less poor

What do Tanzania, Paraguay, Latvia and the twenty-five top-earning US hedge-fund managers (combined) have in common? They all have annual income of 21–28 billion dollars.[16]

	Population	Gross National Income ($billion)
Tanzania	48 million	26.7
Paraguay	7 million	22
Latvia	2 million	28.7
Hedge-fund managers	25	24.3*

*combined income

The first way that massive inequalities of income and wealth can lead to health inequalities is that if the rich have so much, there is less available for everyone else. I don't imagine that anyone has in mind asking the twenty-five top-earning hedge-fund managers to donate a year's earnings to Tanzania, but if they did they would hardly notice, as they would collect their $24 billion the next year, and it would double Tanzania's national income. This could potentially improve the health of Tanzanians in two ways: make individuals a bit richer and improve the public realm. Such money could pay for sewage plants and toilets, provide clean running water and clean cooking stoves, even fund a few school teachers' salaries. No, total fantasy. The critics of aid would say that the money would end up in Swiss bank accounts. I will revisit this question in the next chapter.

For some, it would be no less fanciful to imagine that some of that combined 'earning' of $24 billion could be redistributed within the US. There is an argument, in the past taught to economics students as if it were a fact, that it didn't matter if the top 1 per cent took an increasing slice of the cake, because they are the wealth producers, and setting the wealth producers free enlarges the cake.

Joseph Stiglitz says clearly that is not what the evidence shows. The International Monetary Fund (IMF) is hardly known as a champion of redistribution, but they back Stiglitz.[17] Examining evidence across countries, OECD and non-OECD, the IMF researchers conclude that 'lower net inequality (i.e. after taxes and transfers) is robustly correlated with faster and more durable growth'. There are not even any 'maybes' here. The IMF authors also conclude that redistribution is 'benign' in its effect on growth, so that, in sum, redistribution is pro-growth.

A related argument put out by apologists for inequality is that a rising tide lifts all boats. Swamps, more like. Stiglitz has no patience with this argument either. As quoted above, in the US in particular, the small boats are leaking or capsizing, while the luxury yachts have the freedom of the seas. In Chapter 1, and throughout the book, I laid out why low income was bad for health. In poor countries low income is linked to destitution. In rich countries it is something a bit different. In Chapter 5, when discussing income from work, I said that we had measured deprivation in Europe on the ability to afford:

- to pay rent or utility bills
- to keep the home adequately warm
- to face unexpected expenses
- to eat meat, fish or a protein equivalent every second day
- a week's holiday away from home

- a car
- a washing machine
- a colour TV
- a telephone

This has the air more of deprivation relative to the standards of the society – why otherwise should lack of a colour TV be bad for health? – than to some absolute standard. I said in Chapter 1 that Amartya Sen resolved the debate of absolute or relative poverty by saying that relative inequality with respect to income translates into absolute inequality in capabilities: your freedom to be and to do. It is not only how much money you have, but what you can do with what you have; which, in turn, will be influenced by where you are.[18] If the community provides clean water and sanitation, you don't need your own money to ensure these solutions. If the community provides subsidised public transport, health care free at the point of use and public education, you don't need your own money to access these necessities. The way to understand the importance of income for health is to enquire what people are able to do with the income they have. This relates to the income both of the community and of the individuals within it.

How will this understanding help LeShawn in Baltimore, whose story I told in Chapter 4? To remind you, many of LeShawn's problems arose from his mother's poverty, and the stressful life he had from birth through early childhood, adolescence and young adulthood. One way to intervene in LeShawn's family's poverty is to increase their income, by improving employment prospects and supporting a living wage. Where this is not feasible, in the short term, the state has a clear role to play.

Health warning: I am going to discuss welfare and benefits. Politicians in the US and the UK seem convinced that to reduce welfare spending is self-evidently a good thing. What if every time a politician said he was going to cut benefits to the poor, a little bird whispered in his ear: lower welfare spending means making people's health worse, if not killing people.

One of the NEWS group's conclusions was that good health of the Nordic countries is dependent, in part, on social spending and social protection. As a step in showing this they examined poverty levels before and after taxes and social transfers of various kinds. The benchmark for poverty, as with child poverty in Chapter 4, was having an income less than 60 per cent of the median income. Figure 9.2 illustrates the point.

The height of the bars shows poverty levels in different countries from income gained in the marketplace. The dark bars show poverty after taxes and transfers. First, compare the US

FIGURE 9.2: WHAT WOULD YOU LIKE THE POVERTY LEVEL TO BE?

Proportion below poverty threshold before and after welfare state redistribution around 2000.

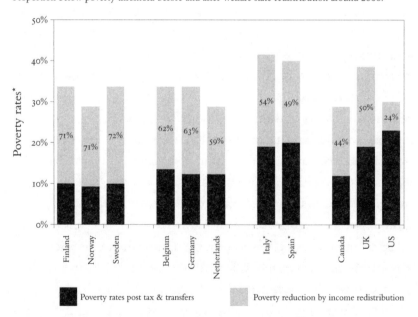

*high rates are an artefact of the way income is measured in Italy and Spain
Source: Lundberg O, Aberg Yngwe M, Kolegard Stjarne M, Bjork L, Fritzell J. The Nordic Experience: welfare states and public health (NEWS). *Health Equity Studies*. 2008; 12.

and UK. Pre-tax, poverty levels are higher in the UK than in the US – the bar is higher. The effect of taxes and transfers is to reduce poverty level by 50 per cent in the UK, and by only 24 per cent in the US (that is what the per cent figures are in the bars on the graph). US poverty rates, post-tax and transfers, are therefore higher than in the UK. If being below the poverty line means not being able to afford items on the list I gave above, health will be damaged and health inequities will be worse. The Treasury Secretary has it in his power to influence the magnitude of health inequities.

In Figure 9.2, look at Finland, Norway and Sweden, where the impact of taxes and transfers is to reduce poverty by more than 70 per cent.

The NEWS group then addressed the question of whether social welfare spending of a country was related to better health. They did this in two ways. First, they used the concept of 'social rights' – legislated social provisions aimed at guaranteeing citizens' welfare and security. They examined two characteristics of social spending to meet social rights, generosity and universality – does it cover everybody? Both were related to good health. The more generous the social spending of a country, and the more universal, the lower is the national mortality rate.

The second way was to examine the impact of social spending, not just on the average health of a country, but on health *inequities*. My Swedish colleague Olle Lundberg reasoned that we should not simply be asking: Nordic, good or bad? If addressing the social determinants of health means empowering people, then one way of giving people more control over their lives is to improve income when it is needed. Therefore look at what is known as social protection – spending by the state on support for old age, bereaved persons, incapacity, health, family, active labour market programmes, unemployment and housing. Then adjust all this for

FIGURE 9.3: SHOCKING NEWS: WELFARE SPENDING IMPROVES
HEALTH AND REDUCES INEQUALITIES

Relative inequalities in health, primary vs. tertiary (women)

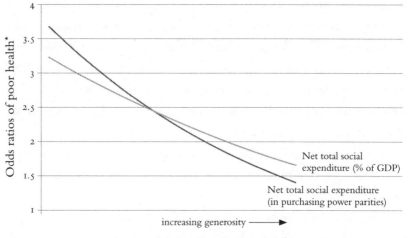

Country Social Expenditure

Note: *primary vs tertiary education
Source: Adapted from data in Dahl 2013 (19).

tax breaks and the amount of direct and indirect taxes paid. Once
they had this measure they looked at its relation to inequities in
health in fifteen European (EU) countries, shown in Figure 9.3, for
women – the results are similar for men.[19]

Women with only primary education are more likely to have
poor health than women with tertiary education; everything
else I've shown you should mean that is not a surprise. But the
greater a country's social spending the narrower the gap in ill-
health between those with least education and those with most.
The graph shows the *relative* health disadvantage of having only
primary compared with tertiary education. There was a big absolute difference as well.

Greater welfare spending improves overall health and narrows
health inequities. There is no question in my mind that it is better
to work than to subsist on benefits, but where work is not possible,

or is not a way out of poverty, spending on social protection makes a difference to people's lives.

The graph shows how much more likely to be in poor health are people with primary education compared with those with tertiary education. It shows that the higher a country's social expenditure, the lower is the health disadvantage of having primary education.

In some Latin American countries, notably Mexico and Brazil, the government's approach to reducing poverty includes conditional cash-transfer schemes, such as Oportunidades in Mexico and Bolsa Familia in Brazil. These schemes are interesting, exciting and problematic. As their name suggests they transfer cash to poor people on certain conditions: that they take their children to health clinics, that they attend health education classes, that older children attend school regularly. I said that cash is given to 'people'. The people are usually women. The assumption is that if the money is given to women it is more likely to be used to support the family's needs than if it is given to people of the male persuasion.

The schemes are exciting because there is little doubt that they have contributed to poverty reduction, in Brazil, for example,[20] and to improved nutrition in Mexico.[21] They are problematic for two reasons. First, it is all very well to insist that girls be in school as a prerequisite for receiving the monthly cash. But what if the schools are hopeless? Transferring cash to poor women is not a substitute for investing in improving institutions and services, such as the health clinics and schools where attendance is required. Second, conditionality is authoritarian. Authorities are saying to women: 'We know what is good for you; we'll give you the money provided you do as we say.' It leaves a bad taste. There is now a move to evaluate whether removing the conditionality component allows the schemes still to function.[22]

. . . because money can be spent in ways
that will improve lives

A second way money can improve the lives of LeShawn and his mother is that the community can spend it in ways that meet their needs while reducing their burden. Transport will serve as example. LeShawn's mother has household income of about $17,000. She spends 23 per cent of that on running a car.[23] Why, you might ask, if you have such low income, would you spend such a vast sum on running a car? I tease my American colleagues that they think public transport is when two people travel in a car at the same time. If public transport is inadequate how else is LeShawn's mother to get to her part-time job, to take her children to hospital, or generally to get about?

We took some visitors to see a Children's Centre in Newham, a deprived part of East London. Childcare provided by the community was charged at £850 a month. How, I wondered, could a woman in a deprived part of London possibly afford to pay that out of her earnings, assuming she could find work? In Britain, for a family with two children in full-time care, the annual cost of childcare is £11,700 ($20,000).[24] Tax credits help, but if their value is being reduced, work is not a way out of poverty. Subsidised childcare might be. A Swedish colleague on the visit pointed out that in Sweden, childcare is state-subsidised. The most you pay per child is £113 a month, £1,356 a year ($2,300).[25] State provision is making working families less poor, and enabling both parents to work.

Similarly, if the community provides the kinds of services for early child development, education, job training and unemployment benefits discussed in earlier chapters, people will not have to pay for them out of their pockets. There is no free lunch, agreed. It takes money. Taxation is a good source of such money. To show that there is a great deal of money about, one-third of the $24 billion income of the top twenty-five hedge-fund managers could fund something like 80,000 New York schoolteachers.

The rich are intolerant of taxation. As mentioned above, when discussing Piketty, in the US and Britain we have made our taxation systems less progressive. The rich, in general, have disproportionate political power. They use it to ensure they pay less tax. If the rich buy their own health care, education, transport, even security, they argue, why should they pay taxes to provide those things for other people? Virtually no one in public life in the UK and US is prepared to have a grown-up discussion in public about whether a more progressive taxation system, with a higher overall tax take, is a price worth paying for improving the quality of people's lives to match that of the Nordic countries.

Before we leave the Nordic countries, it is important to say that there is not an agreed view as to whether health inequalities are narrower there than in other countries less committed to social democracy. The graphs I showed in Chapters 5 and 7, on life expectancy by education, do show overall good health and relatively narrow inequalities in the Nordic countries. Yet other reports dispute this.[26] Our Nordic colleagues point out that overall health is high in Nordic countries, and the health of the most disadvantaged is high. These are major societal advances, while we continue to debate which evidence to believe on the size of the social health gap.

Proportionate universalism

It was the evidence provided by our Nordic colleagues that led us, at the UCL Institute of Health Equity, to come up with the ugly neologism 'proportionate universalism'. Let me explain.

When the British government was planning its Sure Start policy for early child development, I went to a meeting at Her Majesty's Treasury to discuss the proposed programme. It turned out that the initial plans for Sure Start were to target it at the most deprived communities. I showed the group the social gradient in literacy of young people according to parents' education and pointed out that at the top, parents with the highest levels of education, our young people's literacy levels were on a par with Sweden and Japan. But the gradient was steeper in Britain than in Japan and Sweden; the result was that the lower you go in the social hierarchy the worse our young people score compared with Sweden and Japan. The implication was that Sure Start should be for everyone, not only for the worst off (see Chapter 4).

The senior Treasury official, the wonderful Norman Glass (deceased sadly), said:

'Don't come to me with that Scandinavian nonsense about universal interventions. We're Anglo-Saxons. We target and focus on the worst off.'

Anglo-Saxon? Norman was Irish–Jewish, but the point was well made. The default position of British social policy is to target interventions on the worst off. It seems to make sense. Why spend money on those who don't need it? The problem with such 'common sense' is that it ignores the gradient. All the social and related health problems that we see follow a social gradient. The disadvantage of focusing on the worst off is that you miss those, say, in the middle who have worse health than those at the top, albeit better than those beneath them on the ladder.

It is not just from the Nordic countries that we learned the importance of universalist policies. In Chile they talk of Chile Solidario. The aim is to bring the most socially excluded into the mainstream of society, to emphasise their rights and entitlements, not to see the state as a charitable institution handing out help to a grateful poor. Proportionate universalism is an attempt to marry the obvious need to work hardest on behalf of those in greatest need while preserving the universalist nature of social interventions. Services for the poor are poor services. We should want everyone to gain the benefits of universal policies while putting in effort proportionate to need. A key principle is social cohesion.

. . . because inequality damages social cohesion

I was at a meeting in Japan having coffee with a Hungarian colleague. He and I had tried to pursue collaborative research in Hungary, alongside our investigations into poor health in Central and Eastern Europe in the Czech Republic, Poland, Russia and Lithuania. The research did not get going in Hungary, and my colleague was explaining why – personal relations problems. He then passed the comment that Japan was a very stressful country. My reaction was: you have just spent half an hour telling me that things aren't working in Budapest because A is having an affair with B, and her husband is not on talking terms with C, who simply won't work with D and E. You are all pulling against each other. I have the impression that in Japan they are all on the same team. There is, in Japan, a shared commitment to success. We see it in relatively narrow income inequalities, low rates of poverty, low rates of crime, care for older people – and the longest life expectancy in the world.

Richard Wilkinson and Kate Pickett captured public imagination with their book *The Spirit Level*.[27] It contains a simple and powerful idea: inequalities of income damage the health and well-being of all of us, rich, poor, or somewhere in between. I have co-edited books with Richard Wilkinson, and co-written a paper defending his ideas against some of his critics. I agree that social and economic inequalities are bad for health inequalities. There is a 'but'. The evidence that income inequalities are bad for the health of everyone in society was seen only among richer countries, and that evidence is weaker now than it was. In Chapter 7

I included a graph (Figure 7.3, p. 207) showing life expectancy in different countries according to education, and imagined a conversation with a child in Hungary. There were big differences in life expectancy among European countries. But the size of the difference was much smaller for people with university education than it was for people with only primary education. If inequality were damaging the health of everybody you might have imagined big differences between countries for everybody, not only for the most disadvantaged. Inequality damages the health of the poor more than it damages the health of the rich.

That said, I am entirely sympathetic to Wilkinson and Pickett's focus on psychosocial factors. When social and economic inequalities are large, people lower down the social hierarchy are disempowered. Similarly big inequalities mean that we tend more and more to see the poor and socially excluded inhabiting a different world from people in the middle, and the rich inhabiting a different world from everyone else: separate schools, living arrangements, transport, gyms, holidays and attitudes.

Key to living in society is empathy and connectedness – genuine feeling for our fellow members of society. The separate, compartmented lives of people at the top, middle and bottom damage this vital ingredient of society. The previous chapters spell out, in detail, how this lack can damage health through the life course and in communities.

Social hierarchies and health are about much more than income

Robert Sapolsky and I had to get together. We had been introduced by proxy by Robert Evans, a Canadian economist who said in print that he wanted to make comparisons between two long-term programmes of research on primates. They were Sapolsky's studies of baboons in the Serengeti ecosystem and Marmot's studies of civil servants in the Whitehall ecosystem. Both sets of primates, baboons and civil servants, revealed clear social gradients in biological markers of illness and of ill-health.

I met Robert first at his lab at Stanford. His own room there looks a bit like he does, that is if a lab could be described as having scraggly long hair and beard, ruffled, warm, engaging, intellectual and socially committed. Robert and I have reviewed the evidence on social gradients in human and non-human primates to ask what we can learn about human societies and inequalities in health. In primates of the human variety we can speculate whether the social gradient in health might be attributed to lack of access to medical care, to disreputable consumption of fattening foods or alcohol, or to smoking. None of these applies to the baboons, nor is any baboon signed up either to neoliberalism or to social democracy. What does apply, potentially in humans as in baboons, is stress and its physiological effects.[28]

We gave ourselves a caution: apes can be Machiavellian, but no ape was ever Machiavelli; humans are not apes in pinstripe suits; we should not be too literal in reading across from apes to man. That said, the variation among species of non-human primates is instructive for understanding how hierarchies in human societies translate into inequalities in health.

To start with Sapolsky's studies of baboons, there are clear dominance hierarchies, and the major stresses that subordinate animals' experience are psychosocial rather than physical. Food is plentiful and, in the absence of a drought, comes with no more cost than foraging. Luxuries, 'kills', are more available to the dominant animals, but these make up a small proportion of the diet. Dominance in males is seen in access to preferred resting sites, grooming opportunities and access to females. The aggression to which low-status animals are subject is more usually symbolic threats, rather than actual fights. I have in mind the high status baboon, with a leather jacket and a bike chain, cigarette out of the corner of his mouth saying: this piece of savannah ain't big enough for the both of us. The subordinate male beats a hasty retreat, leaving food or female to be enjoyed by the alpha.

We shouldn't jump too quickly to conclusions, but high ranks that enjoy a high degree of social control and predictability, better-developed social relationships (grooming) and access to luxuries, while basics are relatively abundant at all levels of the hierarchy, and aggression symbolic rather than actual, is not a world away from human social hierarchies. In these animal surveys in the wild the 'endpoints' studied have not been disease, or even life expectancy – the numbers involved have simply been too small for precise calculations – but physiological markers of stress. The most frequently studied has been the stress hormone cortisol, which we think is relevant in humans as it is in non-human primates. (You may be wondering how you measure plasma cortisol in a baboon. You hide, then shoot it with an anaesthetic dart, and hurry to get the blood sample before the cortisol level changes. While you go to the field lab, the baboon wakes up and goes about his business.)

Studies of baboons, other than Robert Sapolsky's, have replicated his finding that subordinate males have higher levels of basal cortisol. There is an interesting exception, in conditions of instability. The very top-ranking baboon may engage in real fights to keep his position, as number 2 works to make his move for the top spot. Under these conditions, basal cortisol may be higher in number 1 than in number 2. Even if you are a high-status human male, finding out that you are about to be kicked out of the boardroom or the Cabinet can be stressful.

In some primate species low status is not characterised by frequent episodes of social stress, as described above. In these species the higher cortisol levels in subordinate animals are less marked.

Culture seems important, as well as species differences. Sapolsky and a colleague observed a troop of baboons where, because of historical accident, living too close to humans, 50 per cent of the high-ranking male baboons were killed. What developed next was interesting: a troop emerged that had markedly less aggression related to hierarchy and a greater degree of affiliative behaviour – such as grooming. As with all baboon troops, adolescent males join from outside. Usually the new entrants fight for a place in the hierarchy. In this special troop the new males learned caring behaviour, even treating females without aggression. In this 'caring' troop low status was *not* associated with higher levels of cortisol.

As I said at the start of this section, we should not overstate the read-across from non-human to human primates. That said, it is entirely plausible that low status in humans, as in apes, is associated with higher levels of stress and its physiological correlates. Affiliative behaviour moderates the harmful effects of stress. Social cohesion means trust and social supports from others, or from caring services and institutions, or, as I said in relation to Japan, feeling that you are on the same team. To link back to the discussion on economic and social inequalities, the bigger the inequalities the greater is the threat to social cohesion and hence the greater threat to health equity.

HEALTH OF SOCIETIES IS ALSO ABOUT MORE THAN INCOME

Quoting Amartya Sen, I said it is not so much what you have that is important for health, but what you can do with what you have. Way back in Chapter 1 I pointed to countries that enjoyed good health despite not having high national income. By contrast, in this chapter we have been considering a country, the US, which has relatively poor health, despite high national income.

Let us visit three Latin American countries that have achieved good health despite relatively low national incomes, and in the case of Costa Rica and Chile, strikingly high levels of income inequality.

I start with Cuba. If you've not visited, what do you imagine it is like? Full of Soviet-era apparatchiks dressed in standard-issue

Russian clothes? People anxious, poor and afraid, careful about who they talk to, and about what?

It did not look like that to me, on a recent visit. Among other activities I was invited to give a lecture at the Ministry of Public Health. Not even civil servants looked standard-issue. The women had nail varnish on their fingernails and toenails, and highlights in their hair. They looked like middle-class Latin American women. The men, all dressed appropriately for the hot climate, looked slightly more casual (and fashionable) than an Englishman on his summer holiday – at least they were not wearing sandals with socks.

At one point in my lecture on social determinants of health I described research showing that stress at work was associated with increased risk of heart disease. One way of measuring stress at work, I said, was imbalance between effort and reward. High effort and low reward: has that ever happened to one of you? A titter ran round the audience that rose from a hum to an excited babble. Indeed it had happened to them, and they didn't mind letting me know. And when I showed them the evidence from Europe that the lower the status in the workplace the more common was imbalance between effort and reward, again there was excited acknowledgement. They recognised the phenomenon.

Not a socialist paradise, then, nor lacking social hierarchies.

Cuba could be a Rorschach test. For some, it is a communist pariah. For others, Cuba represents a different model of development: a country that has been able to turn its back on neoliberalism and avoid many of the gross income inequalities that scar Latin America. The political right will frown at this: if there is equality in Cuba, it is because it is uniformly ghastly.

I see it as neither socialist paradise nor communist pariah, but as a poor country with remarkably good health. As when considering Europe, we need to go beyond the ideological battles of the Cold War and try to see what is happening. To see, that is, what we can learn from understanding how Cuba achieved such good health, despite an economy that even its staunchest defenders have

FIGURE 9.4: SOMEONE IS DOING SOMETHING RIGHT

Male life expectancy 1955–2011 in 4 American countries

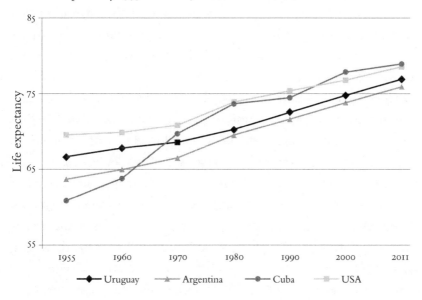

Source: WHO World Health Statistics.

to admit has been a sorry mess. It was dependent on the USSR for everything imported. When the Soviet Union collapsed, so did Cuba's economy. Without petrol for the cars and farm machinery, they went back to using horses and carts and bullocks in the fields – hardly the white heat of modern development.

Despite all this, health flourished. The graph in Figure 9.4 shows life expectancy for Cuba and for three comparison countries from the Americas: Argentina, Uruguay and the USA. Argentina and Uruguay were a good deal more developed in the 1950s than pre-revolutionary Cuba – the revolutionary government of Fidel Castro fought its way to power in 1959. In 1910, Argentina was the eighth-richest country in the world in national income per head, just behind Canada and Belgium, and ahead of Denmark and the Netherlands.

What has happened is simply dramatic. Cuba's life expectancy was ten years shorter than the US in 1955, but by 2011 both countries had the same life expectancy. It had outstripped the two comparison Latin American countries.

The question is: what has Cuba been doing? Cubans tell me that it has much to do with their highly developed health-care system. It is also likely to connect with their emphasis on education and social protection.

Costa Rica's health record looks a great deal like Cuba's, and Costa Rica is *not* a communist country. I asked the Costa Ricans why their health is so good – life expectancy, like Cuba's, similar to the US. The first thing they told me was that they abolished their armed forces in 1948. Why should we have an army? they said. Most countries in this part of the world have armies to suppress their own population; we used the money to invest in education and health care – priorities similar to Cuba's. Figure 9.5 tells an interesting story. It compares Latin American countries in terms of pre-school enrolment and reading scores at 6th grade. Cuba has the most children enrolled in pre-school, and the best reading scores in 6th grade.

FIGURE 9.5: GETTING TO THE CHILDREN EARLY

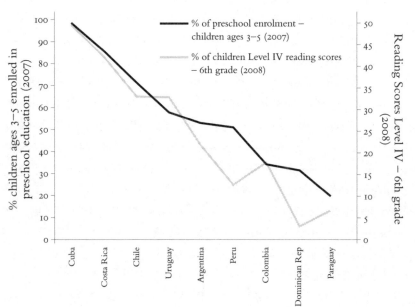

Source: UNESCO.

Next comes Costa Rica, followed by Chile. My 'developed' country examples, Uruguay and Argentina, come lower down on both measures. Paraguay and Dominican Republic do badly.

The truth is that I do not know precisely why Cuba, Costa Rica and Chile, with their remarkably different political histories, all have health up at the same level as the US, despite having only a fraction of the US's income per head. My speculation is that Chile Solidario, with its universalist approach to including the poor, high investment in pre-school and education, and provision of health care, is important. Something similar is at work in the other two countries.

Societies matter. The 'causes of the causes' perspective is relevant. We have a good deal of evidence that we could improve health and health equity by including everyone in society in the implications of Chapters 4–8: early child development, education, work and employment conditions, good circumstances for older people, resilient communities. But we have to want to. Large inequalities of income and social conditions may be a cause of lack of social cohesion, but they may be a symptom, too. Why do we tolerate the incomes of the 1 per cent soaring ever upwards, while apparently not caring that vast numbers of our populations live in poverty? A more socially cohesive society would not want that. To quote Piketty again: 'In a democracy, the professed equality of rights of all citizens contrasts sharply with the very real inequality of living conditions, and in order to overcome this contradiction it is vital to make sure that social inequalities derive from rational and universal principles rather than arbitrary contingencies.' Inequalities exist in all societies. That is how it is. The magnitude and extent of those inequalities, how they come about, and what they mean for the less privileged, is vital to a sense of social justice and to health. We have good evidence that we can do things better.

Living Fairly in the World

Gross National Product counts air pollution and cigarette advertising, and ambulances to clear our highways of carnage. It counts special locks for our doors and the jails for the people who break them. It counts the destruction of the redwood and the loss of our natural wonder in chaotic sprawl . . .

Yet the gross national product does not allow for the health of our children, the quality of their education or the joy of their play. It does not include the beauty of our poetry or the strength of our marriages, the intelligence of our public debate or the integrity of our public officials. It measures neither our wit nor our courage, neither our wisdom nor our learning, neither our compassion nor our devotion to our country, it measures everything in short, except that which makes life worthwhile.

Robert F. Kennedy, University of Kansas, 18 March 1968

At the crowded dinner table of my mind, I have an anarchic Icelandic mayor sitting down with some angry young Greeks, an Irish professor struggling to make ends meet, a Brazilian woman juggling children and poverty, a healthy and well-educated South Korean, a woman from Kerala in South India, a suicidal Indian cotton farmer, a Bangladeshi teenager who loves sweatshops, a Zambian whose children cannot go to secondary school, an irritated Argentinian, an obese Egyptian woman, a young Kenyan chain-smoker and a few randomly chosen Americans and Europeans. The dress is traditional, and/or smart casual.

What the dinner guests all have in common is that their lives, and hence their chances for good health, are all influenced by their country's participation in globalisation. It's my fantasy, so I can structure it how I want. The people serving the food, and listening to moving tales of failure and success, are officials from the International Monetary Fund and the World Bank, the European Commission and the US State Department, and executives from tobacco corporations, food-marketing giants, retail clothing chains and national aid agencies.

Were I Chaucer, and we had a poet's time, each would tell their tale in detail, with brio and wit. But I am not, and we don't, so let's start with the anarchic Icelander. The others will make their appearance in this chapter, as will their clothing and the food on their table. It's a non-smoking environment so the Kenyan chain-smoker has to refrain for a bit.

In 2010, Jon Gnarr was elected mayor of Reykjavik, the capital of Iceland. He was a professional comedian with an anarchist streak. He'd never had anything formal to do with politics, but he formed the 'Best Party' to contest the mayoral election, and campaigned on a promise to break his election promises, which included installing a polar bear in Reykjavik Zoo, free towels at the public swimming pools, and fighting corruption by indulging in it in public.[1] He drove his political opponents bananas by smiling at any and all attacks. We sometimes think our politicians are clowns. Here was a clown who became a politician. He started campaigning as a joke and found himself with a real political job. I met him in June 2013, when I was invited to Iceland by the government to talk to them about social determinants of health. The mayor did what mayors do: he hosted a reception at a special venue in the city and delivered a speech of welcome, albeit you couldn't help feeling that his tongue kept straying towards his cheek. His political adviser told me that they had to take the job seriously and work with City Hall in a responsible way – that was no joke. They did, however, do something very un-politicianlike: decide that one term was enough.

Two pieces of background are relevant. Iceland is a country with a population of just over 300,000, more than a third of whom live in the capital. In Britain, we jest that our country is run by members of an old boys' club who were all at Oxford together. (It's not true; some were at Cambridge.) In Iceland, to say everyone really does know everyone is only a slight exaggeration. Gnarr's wife was a friend of Björk (the singer), and his campaign manager was at university with . . . who knows . . . who is a neighbour of . . . Even if you're an outsider like Gnarr, you have connections all over the place. To illustrate, I was sitting at a fish restaurant outside Reykjavik on a Saturday evening with the Chief Medical Officer and asked him what is the prison population of Iceland. Just a moment, he said, made a quick call, and in three minutes he had the answer: 50 per 100,000. All right, you might expect the Chief Medical Officer to be well connected, but one phone call on a Saturday evening? Incidentally, 50/100,000 is very low, roughly the same as Japan. In the UK the figure is just under 200 per 100,000, and in the US close to 800. In Iceland, if you commit a crime the probability is that the victim will tell your mother next time she sees her in the supermarket. It may be the very cohesiveness of Iceland that is responsible for their low crime rates and remarkably good health.

The second piece of background, more relevant to globalisation and health, is that Iceland had suffered a catastrophic economic meltdown in 2008. It had gone from being a well-organised society based on fishing and huge supplies of geothermal energy – hence aluminium smelting – to housing three private banks that represented everyone's worst nightmare of what reckless cowboys can do when let loose on the global economy.

In Chapter 6, I referred to the debate around the work of Harvard economists Carmen Reinhart and Kenneth Rogoff who showed that when national debt climbs above 90 per cent of GDP, economic growth slows.[2,3] At its peak, Iceland's debt was 850 per cent of GDP! Icelandic banks bought assets round the world, as though all curves go ever upwards without a day of reckoning. The butterfly that flapped its wings might have been the collapse of sub-prime mortgages in the USA, but it caused a hurricane in Iceland and, predictably, the castles in the air were reduced to rubble. The economic collapse was a profound shock to the economic livelihood of Icelanders, not to mention to their self-esteem and to the sense of being part of a small close-knit society. It was against this background that the citizens of Reykjavik, thoroughly fed up with the politicians who had presided over this catastrophe, elected a self-confessed clown.

What happened next?

Iceland appealed to the IMF, who offered help in return for their usual policies of stringent austerity. The general population of Iceland were asked to pay off the debts of a few bankers through taxes and submitting to austerity. In a referendum, they refused – much to the chagrin of those in other countries who had, wittingly or otherwise, found their finances to be tied up with the fate of these lasso-twirling Icelandic bankers. Spending on social safety nets and health care was maintained. Electing a funny man as mayor of Reykjavik was perhaps the population's way of saying that they rejected 'business as usual', including IMF-style economic ortho-doxy. Iceland's response was in sharp contrast to what happened in Greece, Ireland and some other countries. That, and a high degree of social solidarity, were perhaps the reason why Iceland did not see adverse health effects in response to its financial cataclysm, as other countries did.[4]

The first area of globalisation and health that I want to exam-ine, then, is global finance, in various aspects. We will then move on to look at trade; markets and the behaviour of corporations; and at alternatives to the pursuit of economic growth. Each can have a profound impact, for good and ill, on health and health equity.

Asking if globalisation is good or bad is akin to asking if the weather is good or bad. It can be both. A key question is the degree to which globalisation leads to shared knowledge and resources and creates opportunities on the one hand, or is disempowering of individuals and communities on the other.

FAIR FINANCE: THE GLOBAL FINANCIAL CRISIS AND AUSTERITY

The contrast between my anarchist Icelander and angry young Greeks is instructive. Both were disempowered by the global financial crisis, but the response differed markedly. In Chapter 6 I referred to debates between macroeconomists as to whether Keynesian stimulus or austerity was the appropriate response to the global financial crisis. Naively perhaps, I think that economic evidence should determine the outcome of the debate. It turns out that interpretation of the evidence tends to split along political lines – the right embracing austerity, the left more disposed towards Keynesian stimulus. The first is cyclical – when things are tight, cut spending. The second is counter-cyclical – when things are tight, spend. Cross purposes. Politicians then appeal to which interpretation of evidence suits their purpose. Reinhart and Rogoff were quoted by the British chancellor as intellectual justification for the severity of his austerity package. Paul Krugman, a Keynesian economist, tends to be quoted by those who would like to follow a less severe path.

There are several questions here, of which we can isolate three. Which course of action is most likely to lead to the return of economic growth? What is the impact of the different policy choices on people's lives across the socio-economic spectrum? And, related, what do the people want? All could have an impact on health, and on health equity.

On the first, Reinhart–Rogoff say that too much debt slows growth. The IMF, reviewing global experience, says that other things being equal, austerity slows growth.[5] The Reinhart–Rogoff argument was weakened by the mistakes in their spread sheets, but not fatally so. Although a comparison of the two does not settle this issue, it is of interest that the US indulged in a fiscal stimulus, and the UK experimented with austerity. The US economy recovered GDP faster from the 2008 crisis than did the UK. Actually, even that comparison is simplistic, because in the UK the government realised that they were cutting too deeply, so they quietly, with no fanfare, eased off on the austerity after a couple of years of savage squeezing, and gave themselves more time to pay down the debt.[6] A commentator in the conservative *Spectator* magazine said that the chancellor was spending like a 'drunken Keynesian'.[7] One suspects that perhaps there is only one evidence base here: cutting spending in time of recession reduces aggregate demand and delays economic recovery. One cannot but think that enthusiasm for austerity, which has been manifest all over Europe, flies in the face of the evidence, and is pursued for reasons other than presumed economic benefits.

I visited Athens at a time when young Greeks, more than half of whom were unemployed, took to the streets to vent their anger at economic austerity. It was an intense experience. Even the more organised political march was scary, given Greece's history of military coups. Greece had got into a painful muddle with its finances, over years if not decades. Its fellow members of the Eurozone appeared to ignore the mess. The muddle was exposed and inflamed by the global financial crisis. Greece's debts soared and the ability of its government to borrow money plummeted. The country was told that the price of remaining a member of the global financial community in general, and the European currency in particular, was to take the medicine – a powerful cocktail that included drastic cuts to public spending. Public spending sounds abstract. It is not. It may include the indefensible such as early retirement on large pensions for civil servants, but public spending is also jobs and salary levels for teachers and nurses, postal workers and street cleaners. Public spending is also nutrition clinics for children and social care for older citizens, it is health care, unemployment benefits and subsidies to public transport. Predictably, the whole economy suffered under this 'orthodoxy' and spiralled downwards. The response of many disempowered Greeks was to take to the streets and protest.

As Greece was coming up to an election, one German politician watched the unrest on the streets of Athens and mused that perhaps this was not a good time for an election. Wonderful, I thought. Not only are the Greek population to have 'remedies' thrust upon them, they should be deprived of a say. What do Greeks know about democracy, they don't even have a word for it. Oh, they do: δημοκρατία (dēmokratía). Democracy, of course, comes from two Greek words meaning people and power. In Ancient Greece, democracy was an antonym to another word, aristokratia, rule of an elite. Rather than the people, the European Central Bank, the European Commission and the IMF were to dictate what Greece had to do. Here, in the twenty-first century, were European politicians musing that aristocracy was safer than democracy. Safer for whom?

There is already evidence from Greece that the people had legitimate grounds for protest – austerity has damaged health. One obvious mechanism is through unemployment, which, as summarised in Chapter 6, has an adverse impact on mental illness and on suicide rates. It also has an impact on the homicide rate. It is not too melodramatic to say that policies of austerity are leading people to take their own lives, and also to kill each other.

Terminal 2 at Dublin airport is somehow symbolic of what Ireland has been through. The terminal is a wonderful testament to a once booming economy, built to be suitable for a Celtic Tiger, an economy that was going places. When I travel through Terminal 2 now, its echoing halls seem to represent the downside, the hollowness of the promise that the people of Ireland could be rich by lending each other money they didn't have.[8] A taxi driver shakes your hand, so pleased is he to have any business. In Dublin itself, 'To Let' signs on empty office buildings, deserted restaurants and pubs half full are signs of what happens when a growth economy collapses.

In Ireland, as in Iceland, the banks got into all sorts of trouble because they overreached themselves in the apparent belief that there would never be a downturn. Remarkably, the government took the decision to pay the banks' debts. The government, of course, is the taxpayers. The people had to pay the banks' debts, which translated into enormous salary cuts for employed people and damages to employment. The Irish professor at my dinner table found her salary cut by 40 per cent. Cuts in standard of living, cuts in social programmes: the impact on health is likely to be adverse.[9]

Icelanders decided to do things differently from the Irish. I cannot claim that the doctors, academics, civil servants and politicians who talked to me are typical of Iceland, but, to a person, they asked the question: why should all Icelanders be made to pay for the wild excesses of irresponsible bankers? The IMF's remedy was that the Iceland government should assume liability for the bank's losses (as happened in Ireland), which would have resulted in 50 per cent of the national income between 2016 and 2023 being paid to the UK and Dutch governments, holders of much of the debt.[10] The President put it to the people in a referendum and 93 per cent of the population rejected the package. Why did Iceland's health apparently not suffer as a result of their economic crisis? Here is a plausible account:

First, Iceland ignored the advice of the IMF, and instead invested in social protection. This investment was coupled with active measures to get people back into work. Second, diet improved. McDonald's pulled out of the country because of the rising costs of importation of onions and tomatoes (the most expensive ingredients in its burgers). Icelanders began cooking at home more (especially fish, boosting the income of the country's fishing fleet). Third, Iceland retained its restrictive policies on alcohol, again contrary to the advice of the IMF. Finally, the Icelandic people drew on strong reserves of social capital, and everyone really felt that they were united in the crisis. Although extrapolation to other countries should be undertaken with care, Iceland, by challenging the economic orthodoxy at every step of its response, has shown that an alternative to austerity exists.[11]

As Iceland's economy recovers, it is now repaying its debts.

The IMF has a history. I was a member of The Lancet–University of Oslo Commission on Global Governance for Health, chaired by Ole Petter Ottersen, Rector of Oslo University.[12] The starting point for the governance commission was the Commission on Social Determinants of Health (CSDH). The governance commission said in effect: the CSDH has pointed to the causes, and the causes of the causes, of health inequity. We now need to look at what can be done to improve governance at a global level so that effective action can be taken on the social determinants of health.

In light of the experience in Europe with austerity we, the governance commission, went back to an older literature to look at the effect of IMF policies of structural adjustment in low-income countries. It does not make happy reading. In the 1980s the IMF made loans contingent on governments accepting IMF recommendations on how to manage the economy. It was mainstream

Washington consensus: reduce public spending, markets as the default option for public services, economic deregulation, privatise public assets. We concluded:

> the effects of these programmes have been disastrous for public health . . . structural adjustment programmes undermined the health of poor people in sub-Saharan Africa through effects on employment, incomes, prices, public expenditure, taxation, and access to credit, which in turn translated into negative health outcomes through effects on food security, nutrition, living and working environments, access to health services, education.[13]

When discussing the battle between austerians and Keynesians I said that a key criterion should be impact on the lives people are able to lead. Structural adjustment, there is little doubt, led to a great deal of pain in the short term. As an economic policy adviser, how convinced do you have to be that, in the long term, it is worth it, before inflicting such short-term pain on other people?

A SOCIAL PROTECTION FLOOR?

As shown in Chapter 6, unemployment increases national suicide rates. But the greater the spending on social protection – unemployment benefits, active labour market programmes, health care – the more the harm inflicted by unemployment is reduced.[14] Further, when examining the Nordic countries, the message is clear: greater spending on social protection is linked to narrower health inequities.

I have to confess that when I began my involvement as chair of the CSDH, I thought social protection was something that only rich countries could afford. Based on the evidence presented to us, I changed my mind. We made the clear recommendation for universal social protection systems in low-income countries, as in middle and high. These should include people in informal employment. Totally fanciful? The answer is: a bit fanciful. First, the bad news. Currently, globally, only 27 per cent of people are comprehensively covered by social security systems.[15] This means that 73 per cent of people have only partial coverage or none at all. Essentially, lack of coverage means no protection from low income that may arise in a variety of ways: lack of work, sickness or varieties of social exclusion.

The more encouraging news is that the global community wants this to change. The International Labour Office (ILO) convened an Advisory Group on a Social Protection Floor, chaired by Michelle Bachelet, then the former, now the current, President of Chile. Some clarity of language might be helpful. The ILO uses the terms social protection and social security interchangeably, and treats social security as a human right. The term encompasses a broad variety of policy instruments, including social insurance, social assistance, universal benefits and other forms of cash transfers, as well as measures to ensure effective access to health care and other benefits in kind aiming at securing social protection.

The recommendation made by Bachelet's group for a social protection floor was endorsed by 185 countries. The key point for a chapter on globalisation and health is that although social protection is an issue for countries themselves, the global community can play a role in at least two ways: showing what is possible, and using global resources to help countries establish a minimal level, a floor, of social protection for each country. The ILO has weighed into the debate on austerity with a clear statement that social protection systems must be protected and enhanced. The ILO praises the European social model (as described in the previous chapter) but says austerity is putting that under threat to the detriment of the population in Europe – not just Greece and Ireland, but many other countries. It looks with approval at the expansion of social protection in middle-income countries such as Brazil and China. The big question is whether voices such as those from the ILO can be heard above the austerity clamour, and a social protection floor be extended to low-income countries, in addition to preserving social protection in higher-income countries.

ECONOMIC GROWTH, INEQUALITY AND SOCIAL INVESTMENT

Growth is good, isn't it? We scour our daily newspapers to see the GDP figures. If GDP sank by 0.1 per cent in the last quarter it invalidates the government's whole economic rationale; and if it grew by 0.1 per cent the government is triumphant. It's silly. It stretches reason. This is not to deny that growth matters for low-income countries. There is no question that if India's economy is growing at 7–9 per cent a year it has the possibility to do things socially to the benefit of its population's health that it could not when it was a poor country *and* had sluggish growth. There is also no question that if the whole world grew at that rate, the planet would choke.

Economic growth, though, is no guarantee of development, by which I mean the kinds of social goal identified by Robert Kennedy at the head of this chapter, particularly education and health. For the well-being and health of people to be enhanced we must ask how economic growth is used and how equitably it is distributed.

We turn now to the Brazilian and South Korean at my dinner table.

Jean Drèze and Amartya Sen refer to Brazil's growth in the 1960s to 1980s as 'unaimed opulence'.[16] Brazil had rapid economic growth but deplorably low living conditions for large swathes of the population. The Brazilian woman at my table, had the dinner party happened in the 1980s, would have been struggling to raise children in conditions of extreme poverty. By contrast South Korea's growth was more equitably distributed and the proceeds were used for education and the widespread improvement of living conditions.

Since then, say Drèze and Sen, Brazil has changed course. The adoption of a democratic constitution, washing away the vestiges of military dictatorship, the building of social institutions, commitment to free and universal health care, social security programmes, including the conditional cash transfer scheme, Bolsa Familia, which I described in the previous chapter, improved the quality of people's lives and was accompanied by rapid improvements in health. As one indication of how life improved for the Brazilian woman and her children, we can look at stunting – failure to grow adequately in the first year of life. Figure 10.1 illustrates the social gradient.

In 1974–5 that gradient was steep and plain to see: the higher the income the lower the prevalence of stunting. As the years go on, not only does the prevalence of stunting go down for all groups, but the social gradient becomes progressively flatter. By 2006–7 there

FIGURE 10.1: POVERTY IS NOT DESTINY – THINGS CAN GET BETTER

Prevalence of stunting by family income and year of survey: Brazil

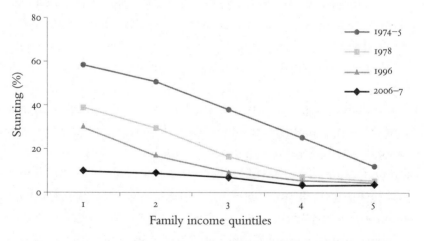

Family income quintiles

Source: Victora CG, Aquino EM, Leal MdC, Monteiro CA, Barros FC, Szwarcwald CL. Maternal and child health in Brazil: progress and challenges. Lancet. 2011; 28(377): 1863-76. And Monteiro CA, Benicio MH, Conde WL. Narrowing socioeconomic inequality in child stunting: the Brazilian experience. Bulletin World Health Organisation. 2009; 88:305-11

is hardly a gradient to be seen. The changes in Brazil improved the lives of children.

Each year the United Nations Development Programme (UNDP) produces a Human Development Report (HDR). The HDR for 2013 expands the insights of Drèze and Sen and identifies what it calls:

> unwelcome types of growth: jobless growth, which does not increase employment opportunities; ruthless growth, which is accompanied by rising inequality; voiceless growth, which denies the participation of the most vulnerable communities; rootless growth, which uses inappropriate models transplanted from elsewhere; and futureless growth, which is based on unbridled exploitation of environmental resources.[17]

The HDR contrasts the Washington Consensus, which argues for getting the economic fundamentals right, with UNDP's own approach, which puts human development first. I love it. Of course I do. This UN agency says that improvement in poor people's lives – and hence, their health – cannot be postponed while the economic fundamentals start to work. It is actually stronger than that. The Washington Consensus, neoliberalism by another name, is likely to make inequalities wider in addition to neglecting the need to build people's capabilities and ensure their meaningful freedoms. Further, consistent with Joseph Stiglitz's arguments outlined in Chapter 9, social protection and enhancing people's capabilities are likely to be good for economic growth and economic productivity.

A way that the UNDP measures progress is with a human development index, and the important thing about this HDI is that it includes health, national income and education. Moving beyond the ideology of whether public spending is good or bad is the evidence shown in Figure 10.2.

FIGURE 10.2: YESTERDAY'S SPENDING LEADS TO TODAY'S
BENEFITS.

Current HDI values and previous public expenditures are positively correlated

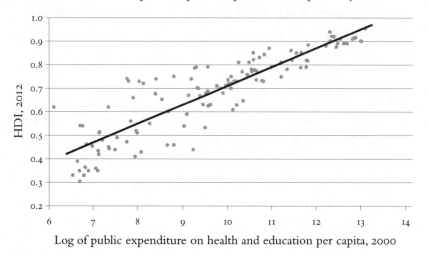

Log of public expenditure on health and education per capita, 2000

Note: HD1 = Human Development Index
Source: UNDP. Human Development Report 2013 – The Rise of the South: *Human Progress in a Diverse World*. New York: United Nations Development Programme, 2013.

Each point on the graph represents a country. It shows that the greater the public expenditure on health (care) and education in the year 2000, the higher the score on the human development index (HDI) twelve years later. If I showed this graph to a class of graduate students they would argue over cause and effect and could come up with any number of competing explanations for this correlation. One of them, though, is the obvious one: if yours is the kind of society that spends more of its public money on schools and health care, yours is likely to be the kind of society that scores better on education, health and income – the components of the HDI.

The HDR 2013 refers to countries that privilege social development rather than simply economic growth as 'development states' and says:

The recent literature on developmental states has grown out of the experiences of the East Asian 'miracle' economies: Japan before the Second World War and Hong Kong, China (SAR), the Republic of Korea, Singapore and Taiwan Province of China in the second half of the 20th century. Recently, China and Viet Nam (as well as Cambodia and Lao PDR) can be seen as developmental states. Common traits include promoting economic development by explicitly favouring certain sectors; commanding competent bureaucracies; placing robust, competent public institutions at the centre of development strategies; clearly articulating social and economic goals; and deriving political legitimacy from their record in development.[18]

Economic development, yes, says the UNDP, but high levels of economic growth alone do not suffice to build a state that is characterised by high levels of health and education. From the 1990s on, Brazil's progress in human development was faster than in the period described as 'unaimed opulence', even though its growth of GDP was slower.

It is the turn of the woman from Kerala, the South Indian state that stands out in relation to India's performance in human development. Life expectancy for women in India has improved, and the improvement is impressive: from fifty-eight in 1990 to sixty-eight in 2012 – although that is still nearly twenty years behind the international top scorer, Japan.[19] In Kerala it is more impressive than in the rest of India. At seventy-seven, it is the one part of India that is up with China and Brazil. The lesson from Kerala is similar to those countries: emphasis on human development, investment in human capabilities . . . and no fear of state intervention. A few comparisons between Kerala and the average for India are instructive (see chart on following page).[20]

When Kerala's good health record first came to attention, thirty or so years ago, one of the puzzles was that if education was so high, why was it one of the poorer states of India? It fuelled speculation that there is a trade-off between involvement of the public sector

in human development and economic success. That scepticism is
no longer valid. Kerala has had rapid economic growth since then,
improvements in living conditions and increases in health, all with
a vigorous involvement of the public sector.[21]

	Kerala	India
Children aged 6–14 in school (per cent)	98	80
Children aged 8–11 who pass a reading test (per cent)	82	54
Female literacy age 15–49 (per cent)	93	55
Proportion below the poverty line (per cent)	20	37
Median income per person 2004–5 (Rs/person)	9,987	5,999

At the beginning of this section, when saying that economic
growth might be helpful in improving development and health,
I stressed that we had to ask both how growth is used and how
equitably it is distributed. Much of the debate in the development
literature concerns whether growth is a cure for poverty. Inequality
is relevant here in at least two ways. First, in the previous chapter I
quoted Joseph Stiglitz, backed up by the IMF, saying that too much
inequality hinders growth. If growth is one route to poverty reduction, then too much inequality hinders that reduction. Second,
the impact may be much more direct. If reduction of poverty was
the main outcome, reduction of economic inequality has a much
bigger impact than simply growth of GDP.[22] I don't think this is
mysterious. Redistribution in the direction of the less well off will
of course benefit the less well off, whether or not the economy is
growing. But growth will only benefit the less well off if its benefits
are inclusive.

Too much inequality is bad for growth and bad for poverty
reduction.

You might be thinking that the way a country chooses to develop is its business: why is it in a chapter on globalisation and health? The answer is twofold. First, bodies like the IMF and the European Central Bank are dictating to countries what they must do if their economies are to be supported. Second, what happens to their economies is heavily affected by global forces. A financial crisis that began in Wall Street and the City of London had profound effects round the world.

There is a further answer. What one country does in relation to trade and aid is a potentially powerful driver of its own and other countries' development.

TRADE

Dying to trade

Next as we go around the table we come to the Indian cotton farmer. He is pleased to be with us. With good reason. Every half an hour an Indian farmer commits suicide, in excess of 16,000 per year. Cotton farmers seem to be particularly vulnerable – 270,000 suicides since 1995.[23] India is so enormous that any statistic sounds large. There are about 3,000 births every hour. Are two suicides an hour a lot? It turns out that they are. In one contiguous group of states – Maharashtra, Karnataka, Andhra Pradesh, Chhattisgarh and Madhya Pradesh – the suicide rate among farmers is nearly three times the average rate for all India (farmers and non-farmers).[24]

Our Indian dinner guest is all in favour of globalisation – well, mostly. He attributes his children's improved chances of survival to advances in Western medical science that India enjoys. He watches World Cup football on television and, poor as he is, he uses a mobile phone, which he loves. Always in debt, though, our farmer is on the edge of disaster. Drought, and resultant crop failure, can do him in. There is a question of whether variability in the climate, a feature of climate change, is making both floods and drought more common. Not much that he, or any one government, can do about that – although all of us together could.

There is another kind of shock, much more amenable to change: subsidies to US cotton farmers. US cotton farmers, many of them giant corporate farms, receive substantial subsidies from the US government – more than $3 billion in 2008–9 – to support their economic livelihoods.[25] The effect of these subsidies is to lower the world price of cotton. In turn, a lower world price undercuts the ability of cotton farmers in India and Africa to sell their produce at an economic price. The US may be subsidising domestic producers for good political reasons, but the removal of these subsidies would allow the world price of cotton to rise by 6–14 per cent. Is it stretching the causal chain implausibly to suggest that subsidies of US cotton producers are leading to suicides of Indian cotton farmers? It is entirely plausible that US subsidies are making a difference to the livelihood of Indian cotton farmers. It is also entirely plausible that inescapable debts are leading Indian cotton farmers to take their own lives.

A newer feature that is affecting Indian cotton farmers is the marketing of genetically modified cotton crops. Sold to farmers on the grounds of increase in yields, because of resistance to boll worms, these seeds raise costs in a variety of ways: increased, not decreased expenditure on pesticides to control other parasites; the seeds cannot be propagated, so farmers have to buy new seeds every year; costs that are higher than conventional seeds – the company claims the high prices are necessary to cover the costs of meeting regulatory standards.

Brazil, India, China and several West African countries have appealed to the US to remove their cotton subsidies and allow free trade. The lack of success of this appeal led to Brazil pursuing the US through the World Trade Organization. The US did not budge.[26] One might respect the argument for free trade somewhat more if those who argue for it obeyed its rules.

Not just the US, and not just cotton: subsidies to European agriculture in one week equal subsidies to African agriculture in one year.[27] In a globalised world, we should want all countries to develop economic self-sufficiency. One should not rig the conditions so that they always favour the rich and disempower low-income countries.

Trading to live

Next to the – thankfully not suicidal – cotton farmer sits the Bangladeshi teenager who likes sweatshops. She looks around the table at the Americans and Europeans wearing clothes – smart casual, remember – from Benetton, Primark, C&A, Mango and others and she says: I made those garments. Well, perhaps not literally those very garments, but ones very much like those were made in the factories where my friends and I work.

Cue guilt feelings on the part of the Americans and Europeans. It is difficult not to feel that our liking for cheap clothes is somehow linked to the collapse, in April 2013, of the garment factory at the Rana Plaza complex that killed 1,100 people and injured 2,500 more. Cheap clothes in London and New York mean rotten factory conditions and low pay in Dhaka, in Bangladesh. Like it or not, we are involved.

The simple version of this is that we, in high-income countries, export low pay and sweatshop working conditions to Bangladesh and Bangladesh exports affordable clothing to us – globalisation at work. It is not, though, a simple case of good and evil.

First, Bangladesh as a country is a willing participant. It has in excess of 5,000 garment factories. The industry earns $20 billion a year in exports and it is the second-biggest exporter of garments after China. Second, what about the people? My mantra is: put health equity at the heart of all policy-making. The garment industry employs 4 million people in Bangladesh, 90 per cent of them women. Dangerous factory conditions, low pay: is

this just another way to do women in? Are these not precisely the
sort of working conditions that I described as disempowering in
Chapter 6?

The answer is that they are, but young Bangladeshi women
consider the alternative available to them. The alternative, so far,
is not better working conditions. These young women, coming
from the countryside, have swapped a life of early marriage and
rural poverty for earning their own money, controlling the decision of when and if to marry, and having a desirable skill.[28] Shaina
Hyder, while a young scholar in the Law Faculty of the University
of California Berkeley, interviewed Bangladeshi garment workers.
Hyder reports that 90 per cent of her interviewees thought that
working was better than being a housewife, and could see the
opportunities it brings. One garment worker, a woman in her
forties from a rural background, saw her daughter go to college.
Three generations: rural poor, urban factory worker, college
graduate.

That is not to say that any of us who has bought a garment
made in Bangladesh should be relaxed about the working
conditions in which it was produced. The Rana Plaza incident
brought much-needed attention to the question of working
conditions in Bangladesh's garment industry. There are power
asymmetries at work here. If Bangladesh starts to get more
organised about pay and working conditions, multinational
corporations can simply shift their business elsewhere, to the
detriment of Bangladesh's economy and of the women who
gladly see the work as empowering them. There is not a well-
developed mechanism for enforcing global working standards,
although ILO is trying to help. Shaming individual corporations into acceptable practice can only go so far. That said, there
are signs that a concerted effort is being made by the government in Bangladesh to recognise trade unions and pay attention
to working conditions.[29]

Winners and losers

As my two examples show, there are winners and losers from international trade – Indian farmers suffering, Bangladeshi women having the chance to transform their lives. I led a European Review of Social Determinants and the Health Divide.[30] As part of that Review we invited Ron Labonté of the University of Ottawa to update the work he did for the CSDH on globalisation and health. Ron commented that the relationship between trade policies, poverty and inequalities is a huge field of policy research, but two significant pointers emerged.[31] The first relates to the long, and I mean very long and protracted, Doha development round negotiations conducted under the auspices of the World Trade Organization. Assuming the talks ever reached a conclusion, analysts modelled four different outcomes. Their work suggested that there would be annual real income gains of between $6 and $8 billion each for Japan, the USA and the EU 15 group of countries, and losses of about $250 million for Sub-Saharan Africa. Free trade sounds like a good thing. As we saw above, when it works against the interests of Europe and the US, the rich countries have no compunction in discarding it. If it is to the benefit of the rich countries at the expense of the poor, we hear pious exhortations on how free trade benefits everyone. But not equally.

Ron's second observation was that if trade liberalisation does occur, and there are adverse impacts on income and employment in rich countries and in poor, the kind of safety nets that I alluded to above, with a social protection floor, are viable options.

Should there be a 'should'?

Running through the discussion above there is an implicit concern that decisions taken for one reason may have adverse impacts on the health of disadvantaged people in other countries. The purpose of the original decision may have been entirely admirable. If you are an elected politician for a rural community in Europe or the

US, you may take a view that your primary responsibility is to your constituents. If subsidies to your farmers hurt farmers in India or Africa, that is unfortunate, but not your chief concern. If you are the leader of a country you may well say that your motivation is not in being 'fair' to other countries but in pursuing your country's national interest. I explored in Chapter 3 what social justice meant for health inequities. I didn't say it, but I was in a sense assuming that if we are a big interconnected globalised world community, then concerns with social justice should be global rather than simply national. It slipped out, I just used 'should'.

If I enjoy cheap clothes, I should care, shouldn't I, if workers are benefiting or suffering in providing them. After all, if I were the factory owner, I should have a responsibility for the health of my workers, shouldn't I? If they go home happy and well fed because of their work with me, I can feel I am doing the right thing. If I get rich on the back of their ill-health, do I not have some sense of responsibility? If I am not the factory owner but the user of the products that the factory produces, my sense of responsibility is weakened, probably rightly, but should it disappear all together?

The reason for coming back to this discussion here, is because I want to talk about aid, overseas development assistance. Is there a 'should' we can recognise? Should the money of taxpayers in high-income countries be used to help the livelihood of people in low-income countries? If aid were ineffective, there cannot be a 'should'. There can be no obligation on us to do something that is useless or even harmful. We'll come to that in a moment.

DEBT AND AID

Paying one's debts

Our Zambian dinner guest is angry, and the Argentinian thoroughly fed up. The first feels let down by everyone, from his

own government to the international community; the second is
profoundly annoyed that just when he was getting his self-esteem
back, he has been undermined all over again. What unites these
dinner companions is concern over their countries' debt. They
would like us to put aid in the context of debt, which is what I do
in Figure 10.3 overleaf. The figures come from before the global
financial crisis.

The first observation, looking at this graph, is that when it comes
to aid, development assistance, the amounts of money are trivial in
the context of the economies of rich countries. An agreed benchmark was 0.7 per cent – rich countries would give 0.7 per cent of
their GDP to overseas development assistance.[32] We are way below
that. For example, the US economy turns over about $13 trillion a
year; 0.7 per cent of that is about $90 billion a year. If we add Japan,
and the richer European countries . . . the sum comes to a good
deal more than the amounts currently going out in aid.

Second, in every region of the world, except Sub-Saharan Africa,
the amount coming back to rich countries in debt repayment far
exceeds receipts of aid. Latin America and the Caribbean are a
cash cow for the rich countries. Some of these debt repayments
are entirely reasonable. Countries need to borrow to make their
economies work. Some are not.

As an example of unreasonable debt repayment, take Zambia. In
the 1980s, when the cold war was still in progress, Zambia borrowed
from Romania for agricultural equipment and services. In 1999
Zambia was having difficulty paying its debts, and was in the process of renegotiating its loans. Enter vulture funds – hedge funds that
behave like vultures. A vulture fund registered in the British Virgin
Islands and run by a US businessman bought Zambian debt at the
knockdown price of $4 million. How is this possible? Let's say a
bank has loaned Zambia $50 million. There can then be a second-
ary trade in that debt. One bank 'sells' that debt to some other kind
of investor, who trades it further, and so on. When it turns out,

FIGURE 10.3: WHO IS HELPING WHOM

Debt service and development assistance by region, 2000–2008
(developing countries only)

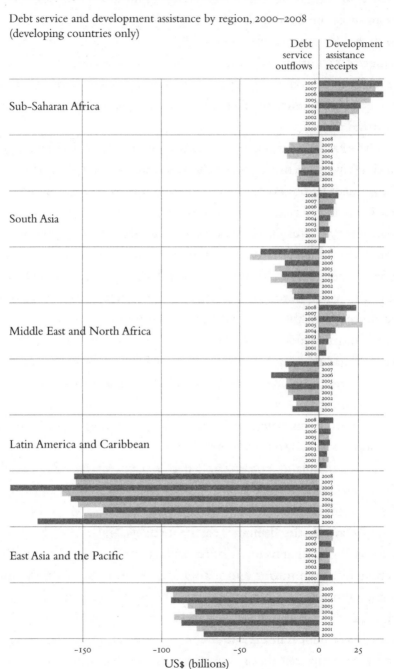

US$ (billions)

Source: updated from WHO Commission on Social Determinants of Health

what a surprise, that Zambia is having difficulty paying its debts, the price of the debt on this secondary market tumbles. It could be, for example, that $50 million of debt gets sold for $4 million. The owner of $50 million of Zambian debt calculates that he is never going to be repaid, so he gets rid of his 'worthless' holding for any money at all. The buyer of this 'worthless' debt makes the calculation that, eventually, he will make a killing. Our Zambian guest wants to know how any of these financial shenanigans is going to make it easier for his children to go to secondary school.

A decade later, having paid $4 million for Zambia's debt, the vulture fund claimed debt repayments from Zambia of $55 million and, when it refused, pursued it through the courts.[33] Morality? Candy from a baby, more like. Selfish to take candy from a baby? Not a bit of it. I'm doing it for the baby's own good: bad for its teeth, laying the seeds of bad habits that would lead to obesity. I'm not a greedy vulture, I'm a public benefactor, saving babies everywhere from themselves. What's more it is perfectly legal, and the corrupt leaders who rule Zambia would probably have stolen the money – it is much better off in the hands of the businessmen who control the vulture fund.

Happily, in this particular case, the Royal Courts of Justice in London took a different view, not so much on the morality or legality of the claim, but on the nature of the evidence presented. 'Put at its kindest . . . some of the witnesses [for the fund] were less than candid,' said the judge.

I remember the feeling I had after the Gleneagles Summit in 2005. Tony Blair was UK Prime Minister and hosted the G8 summit. Shamed into it by rock stars, perhaps, the world's leaders declared that they would give debt relief for the poorest countries as a significant step in abolishing world poverty. Zambia was a recipient of debt relief. In theory, at least – I know, there is a great deal of corruption about – instead of paying interest on debts, Zambia could use the money for education and health care. But along comes this vulture fund, which voluntarily bought the debt for a pittance, pursuing Zambia for more in debt repayment than it would receive in debt relief.

It is not only the poorest countries that have got into trouble with their debt. As I write, Argentina is at the mercy of a vulture fund. Its case is different from Zambia's because Argentina is not one of the poorest countries that qualify for debt relief, but its ability to solve its problems is strongly affected by debt. I do not for one moment suggest that there is only one side to this story and that Argentina was a model of good financial management before it defaulted on its debt in 2001. But Argentina's virtues or otherwise do not justify the role of a vulture fund. Prior to its default in 2001, Argentina's debt was being traded as if it were sardines. It is hard to think of a way that any one Argentinian benefited by having one person in The Hague buy a chunk of Argentinian debt from another in Frankfurt, but no doubt a trader somewhere can explain why it was good for the people of Buenos Aires. No, I wouldn't believe him either.

When Argentina could not pay its debts in 2001, its creditors agreed, or felt they had no other option but to write down the value of their debts by up to 70 per cent – known in the trade as a 'haircut'. Enter a vulture fund that bought up some Argentinian debt cheaply, which was not subject to the haircut, it was a holdout. Argentina's debt in the subsequent decade was at manageable level, and it was paying off the holders of its (reduced) debt, the ones who took the haircut. Once again, the vulture fund entered the scene and demanded full repayment, of the whole value of the debt – debt that they had purchased at a bargain-basement price, but was a holdout from the original haircut agreement. (Are you following this?)

Remarkably, a US court ruled that Argentina was *not* allowed to continue to repay its creditors, the haircut crowd, on the reduced debt, unless it also 'repaid' the vultures on the full value of the debt at the same time, the holdout. Argentina argued, reasonably enough it seems to me, that had they the prospect of repaying the full value of the debt, they would not have demanded haircuts of the rest, and they simply could not do it. The court was adamant: pay the vulture fund at the same time, or pay nobody. Argentina defaulted with who knows what knock-on effects in Brazil, other Latin American countries, global finance, let alone Argentina's ability to spend on national programmes. And failure to spend on national programmes has the potential to damage health, for all the reasons that I have covered in the previous chapters.

There is a serious failure of global financial governance when the interests of hedge funds, legally if not morally, trump the ability of nations to decide their own future.

Does aid work?

The medieval Jewish scholar Maimonides wrote of eight levels of charity. The lowest is to give unwillingly. Skipping through the levels, the second-highest is to give anonymously without knowing to whom you give. The highest is to help the needy with employment or other arrangements so that they progress to the point of no longer needing help.

Maimonides seems to be arguing from the point of view of the donor – give unwillingly is the donor's perspective. But he also takes in the recipient. While there may be a tiny proportion of people who would prefer charity to self-sufficiency – exaggerated by the right, minimised by the left – the highest level of charity from the recipient's viewpoint is also to be in a position not to need charity. Which is where we want to be as a global community, surely: to create the conditions for the poor and disadvantaged to be empowered to control their own destiny. With 49 per cent of people in Sub-Saharan Africa and 31 per cent in South Asia living on $1.25 a day or less, we are not there yet. There is little doubt that the Indian cotton farmer would rather be able to grow and sell his cotton at a profit, than have to subsist on a lowly government handout. The Zambian at our table would like there to be schools for his children to attend. If, in the short term, that takes external assistance, he accepts that as a stage in a process.

It would seem obvious that if a country lacks the resources to employ nurses and teachers, to buy medicines and textbooks, to build latrines and a clean water supply, to provide pensions and social protection, then international assistance would help. Critics say of the advocates of aid that part of what they say is obvious and part is true; unfortunately these two do not overlap. Aid may distort a country's priorities, create dependencies, have much more to do with the priorities of the donor than the needs of the recipient, act as a kind of resource curse for a country, thus hindering the climb out of poverty. And then of course there is corruption: aid money can end up in shady places, and not used for its intended purpose. In the end, say the critics, it just does not work.

Banerjee and Duflo, who we met previously as the authors of *Poor Economics*, contrast the positions of Jeffrey Sachs of Columbia University, who says aid is effective, and William Easterly, New York University and previously a World Bank economist, who says it is not.[34] Princeton economist Angus Deaton is much more with Easterly than with Sachs.[35] Parenthetically, reading their views of each other is a great spectator sport, if offering few lessons in politeness. Banerjee and Duflo say that, at heart, this is an ideological debate between left (Sachs) and right (Easterly). They say that there is not a BIG answer to whether aid works, but small answers as to whether specific forms of aid work under which circumstances. Much of the answer to when and whether, they say, will come from randomised controlled trials. Deaton is not only critical of aid, he is critical of what he calls randomistas who think the answer to what works will come from such trials. It would all be good knockabout intellectual fun, were it not such a vitally important question.

Banerjee and Duflo use the example of impregnated bed nets to protect against mosquito bites and consequent malaria. Sachs says provide bed nets, children won't get malaria, and their earning power will grow by 15 per cent. Easterly says that unless people pay for the nets, they won't value them and will not use them for the intended purpose. It will be a waste of money and ineffective in the control of malaria. Banerjee and Duflo don't quite say: a plague on both your houses. They say that Sachs exaggerates the economic benefits. But Easterly is wrong. They point to evidence that use of bed nets, *for the purpose intended*, is increased by making them cheaper, or free to the recipient.

Whether aid can help in poverty relief and economic growth remains a vexed question.[36] Particularly so, in the context of debt repayment shown in Figure 10.3 and trading and financial arrangements that can work to the disbenefit of low-income countries. Aid for health care and disease control can be effective, as Banerjee and Duflo say, under particular circumstances. In our European Review we pointed to the fact that, in 2009, external assistance for health made up about half of government expenditure on health care in low-income countries.[37] Were this to be summarily removed it would create great hardship. It is vital though to be satisfied that the money is being used to good purpose.

FOOD GLORIOUS FOOD

When, at the dinner table, we come to the obese Egyptian woman, I tell her about my recurring nightmare. I dream that I am attending a board meeting of a corporation whose main product is fizzy drinks. The strategic analyst addresses the board:

'Gentlemen [it's my nightmare – they are all men in my nightmare]. We are in trouble. We are in the business of selling calories – flavoured sugary water. But globally people are doing less physical activity. They need fewer calories. Trouble looms. [The board has a collective vision of their private jets taking off without them.] But, I have a solution. [The private jets come back into view.] There are two main drivers of an individual's calorie consumption: physical activity and body mass. In general the more an individual weighs, the more calories they need to stay in balance. So we promote obesity. How do we do that? Increase portion size. Offer twenty per cent more for "free". It costs us next to nothing. All our costs are in processing, distributing and marketing. That way we get a fatter population who will need more calories. [Bigger and better private jets.]'

At this point in my nightmare, I wake up screaming. Thank goodness real life is nothing like that. Purveyors of soft drinks may not set out to make people obese; it happens to be the effect of their products. Of all the proposed contributors to obesity, the one for which the evidence is strongest is consumption of fizzy drinks.[38] It is highly likely that fast foods, rich in fat and sugar, are also fuelling obesity, although the evidence is not quite as secure as with sugary drinks.

From the time that my concern with social determinants of health came out of the academic environment into the policy sphere, I have been told that we must collaborate with the private sector, in food as in other areas. I am sure we must. The problem is that we have different aims. Mine is health equity. Theirs is profit. If they coincide, fine. But, if not, we get into the kind of battles that I regaled you with in Chapter 2. There I produced three graphs of the alarming increase in obesity in the US. As goes the US, so goes the world, as the two graphs in Figure 10.4 show.

The standard for measuring overweight and obesity is Body Mass Index – weight in kg divided by height in metres, squared. A BMI of 25 or greater is called overweight; of 30 or over is obesity. It's hard to see my Egyptian dinner guest on this graph. Not so

FIGURE 10.4: SMALL WORLD, BIG PEOPLE

Global mean BMI, ages 20+, male 1980

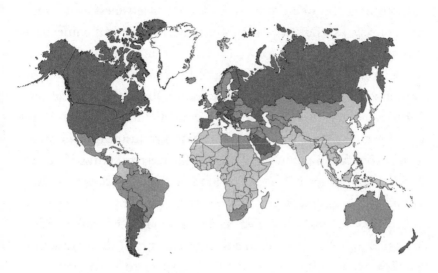

Global mean BMI, ages 20+, male 2008

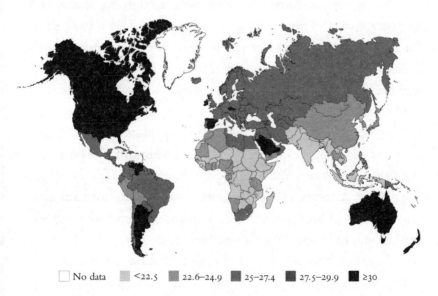

☐ No data ▨ <22.5 ▩ 22.6–24.9 ▦ 25–27.4 ▤ 27.5–29.9 ▪ ≥30

Source: World Health Organization. *Mean Body Mass Index (kg/m2), ages 20+, age standardized, 1980–2008, 2014* [07/01/2015]. Available from: http://gamapserver.who.int/gho/interactive_charts/ncd/risk_factors/bmi/atlas.html.

hard to see her in real life. An Egyptian woman in her late forties has a 90 per cent chance of being overweight, and a two-thirds chance of being obese.[39] If we had a Mexican guest at the table, the chances are the same as in Egypt. Overweight is the norm, and obesity almost so.

Of course, the food industry argues that it is not their foods that are making people fat, it is people's pattern of eating. It's a bit like the gun lobby arguing that guns don't kill people, people do. It is true that if you didn't consume fast foods they wouldn't make you fat. Beyond that astonishing insight is the fact that food corporations are trying as hard as they can to get as many of us to consume as many of their products as possible. They are succeeding. Global sales of packaged foods grew by 92 per cent to $2.2 trillion in the decade to 2012.[40] The Coca-Cola Corporation publishes figures of sales of their beverages. Mexico tops the world league: 675 servings (of 8 US oz, 237 ml) per person per year. The US is a laggard. It comes in fourth with (only!) 394 servings per person per year. There is some pressure to make processed foods 'healthier' in richer countries, less so in other countries. Diet sodas make up 22 per cent of Coca-Cola's sales by volume in Europe and nearly one-third in North America but just 6 per cent in Latin America.[41]

It is not fanciful to link Mexico's top billing on the obesity league with their top spot in Coca-Cola consumption. To repeat, the more sugary drinks you consume the more likely are you to be overweight or obese. To be sure, other foods make a contribution, and the sales of highly processed foods are growing sharply in low-middle and middle-income countries.[42]

What we are seeing is a globalisation of food patterns. In high-income countries we have already seen the impact of processed foods on eating styles. It has gone a long way in the UK. A survey in England revealed that 30 per cent of households use their table for meals barely a few times a year. Nearly two-thirds of people eat at their table less than once a week. Just 18 per cent of people have one or more meals a day at their table. (Three per cent have no table.) With the growth in sales of highly processed foods globally, we will be exporting this pattern of eating.[43] The consequence will be not only obesity, diabetes and other non-communicable disease, but a different way for families and friends to relate to each other.

Earlier (Chapter 2), I pointed out that a majority of the world's population are urban, and do not grow their own food. Markets are vital in matching people to food. Processed food will play a part in meeting people's nutritional needs. But, I said, there are market failures. In one sense the growth of Nestlé, Coca-Cola, PepsiCo, Kraft, or its successor, and the retail fast food chains is a fantastic market success. Sales grow because these companies bring food to people. Shareholders must be happy. From the point of view of overnutrition it has to be counted a failure.

I am not much given to wringing my hands at the lack of solutions, but if there were a ready way to limit the reach of transnational food corporations and reduce their impact on obesity, we might be doing it. Knowledge helps, in two ways. The more it is recognised what a potentially profound effect food corporations are having on global food patterns, the greater the pressure to do things differently, and the more the spread of fattening food and beverages can perhaps be controlled. Second, the evidence I reported in Chapter 2 showed that other factors can prevent or mitigate the growth of obesity. Just as in high-income countries obesity growth is becoming less extreme in people with high status, so in low-income countries there is less obesity among those with higher levels of education. If the Egyptian woman at our table had gone to university, she would be less likely to be obese than her sisters with less education.

The experience with tobacco is relevant, in part. We come at last to the chain-smoking Kenyan, whose habit reflects the widespread activities of tobacco companies to recruit globally to their deadly habit. With use of tobacco products declining in some high-income countries, the tobacco industry has shifted its focus to low- and middle-income countries where 80 per cent of the one billion smokers in the world now live.[44] We actually know a good deal about how to make progress in reducing smoking. It involves much more than simply exhorting people to look after themselves. Tobacco control measures include pricing, bans on advertising, restriction of sports sponsorship, restrictions in public places and health warnings on packets. Much of this has been enshrined in a Framework Convention on Tobacco Control (FCTC), coordinated by WHO and endorsed by most countries.

The FCTC ought to be showing the way for what global coordination can do. The problem is that the tobacco industry has profits to make, and is challenging it wherever it can. The case of Uruguay is instructive. Uruguay signed up to the FCTC and wanted to increase the size of the health warnings on its packets. Philip Morris challenged them through the courts. Similarly, Australia's initiative in introducing plain packaging is being challenged by Philip Morris. In both cases the cigarette company is arguing violation of trade agreements.

I think the global health community will win this one. The case of smoking is so open and shut. Smoking could kill a billion people this century if it is not curbed. The tobacco industry is on the wrong side of this issue. It will be difficult for courts or arbitrators to fly in the face of public opinion and continue to find that trade agreements mean that selling tobacco should trump the public's health.

That said, it will take global action, as it will with food. Until this point in the book, despite the uncertainties that are fundamental to my life as an academic, I have been rather sure of what the evidence shows we can do to advance the cause of health equity. I have been clear that models of good practice exist that show the rest of us how things could be done. With this global terrain, I am less sure how we get from where we are now to where it would be desirable to be. And there are many other guests I could have had at my dinner table. The Malian nurse working in Manchester rather than Mali, representing the flow of health workers from poor countries to rich; the Indian with cancer who could not afford the price of the drug because intellectual property protection did not allow a generic version to be made and sold at a fraction of the cost; the illegal migrant from Africa, fleeing poverty and making his way through Southern Italy and Spain into Europe, facing uncertainty and worse at both ends of his journey. They are all clamouring for our attention.

Our Commission on Global Governance for Health has made an important step in the direction of identifying how to make progress. First is to recognise the problems of power asymmetry and the fact that for global health equity to improve, action will be needed across all the important social areas that I have described. Second, and related, there should be independent monitoring of progress made in redressing health inequities, and in countering the global political forces that are detrimental to health. Third, whatever improvement there is to be in global institutions and the way they are governed, fundamental is a commitment to global solidarity and shared responsibility.

Here's one optimistic view of globalisation from Thomas Friedman: 'Holy mackerel, the world is becoming flat. Several technological and political forces have converged, and that has produced a global, Web-enabled playing field that allows for multiple forms of collaboration without regard to geography or distance – or soon, even language.'[45] It is a wonderful rosy picture. We all benefit from this global interconnectedness.

Here is a more nuanced, and I would judge a more accurate, view from the economist Nancy Birdsall: 'But the world is not flat. Those of us on the top, with the right education and in the right countries, can easily overlook the countries and the people stuck in deep craters across the global landscape.'[46] Progress will come only from recognising the peaks and troughs and dealing with them.

The Organisation of Hope

I will give you a talisman. Whenever you are in doubt, or when the self becomes too much with you, apply the following test. Recall the face of the poorest and the weakest man [woman] whom you may have seen, and ask yourself, if the step you contemplate is going to be of any use to him [her]. Will he [she] gain anything by it? Will it restore him [her] to a control over his [her] own life and destiny? In other words, will it lead to swaraj [freedom] for the hungry and spiritually starving millions?

Then you will find your doubts and your self melt away.

Mahatma Gandhi

'You are the first white man who spoke to me in a way I could believe in; what you said: did it include me?' Then the Maori woman, in traditional Maori fashion, introduced herself by saying who her grandparents and parents were. She finished: 'I think what you said includes me, but I want to hear from you that it is so.'

I had just given a lecture, covering some of the material in this book, at a big meeting in Auckland organised by the New Zealand Medical Association. When the Maori woman spoke, the watery condition of my eyes that I reported in the Introduction made a nuisance of itself. Finally, in a small voice, I said that when I was at a People's Health Assembly in Thailand, the Thais told me about the 'triangle that moves the mountain'. The three corners of the triangle are: government, knowledge/academia and the people. Get the three working together and we can move mountains. Then I recalled how at the Thai assembly a group of children, each one more gorgeous than the next, sang:

> We are all waves of the same sea
> We are all stars of the same sky
> It's time to learn to live as one.

I said to the Maori woman: if what I said did not include you, the people, then I am doing something terribly wrong. Of course, it includes you, as it does the people of the Kokiri Marae I described in Chapter 8.

'We opened our minds. More important we opened our hearts.'

Who do you imagine might say something like that? A social worker? A New Age traveller? A cleric of one or other faith? How about a Deputy Chief Fire Officer at West Midlands Fire Service in Birmingham, England. He was launching their report 'Improving Lives to Save Lives – the role of West Midlands Fire Service in contributing to Marmot objectives'. He said that they opened their minds to the Marmot Review, *Fair Society, Healthy Lives*, and they opened their hearts to what they could do to help the poor and the needy in the communities they serve and of which they form a vital part.[1]

A woman fire officer told the story of 'David', an octogenarian, living alone. Fire officers had been called because he was burning rubbish in his living room to stay warm – his gas had been cut off. The fire officer said it took her three weeks of coaxing for David, finally, to let her in the door. She asked how he spent his time. He didn't 'do' anything. He didn't watch TV because his electricity had been cut off twenty-six years ago. His only outings were to the corner store to buy a few things to eat. He saw no one.

The fire officer brought him clothes, Christmas dinner, located his sister, and finally got him on needed medication and into sheltered accommodation. He was in a good deal better state than when they found him. A fire officer did that!

At my visit to the West Midlands Fire Service, it was quite something as one burly fire fighter after another told moving stories of how they were working with children, with older people, and those in need, to improve people's lives. For most of my day with the fire fighters, one or other of us was in tears. That watery ocular condition is catching.

These fire fighters in Birmingham England had picked up on the activities of the Merseyside Fire and Rescue Service that I described in Chapter 8, and said: we want to use our capacity out in the community to improve people's lives. Their principles are Prevention, Protection and Response. They have given an undertaking to respond within five minutes to a call for a fire. They spend between 6 and 10 per cent of their time responding to fires. With training, shifts and preparation, that comes to about half their time; they have been innovative, creative and committed in using the other half to enhance the communities they serve. They quote my English Review in pointing out that both health and fires follow the social gradient. Prevention of one is likely to help in preventing the other.

One important principle is Making Every Contact Count. A fire fighter goes into a home to check fire risks and talk about making the home safer. He sees hoarding of 'stuff' which contributes to risk; deprivation; isolation of an elderly person. He doesn't then say: bad luck, but it's not my problem. He either works on the problem himself or works with colleagues to figure out who they should be working with. If the fire fighter has reason to suspect domestic violence, for example, he contacts the relevant experts.

They have 'Marmot Ambassadors' who are the front-line staff whose role is acting on the six domains of recommendations in our English Review, *Fair Society, Healthy Lives.* They call them the Marmot Six. I say to general practitioners: this is what the fire fighters are doing to prevent fires and reduce health inequalities. What are *you* doing? The answer is: more and more, we are doing quite a bit.

After my bicycle accident left me with a fractured femur, the first trip I made was to Stockholm, in January 2013. With my walking stick (happily, long since discarded), I struggled through the snow to the Royal Swedish Academy of Science for a meeting on social determinants of health. Among many others, a member of the Swedish parliament spoke about the WHO Commission on Social Determinants of Health (CSDH). He said that most reports of international commissions are scarcely read and mostly ignored. Emphatically, this was not the case with *Closing the Gap in a Generation*, the final report of the CSDH. He said it is much discussed, still, in the Swedish Parliament, five years after publication.

At his invitation I went to the Swedish Parliament a few months later. I told the parliamentarians that the Swedish Association of Local Authorities and Regions had galvanised its members, with great enthusiasm, to take action on social determinants of health. What were they, the Parliament, doing? Should all the action be at local level?

The City of Malmö was the vanguard. They took *Closing the Gap in a Generation* as a starting point and asked: how, using the recommendations of the global Commission on Social Determinants of Health, can we work together for a socially sustainable Malmö?[2] Other Swedish cities are following suit: Linköping, Göteborg, Östersund, and perhaps others. As I write, the Swedish government has taken the decision to set up a Swedish Commission on Equity in Health.

In Göteborg, local government set up their city Commission. The leitmotif of this Göteborg activity is inclusion: 1,100 people, mainly employees of the City of Göteborg, came to a conference on socially sustainable Göteborg. I have been to meetings of various kinds in London, but never a thousand people engaging with how to make London a more socially sustainable place. Per capita, to match Göteborg, such a London meeting would have to have numbered 11,000. The day after my visit, 400 of these 1,100 were to sit down to work together to plan a more socially sustainable Göteborg, with health equity and sustainable development at its heart.

In England, local governments now have 'health and well-being' boards whose job description is in the name. The King's Fund, a health think tank, did a survey of their priorities. Out of sixty-five local authorities in the survey, three-quarters said that their number one priority was 'Marmot Principles' – referring to the Marmot Review, *Fair Society, Healthy Lives.*

I met one local councillor from Manchester who said: 'You're Marmot! I didn't realise that Marmot was a person. We talk about implementing Marmot.'

In the US, particularly, I hear the cry of anguish that health equity is a fine goal, and social determinants are fine principles of action, but what if the central government seems unwilling to act, or unable, given Washington deadlock? I point to the action at local level. Not just in the UK, but in the US, too. Come to Lexington Kentucky, I am urged, come to Baltimore, come to Los Angeles, and see what we are doing. We need central government, of course, but we also need action where people are born, grow, live, work and age – at local level.

'We offer our patients up to one hundred different programmes. In the same community centre where the general practice is located we have language classes, occupation skills, how to do a job interview, a children's centre, counselling, and so many more,' said Sam Everington, a GP from Bromley-by-Bow in East London.

'But that's not your job,' said the BBC interviewer. 'Surely you are supposed to treat sick people, not teach them how to be more employable.'

But if people can't get a job, how can their health improve?

Building on inspiring examples, such as Bromley-by-Bow, not to mention the fire fighters, it seemed reasonable to ask what doctors and other health professionals can do on social determinants of health. It is not quite as obvious as it sounds. Doctors treat sick people, they don't address child poverty or fear of crime. If, as I have been arguing, the key determinants of health lie outside the health-care system, is there a role for doctors and other health professionals in promoting health equity, apart, that is, from their vital role of treating the sick? It is certainly the question put to me by the doctors at the British Medical Association when I spent time there.

Working with Vivienne Nathanson at the BMA, and my colleagues at the UCL Institute of Health Equity, we produced a report on what doctors and others could do on social determinants of health.[3] We grouped recommendations under five headings: education and training – make sure medical students and doctors understand the insights on social determinants of health; seeing the patient in a wider context – don't treat illness in the homeless, for example, without trying to deal with their homelessness; the health service as employer – ensure good conditions of work for health service employees; working with others – Bromley-by-Bow illustrated the importance of cross-sector working, as did the fire fighters; advocacy – doctors and other health professionals advocating for policies that would improve conditions for their patients.

Empty words? Nice document, but . . . ? Emphatically not. We got commitments from twenty-two medical and health-care

organisations: medical Royal Colleges, nurses, midwives, physio-
therapists, more or less everyone we approached embraced these
ideas. More, they worked to incorporate practice on social determinants of health into the day jobs of their professional groups.

Advocacy is central. I ask the doctors: who cares more about
health than we do? We should therefore be concerned about the
causes of health inequity. Remember the words of Rudolf Virchow,
the great nineteenth-century pathologist: physicians are the natural
attorneys of the poor. In Moldova, doctors told us that they are
anti-poverty campaigners, so clear is the link between poverty and
ill-health.

As with the BMA, I have the same compact with the World
Medical Association: they agree to get doctors active on social
determinants of health, and I agree to stand for election as
President. They did, and I did. I appealed to doctors' finer instincts.
Remember why we went into medicine? I asked representatives
of medical associations from round the world. If any of us have
forgotten, we should spend time with today's medical students
and imbibe their enthusiasm for changing the world to reduce
avoidable inequalities in health. We have at least a dozen National
Medical Associations, with the Canadians and British in the lead,
exploring with us what doctors can do on the social determinants
of health. The first twelve are the hardest. Doctors, too, are joining
the global movement.

THE TRIANGLE THAT MOVES THE MOUNTAIN

We are on the move. The five vignettes that I have just touched on
illustrate the Triangle that Moves the Mountain. We need governments to be involved – local, national and global. We need people
to be involved. The 'people' include civil society groups. The West
Midlands fire fighters, employees of local government, had in effect
become a civil society group, representing and serving their local

population. Yes, and we need health professionals. And we need knowledge, involvement of academics and experts. The review of social determinants of health for a socially sustainable Malmö, for example, involved academics who reviewed the evidence, as well as politicians and representatives of the city population. The evidence in this book builds on the scores, no hundreds, of experts who contributed their knowledge to the syntheses of evidence that were the bases of my three reports, *Closing the Gap in a Generation, Fair Society, Healthy Lives* and the *European Review of Social Determinants and the Health Divide.*

I am excited and embarrassed. Excited, because at the start of the Commission on Social Determinants of Health, we said we wanted to foster a social movement. That movement is alive and well. To the vignettes from New Zealand, Sweden and England, I could add Brazil, Chile, Costa Rica, Cuba, Canada, various US cities, Slovenia, Italy, Peru, Colombia, South Africa, Norway, Denmark, Finland, Iceland, Egypt, Taiwan . . . and many more.

Embarrassed, because my vignettes make it sound like I am driving it – changing the world one flight at a time. I have been not so much driving it as being the advocate, but it is taking off. We have a movement. As one of the members of the WHO Commission on Social Determinants of Health said, quoting Harry Truman I think: it's amazing what you can achieve if you don't care who gets the credit. People are claiming their own insight into the effect of society on health – a good development.

The report of the global commission was taken to the World Health Assembly, initially by the Nordic countries and Brazil. When it was debated, representatives from thirty-eight countries spoke supporting the recommendations of *Closing the Gap in a Generation*. All over the globe I am hearing the language of social determinants of health and health equity. When the UN Secretary-General used the language of *Closing the Gap* – the conditions in which people are born, grow, live, work and age – at Ecosoc, the Economic and Social Council of the UN in 2009, I asked the Chair of Ecosoc if Mr Moon knew he was quoting from our report. Her response: that language is out there.

Parenthetically, I thanked representatives of the Nordic countries and Brazil for taking the initiative in supporting the recommendations of *Closing the Gap*. Their response: we are not doing it for you; we are doing it for the cause of a more just distribution of health in the world.

I am excited.

A BBC journalist who chaired a BBC Festival of Ideas at which I spoke said:

'You're a professional optimist, aren't you?'

'Of course,' I told him. 'There are a hundred and ninety-four member states of the World Health Organization. Suppose only twenty countries had taken seriously *Closing the Gap in a Generation*. I wouldn't be saying on the BBC that a hundred and seventy-four countries were ignoring us. I would say that perhaps next week there will be twenty-two countries, and the month after that thirty. We are on the move. In fact, depending how you count, many more than twenty countries are acknowledging the importance of social determinants of health.'

'What about the global level?' he asked.

In *Closing the Gap in a Generation* one of our recommendations was that there be a global meeting where all countries report on progress on social determinants of health and health equity. Be careful what you wish for. When our report was discussed at the World Health Assembly, the governing body of the World Health Organization (WHO), Brazil, said, in effect: great idea! We'll host the global meeting. The government of Brazil has put arrangements in place for it.

It happened. In October 2011, the First World Conference on Social Determinants of Health was held in Rio de Janeiro, hosted

by the Brazilian government and organised by WHO. More than
120 countries were represented, with more than sixty ministers of
health. I know, you cynics, you are thinking what minister would
not want a trip to Rio. The fact is that it happened. To be sure, it
was not perfect. Not all the ministers who attended had a keen
understanding of social determinants of health. Some could not
wean themselves away from talking about medical care. Medical
care is of vital importance, but this meeting was about social determinants of health.

It is so remarkable, that I'll say it a third time: it happened. It is
remarkable because global health meetings have either been about
control of specific diseases – malaria, tuberculosis, AIDS, non-
communicable diseases – or about health systems. Here was a third
strand to global health: social determinants of health. We didn't talk
only about vaccination and bed nets, about tobacco and alcohol,
important as they are. We talked of empowerment of women, of
early child development and education, of employment and work,
of income and poverty. As one colleague after another came up to
me and said this could not have happened five years ago, symboli-
cally, we rubbed our eyes.

As with all international meetings, there was some low politics,
and even some high politics, some laughable in its triviality, some
more serious. Among the more serious was the Rio Declaration that
emerged from the meeting. It was quite bland. The Commission on
Social Determinants of Health made a clear statement that inequities
in power, money and resources were driving inequities in conditions
of daily life, which in turn were responsible for health inequities. As
the International Federation of Medical Students' Associations pointed
out, inequities in power, money and resources were airbrushed out of
the Rio Declaration – too strong for some ministerial stomachs. That
said, there was passion, excitement and encouragement among the
representatives of government, civil society and academics who took
part. Governments, and others, declared their commitment to act.

And act they have, with enthusiasm and moral fervour.

The moral commitment is important. I was introduced to the head of one of the large global management consultancies. I sought his help, pro bono, in implementing social determinants of health globally. I explained what we were about. He listened.

'Tell me, when you visit a country, urging take-up of your recommendations, do you have resources to offer the country?' he said.

'No. No resources.'

'Do you have a large cadre of trained personnel that can be sent in to help?' he continued.

'No. Not really.'

'What can you offer, then?' was the next question.

'The opportunity for a country's leaders to improve the health and well-being of all their citizens and to reduce unjust inequalities in health. In short, to create a more just society.'

'You really do need help!' he said.

THE BEST OF TIMES, THE WORST OF TIMES

Back to excitement. In Chapter 1 I quoted Dickens. It is the best of times: the evidence laid out in chapters 4–10 shows that we know what to do to reduce inequities in health between and within countries. Many people – governments, civil society organisations, health professionals, international bodies, fire fighters (!) – are listening to that evidence and acting on it.

Perhaps the worst of times is too strong. There are, though, major challenges to health equity, prominent among them increasing economic and social inequalities and the lack of political response to them. Jean Drèze and Amartya Sen entitled their latest book on India *An Uncertain Glory*. It was a reflection that there are things both glorious and not so glorious about India's progress. They identify inequality in India as a cause of major unsolved problems. They do not, however, think that it is well captured by a simple measure of income inequality such as the Gini coefficient (in which everyone's income is ranked from lowest to highest, and a calculation made of dispersion; if everyone had the same income the Gini would be 0; if one person had all the income the Gini would be 1; the greater the inequality the higher the Gini in the range 0 to 1).They write:

> First, when the income levels of the poor are so low that they cannot afford even very basic necessities, the gulf between their lives and those of the more prosperous has an intensity – indeed an outrageousness – that aggregate inequality indicators cannot capture . . . Second, measures of private incomes miss the role of public services, in such fields as education, health care, social facilities and environmental support.[4]

Banerjee and Duflo, whose work on poverty we met earlier, write that, in effect, the poor are being asked to bear too much responsibility.The richer you are, the more things are done for you. You can depend on clean water, get your daily vitamins from fortified breakfast cereals, assume that your food is microbiologically safe, that the building you work in won't collapse and that pension plans will be arranged for you. Individual decisions about how to organise all of these features of our lives would be difficult for anyone, let alone the poor. Especially so, as the poor lack information.[5] I would add that these features follow the social gradient.

As with India, so with the world. Poverty in high-income countries may not have the intensity of poverty in India, but we need to rediscover some of our outrage.When in Britain, the fifth-richest county on the planet, nearly a million people have to resort to food banks because they cannot afford to feed their families, it is time to ask how we can do things differently. Similarly, some outrage would not come amiss when we realise that young men in the US have less chance of surviving to sixty than young men in forty-nine other countries. There has been outrage, of course, on the streets of Madrid and Athens among unemployed young people, and by the 99 per cent in opposition to the 1 per cent. Such outrage needs to be channelled into producing fairer societies.

As with India, so with the world, inequities in power, money and resources are working against action to promote health equity. As one example, a 2014 report from the OECD, the rich country club, shows that income inequality increased in almost all OECD countries – Figure 11.1. The most unequal of the rich countries is Mexico, followed by Turkey and the US.[6]

For all the reasons reviewed earlier, and reprised by Drèze and Sen (although they think that this Gini measure doesn't adequately capture the ill-effects on the poor), increases in income inequality will have an adverse effect on living standards, and hence on the health of those lower down the social scale. But won't redistribution

FIGURE 11.1: GINI COEFFICIENTS OF INCOME INEQUALITY, OECD COUNTRIES, MID-1980S AND 2011/12

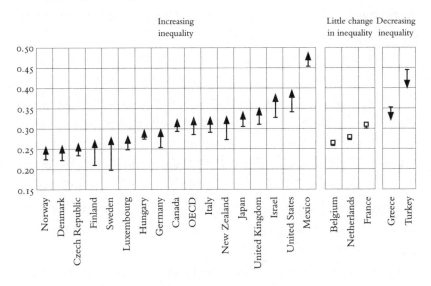

Note: Incomes refer to household disposable income, adjusted for household size.
Source: OECD Income Distribution Database.

of income harm economic growth? Don't we hear, time and again, that setting the wealth producers free is good for everyone? The OECD is unequivocal on what the evidence shows: the *greater* the income inequality, the *less* the growth. Why? Because if the poor have little money, they can't buy things. Further, the OECD empha- sises that the negative effect on growth arises not just because of the low purchasing power of the bottom 10 per cent, but of the bottom 40 per cent. Of course, saying that we need to pay atten- tion to the bottom 40 per cent, not only to the very poorest, moves towards the gradient. Music to my ears. Even were you concerned only with economic growth, greater equality makes sense, but as I have tried to make plain, exorbitant inequality damages our lives, and has impact on the social gradient in health. There are strong moral and practical reasons to be concerned.

If we turn from income to wealth, again we see enormous inequalities. According to the *Economist*, global wealth grew from $117 trillion in 2000 to $262 trillion in 2014.[7] That comes to $56,000 for each adult on the planet. But half the people in the world have less than $3,650 each; and the richest 20 per cent have 94.5 per cent of all the wealth.

What the figures on income and wealth show is that there are oceans of money sloshing about. It is not easy to maintain the fiction that we do not have enough money to do good things. The problem is that, within countries, the concentration of wealth is becoming more extreme. That was the message of Piketty's *Capital in the Twenty-First Century*. At the same time as wealth concentration is increasing, all across Europe and the US we are being lectured to on the dire importance of austerity. Public services have to be cut back because . . . because . . . we cannot afford them?

John Maynard Keynes, immediately after the Second World War, wrote: 'The day is not far off when the economic problem will take the back seat where it belongs, and the arena of the heart and the head will be occupied or reoccupied, by our real problems – the problems of life and of human relations, of creation and behaviour and religion.'[8] In country after country, too much of our public conversation is about how we can grow national income, too little about how we can improve society.

Keynes's message is similar to that of Bobby Kennedy, with which I began Chapter 10. To remind you, he called for going beyond Gross National Product as a measure of progress and emphasising: 'the health of our children, the quality of their education or the joy of their play . . . the beauty of our poetry or the strength of our marriages, the intelligence of our public debate or the integrity of our public officials. . . our wit [and] our courage . . . our wisdom [and] our learning . . . our compassion . . .'

These are all good things, but not all are so easily measurable. My simple proposal is that health and health inequity are good measures of how we are doing as a society. They are outcomes and they are indicators. By that I mean that health and health equity are valued in themselves. Given the choice, other things being equal, most of us would choose to live in a society characterised by general good health. We value good health. As indicators they form another function. I have argued through the book that health and health equity tell us something more about the quality of the society in which we live: perhaps not directly about the quality of our poetry, or our wit and courage, to quote Bobby Kennedy, but certainly about the quality of our education, our social life, our institutions. Get those right, and not only will health flourish, we are likely to reduce crime, and have a better-functioning society.

MOVING FORWARD

Based on its health record, there are grounds to be concerned about US society. Joseph Stiglitz, who I quoted on inequality, is concerned that increasing economic inequality in the US poses all sorts of burdens. No other country should be complacent that it has it right. The problem is, says Stiglitz, that we have been pursuing economic policy that benefits the 1 per cent. Trickle-down economics is defunct and does not work. Time is running out, but there are solutions. He lays out an economic reform agenda that curbs excesses at the top and invests in the rest of the population.[9] While I have not addressed economic policy directly, many of his suggestions for social protection and investing in the population are entirely consistent with my recommendations in earlier chapters in this book.

Policies to address inequities quickly move into the political realm. I maintain the fiction that I am not political ... and have been criticised for it. A criticism I accept. For example, Vicente Navarro, of Johns Hopkins and Barcelona, praised the report of the Commission on Social Determinants of Health. He particularly liked our phrase: social injustice is killing on a grand scale. But then he said: we know who the killers are – name them and shame them.[10]

I offer two reasons for my 'non-political' position, in mitigation if it were needed. First, a political level of analysis requires research all of its own.[11] For example, Jacob Hacker, American political scientist, and his collaborator Paul Pierson have written an excellent book on how the growing inequality of income in the US can be accounted for by the disproportionate political power of the very rich.[12] I am delighted for others to pursue analysis of the politics. Second, I want political parties of whatever complexion to take on the agenda that I am promoting. We are talking about creating societies that meet the needs and create the opportunities for flourishing of all their members. That should not be the province of one political party. At the global level, if the CSDH report started to name and shame presidents and prime ministers we would not have had representatives of thirty-eight countries praising it at the World Health Assembly and support from Africa, India, China, the USA and many European countries.

Politics quickly departs from evidence into the realm of ideology. As I said right at the beginning, I do have an ideology: inequalities in health that are avoidable by reasonable means, and are not avoided, are unjust, inequitable. But the evidence must be a key part of the conversation. We know that ideology shapes views of the evidence, but that is not a reason to stop arguing from the evidence and simply surrender to prejudice. If someone 'believes' that the poor of India brought their ill-health on themselves, we need to show the evidence to the contrary. My own view is that the truth will win out against prejudice, eventually – and I would support that view with evidence.

I am not sure how, politically, you get from here to there. But I am sure that knowledge is an important part of the process. In case you thought that the political leaders in your country, whichever that is, are uniquely 'economical with the truth', here is George Orwell: 'In our time, political speech and writing are largely the defence of the indefensible.'[13] Or go further back and listen to Dickens's savage mockery of political leaders in Victorian times.

Routinely, in surveys of who the public trusts on scientific issues, politicians vie with journalists for the bottom rank. That gives me faith in democracy. The public can tell when they are being lied to. But we need to be informed. For example, in Britain in 2015 an economic recovery is being trumpeted. We are the envy of the rich world, we are told. The actual figures are in Figure 11.2. Real wages in 2013 in the UK were 7 per cent lower than they were in 2007 – the worst performance of any of the rich countries. Is there not something of a gap between the rhetoric and the reality?

As a member of the general public, perhaps you are not given to looking at reports from the International Labour Office, but you know that your living standards have declined simply by doing the family shopping and paying your energy bills.

In Britain, where there is a tradition of respect for evidence, data tend to be used as weapons in political debate rather than for

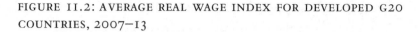

FIGURE 11.2: AVERAGE REAL WAGE INDEX FOR DEVELOPED G20
COUNTRIES, 2007–13

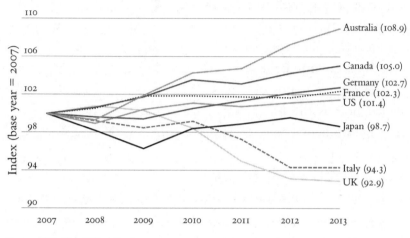

Source: ILO Global Wage Database.

reasoned argument. If one set of figures don't make your political case, chose another. 'Lies, damn lies, and statistics' has a long
history.

A major reason for writing this book is to share knowledge
on how the working of society impacts on health and the unjust
distribution of health and what we can do about it.

One senior Conservative politician in Britain put it to me that
my agenda is closer to social democratic than to Conservative
thinking. I have tried studiously in public, and in this book, to
make my case on the evidence, not on prior political beliefs. My
response to this politician was that avoidable health inequality,
health inequity, was the deepest injustice in our society. Was he
saying that only social democratic politicians cared? I hoped
not. Further, showing that politicians distort the evidence to
suit their political ends was not a party-political act; it should
be aimed at all our political leaders whatever their makeup.
No political party has a monopoly on purveying misleading
information.

A PLANET–SHAPED HOLE

It is tempting to want to try to write about everything. Tempting but foolhardy. I have written this book about what I know and what I have been doing in research and policy. I am aware of a big hole here. Environment has made only fleeting appearances, and climate change stands out for having gone missing. The planet-shaped hole is the book that needs to be written on bringing the environmental and social determinants of health agendas together.

Sustainable development has taught us the importance of equity between generations as well as within. And I would argue that discussions on preserving the planet must take equity within this generation into account – within and between countries. For example, congestion charging – charging you if you drive your car into the central city – is a good 'green' tax. But like all consumption taxes it tends to be regressive, in that it takes a higher proportion of a poor person's income than of a rich person's. I have raised this in environmental circles and been told: don't spoil a perfectly good tax by worrying about equity. I am tempted to retort: don't damage equity with your perfectly good taxes. We need to bring the environmental and health equity agendas together.

Similarly, as low-income countries develop, their use of carbon increases. Carbon trading can be seen as a way for rich countries to buy the rights of poor countries to pump out carbon dioxide. It has the effect of allowing people in rich countries to enjoy their lifestyles and hindering the economic development of low-income countries – a deep social injustice. We need to bring the environmental and health equity agendas together.

After all, sustainable development means a balance of the three pillars: economic, social and environmental. These three pillars are vital for health equity. Attending both to climate change and to health equity requires acting on evidence to produce the kind of society we want – one that meets the needs of the present generation without hazarding the lives of future generations.

ACROSS THE SPECTRUM FROM
LOW- TO HIGH-INCOME COUNTRIES

I have argued that disempowerment, material, psychosocial and political, damages health and creates heath inequities. Such disempowerment may take different forms in low-, middle- and high-income countries. But the general approach to promoting a just distribution of health is similar. When we conducted the European Review of Social Determinants and the Health Divide we were concerned with countries from Central Asia to Scandinavia. We said that there was something for everyone in our recommendations. If you are in a country with poorly developed social systems, do something. It will make a difference. If your country is on the way, do more. And if you are in the Nordic countries, do it better.

Do something. Do more. Do it better.

Notes

INTRODUCTION

1 Chesney E, Goodwin GM, Fazel S. Risks of all-cause and suicide mortality in mental disorders: a meta-review. *World Psychiatry: official journal of the World Psychiatric Association.* 2014;13(2):153–60.

2 Gordon T. Further mortality experience among Japanese Americans. *Public Health Report.* 1967; 82: 973–84.

3 Committee on Medical Aspects of Food Policy. *Nutritional Aspects of Cardiovascular Disease.* London: HMSO, 1994. 1–186.

4 Nichaman MZ, Hamilton HB, Kagan A, Sacks S, Greer T, Syme SL. Epidemiologic studies of coronary heart disease and stroke in Japanese men living in Japan, Hawaii and California: distribution of biochemical risk factors. *American Journal of Epidemiology.* 1975; 102: 491–501; Yano K, Rhoads GG, Kagan A, Tillotson J. Dietary intake and the risk of coronary heart disease in Japanese men living in Hawaii. *American Journal of Clinical Nutrition.* 1978; 31: 1270–9.

5 Matsumoto YS. Social stress and coronary heart disease in Japan: a hypothesis. *Milbank Mem Fund Qtly.* 1970; 48: 9–36.

6 Marmot MG, Syme SL. Acculturation and CHD in Japanese-Americans. *American Journal of Epidemiology.* 1976; 104: 225–47.

7 Marmot MG, Shipley MJ, Rose G. Inequalities in death – specific explanations of a general pattern? *Lancet.* 1984; 1(8384): 1003–6.

8 Syme SL, Berkman LF. Social class, susceptibility, and sickness. *American Journal of Epidemiology.* 1976; 104: 1–8.

9 Navarro V. *Medicine under Capitalism.* Croom Helm, 1976.

10 Van Rossum CTM, Shipley MJ, Van de Mheen H, Grobbee DE, Marmot MG. Employment grade differences in cause specific mortality. A 25 year follow up of civil servants from the first Whitehall study. *Journal of Epidemiology and Community Health.* 2000; 54(3): 178–84.

11 Karasek R, Theorell T. *Healthy Work: Stress, Productivity, and the Reconstruction of Working Life*. New York: Basic Books, 1990.

12 Marmot M. *Status Syndrome: How Your Social Standing Directly Affects Your Health and Life Expectancy*. London: Bloomsbury Publishing, 2004.

13 Rose D, O'Brien K. *Constructing Classes: Towards a New Social Classification for the UK*. Swindon: ESRC, 1997.

14 Marmot M, Bosma H, Hemingway H, Brunner E, Stansfeld S. Contribution of job control to social gradient in coronary heart disease [authors' response letter]. Whitehall II Study. *Lancet*. 997; 350: 1405.

15 Marmot Review Team. *Fair Society, Healthy Lives: Strategic Review of Health Inequalities in England Post 2010*. London: Marmot Review, 2010.

16 The Price of Being Well. *The Economist*. 28 Aug 2008.

17 Navarro V. What we mean by social determinants of health. *Global Health Promotion*. 2009; 16(1): 5–16.

1 THE ORGANISATION OF MISERY

1 Deaton A. *The Great Escape: Health, Wealth, and the Origins of Inequality*. Princeton: Princeton University Press, 2013.

2 Yellen JL. Perspectives on Inequality and Opportunity from the Survey of Consumer Finances: Federal Reserve; 2014 [22/12/2014]. Available from: http://www.federalreserve.gov/newsevents/speech/yellen20141017a.htm.

3 Hutton W. Banking is changing, slowly, but its culture is still corrupt. *The Guardian*, 2014 [updated 16/11/2014]. Available from: http://www.theguardian.com/commentisfree/2014/nov/16/banking-changing-slowly-but-culture-still-corrupt.

4 Commission on the Social Determinants of Health. *Closing the Gap in a Generation: Health Equity through Action on the Social Determinants of Health. Final Report of the Commission on Social Determinants of Health*. Geneva: World Health Organization, 2008.

5 Hanlon P, Walsh A, Whyte B. *Let Glasgow Flourish*. Glasgow: 2006.

6 Ibid.

7 Scottish Public Health Observatory. Comparative Health Profiles 2010. Available from: www.scotpho.org.uk/home/Comparativehealth/Profiles/2010CHPProfiles.asp.

8 City of Westminster. Area Profiles 2013 [15/09/2013]. Available from: http://www.westminster.gov.uk/services/councilgovernmentanddemocracy/ward-profiles/.

9 Marmot Review Team. *Fair Society, Healthy Lives: Strategic Review of Health Inequalities in England post-2010*. London: Marmot Review, 2010.

14 Maes HH, Neale MC, Eaves LJ. Genetic and environmental factors in relative body weight and human adiposity. *Behavior genetics*. 1997; 27(4): 325–51.

15 Stamatakis E, Zaninotto P, Falaschetti E, Mindell J, Head J. Time trends in childhood and adolescent obesity in England from 1995 to 2007 and projections of prevalence to 2015. *Journal of Epidemiology and Community Health*. 2010; 64(2): 167–74.

16 Aitsi-Selmi A, Chandola T, Friel S, Nouraei R, Shipley MJ, Marmot MG. Interaction between education and household wealth on the risk of obesity in women in Egypt. *PLoS One*. 2012; 7(6): e39507.

17 CDC. *Health Behaviors of Adults: United States, 2008–2010*. 2013.

18 Pear R. Insurance Rolls to Rise in State Fighting Plan. *The New York Times*. 06.09.2013.

19 Banks J, Marmot M, Oldfield Z, Smith JP. Disease and disadvantage in the United States and England. *Journal of the American Medical Association*. 2006; 295: 2037–45.

20 Crimmins EM, Preston SH, Cohen B, editors. *Explaining Divergent Levels of Longevity in High-Income Countries*. National Research Council; Panel on Understanding Divergent Trends in Longevity in High Income Countries; Committee on Population, Division of Behavioral and Social Sciences and Education. Washington, DC: The National Academies Press, 2011; Woolf SH, Aron L, editors. *U.S. Health in International Perspective: Shorter Lives, Poorer Health*. National Research Council; Institute of Medicine. Washington, DC: The National Academies Press, 2013.

21 Deaton A. *The Great Escape: Health, Wealth, and the Origins of Inequality*. Princeton: Princeton University Press, 2013.

22 World Health Organization. *World Health Statistics 2014*. Geneva: WHO, 2014.

23 Singh GK. U.S. Department of Health and Human Services, Health Resources and Services Administration, Maternal and Child Health Bureau. *Maternal Mortality in the United States, 1935–2007: Substantial Racial/Ethnic, Socioeconomic, and Geographic Disparities Persist*. 2010; Chang J, Elam-Evans LD, Berg CJ, Herndon J, Flowers L, Seed KA, et al. Pregnancy-related mortality surveillance – United States, 1991–1999. Morbidity and mortality weekly report Surveillance summaries. 2003; 52(2): 1–8.

24 Johnson D, Rutledge T. Maternal Mortality – United States, 1982–1996. The Morbidity and Mortality Weekly Report. 1998; 47(34): 705–7.

25 Allen M, Allen J, Hogarth S, Marmot M. *Working for Health Equity: The Role of Health Professionals*. London: UCL Institute of Health Equity, 2013.

26 Harvard School of Public Health. Making health choices easy choices: Harvard University, 2014 [07/04/2014]. Available from: http://www.hsph.harvard.edu/obesity-prevention-source/policy-and-environmental-change/.

27 Sen A. *Development as Freedom*. Oxford: Oxford University Press, 1999.

3 FAIR SOCIETY, HEALTHY LIVES

1 Rawls J. *A Theory of Justice*. Harvard: Harvard University Press, 1971.
2 Daniels N. *Just Health Care*. Cambridge University Press, 1985.
3 Sen A. *Inequality Reexamined*. Oxford: Oxford University Press, 1992.
4 Sandel MJ. *Justice: What's the Right Thing to Do?* New York: Farrar, Straus and Giroux, 2010.
5 UCL Institute of Health Equity. *Local Action on Health Inequalities: Understanding the Economics of Investments in the Social Determinants of Health*. London: Public Health Equity, 2014.
6 Murphy KM, Topel RH. The Value of Health and Longevity. *Journal of Political Economy*. 2006; 114(5): 871–904.
7 Singleton N, Meltzer H, Gatward R. *Psychiatric Morbidity among Prisoners*. London: ONS, 1999.
8 Mental health statistics: Prisons: Mental Health Foundation, 2014 [23/12/2014]. Available from: http://www.mentalhealth.org.uk/help-information/mental-health-statistics/prisons/.
9 Marx K. *The 18th Brumaire of Louis Bonaparte*. Wildside Press, 2008 [1851].
10 Violence Reduction Unit. Retirement of DCS John Carnochan 2013 [14/04/2014]. Available from: http://www.actiononviolence.co.uk/content/retirement-dcs-john-carnochan-0.
11 Marmot MG, Davey Smith G, Stansfeld SA, Patel C, North F, Head J, et al. Health inequalities among British Civil Servants: the Whitehall II study. *Lancet*. 1991; 337(8754): 1387–93.
12 Ibid.; Bosma H, Marmot MG, Hemingway H, Nicholson AC, Brunner E, Stansfeld SA. Low job control and risk of coronary heart disease in Whitehall II (prospective cohort) study. *British Medical Journal*. 1997; 314(7080): 558–65.
13 Marmot et al. Health inequalities; Bosma et al. Low job control.
14 Sen A. *Development as Freedom*. New York: Alfred A. Knopf, Inc, 1999.
15 Sen A. *The Idea of Justice*. London: Allen Lane, 2009.
16 O'Neill O. Reith Lectures: A Question of Trust 2002 [14/04/2014]. Available from: http://www.bbc.co.uk/radio4/reith2002/.
17 Saez E. Striking it Richer: The Evolution of Top Incomes in the United States (Updated with 2012 preliminary estimates) 2013 [14/04/2014]. Available from: http://elsa.berkeley.edu/~saez/saez-UStopincomes-2012.pdf.
18 OECD. OECD Stat Extracts: Income Distribution and Poverty – Poverty rate after taxes and transfers, poverty line 60% 2013 [14/04/2014]. Available from: http://stats.oecd.org/Index.aspx?DataSetCode=IDD.
19 Galbraith JK. *The Affluent Society*. New York: Houghton Mifflin Company, 1998.

20 Wilkinson RG, Pickett K. *The Spirit Level: Why More Equal Societies Almost Always Do Better.* London: Allen Lane, 2009.

21 Lewis M. *The Big Short: Inside the Doomsday Machine.* London: Allen Lane, 2011.

22 Hampshire S. *Justice Is Conflict.* Princeton NJ: Princeton University Press, 2000.

23 New Policy Institute, MacInnes T, Aldridge H, Bushe S, Kenway P, Tinson A. *Monitoring Poverty and Social Exclusion 2013.* Joesph Rowntree Foundation, 2013.

24 Hacker J, Pierson P. *Winner-Take-All Politics.* New York: Simon and Schuster, 2010.

25 Park A, National Centre for Social Research. *British Social Attitudes: the 25th Report.* Los Angeles, London: SAGE, 2009.

26 Hutton W. *Them and Us: Changing Britain – Why We Need a Fairer Society.* London: Abacus, 2011.

27 Bell R, Britton A, Brunner E, Chandola T, Ferrie J, Harris M, et al. *Work, Stress and Health: The Whitehall II Study.* London: International Centre for Health and Society/Department of Epidemiology, 2004; Bosma et al. Low job control; Marmot et al. Health inequalities.

28 Kelly Y, Sacker A, Del BE, Francesconi M, Marmot M. What role for the home learning environment and parenting in reducing the socioeconomic gradient in child development? Findings from the Millennium Cohort Study. *ArchDisChild.* 2011; 96(9): 832–7.

29 Mullainathan S, Shafir E. *Scarcity: Why Having Too Little Means So Much.* New York: Times Books, 2013.

30 Blinder AS. What's the Matter with Economics? *New York Review of Books.* 2014; December 18: 55–7.

31 Marmot M. A continued affair with science and judgements. *International Journal of Epidemiology.* 2009; 38: 908–10.

32 Various. Fair Society, Healthy Lives Reviews. *Social Science & Medicine.* 2010; 71(7).

33 Marmot M. *Status Syndrome: How Your Social Standing Directly Affects Your Health and Life Expectancy.* London: Bloomsbury, 2004.

4 EQUITY FROM THE START

1 Gladwell M. *Outliers: The Story of Success.* London: Penguin, 2009; Epstein D. *The Sports Gene: Talent, Practice and the Truth about Success.* London: Yellow Jersey Press, 2013.

2 Grantham-McGregor SM, Cheung YB, Cueto S, Glewwe P, Richter L, Strupp B. Development potential in the first 5 years for children in developing countries. *Lancet.* 2007; 369(9555): 60–70.

3 Jeremiah 31:29. *The Holy Bible: Containing the Old and New Testaments.* London: Collins, 2011.

4 Hertzman C, Boyce T. How experience gets under the skin to create gradients in developmental health. *Annual Review of Public Health.* 2010; 31: 329–47 3p following 47; Adler NE, Ostrove JM. Socioeconomic status and health: What we know and what we don't. In: Adler NE, Marmot M, McEwen B, Stewart J, editors. *Socioeconomic Status and Health in Industrial Nations.* New York: New York Academy of Sciences, 1999; 896: 3–15.

5 Hertzman and Boyce. How experience gets under the skin.

6 Power C, Hertzman C. Social and biological pathways linking early life and adult disease. *British Medical Bulletin.* 1997; 53: 210–21.

7 Barker DJ. Fetal origins of coronary heart disease. *British Medical Journal.* 1995; 311: 171–4; Barker DJP. Fetal nutrition and cardiovascular disease in later life. *British Medical Bulletin.* 1997; 53(1): 96–108.

8 Felitti VJ, Anda RF, Nordenberg D, Williamson DF, Spitz AM, Edwards V, et al. Relationship of childhood abuse and household dysfunction to many of the leading causes of death in adults. The Adverse Childhood Experiences (ACE) Study. *American Journal of Preventive Medicine.* 1998; 14(4): 245–58.

9 Norman RE, Byambaa M, De R, Butchart A, Scott J, Vos T. The long-term health consequences of child physical abuse, emotional abuse, and neglect: a systematic review and meta-analysis. *PLoS Med.* 2012;9(11):e1001349.

10 Smith Z. *NW.* London: Hamish Hamilton, 2012, pp. 270–1.

11 Plomin R. Genetics and children's experiences in the family. *Journal of Child Psychology and Psychiatry.* 1995; 36: 33–67; Plomin R. *Nature and Nurture: An Introduction to Human Behavioral Genetics.* Pacific Grove, CA: Brooks-Cole, 1990.

12 UCL Institute of Health Equity. Marmot Indicators 2014 [10/11/2014]. Available from: http://www.instituteofhealthequity.org/projects/marmot-indicators-2014.

13 Hart B, Risely TR. The early catastrophe: the 30 million word gap by age 3. *American Educator.* 2003; 27(1): 4–9.

14 Williams Z. Do stay-at-home mothers upset you? You may be a motherist. *The Guardian.* 21 October 2013.

15 Chatterjee M, Macwan J. *Taking Care of Our Children: The Experiences of SEWA Union.* Ahmedabad: Self Employed Women's Association, 1992, p. 5.

16 McMunn A, Kelly Y, Cable N, Bartley M. Maternal employment and child socio-emotional behaviour in the UK: longitudinal evidence from the

UK Millennium Cohort Study. *Journal of Epidemiology and Community Health*. 2012; 66(7): e19.

17 Heymann J, McNeill K. *Changing Children's Chances: New Findings in Child Policy Worldwide*. Cambridge, Mass.: Harvard University Press, 2013.

18 Pinker S. *The Blank Slate: the Modern Denial of Human Nature*. London: Allen Lane, 2002.

19 Schonbeck Y, Talma H, van Dommelen P, Bakker B, Buitendijk SE, HiraSing RA, et al. The world's tallest nation has stopped growing taller: the height of Dutch children from 1955 to 2009. *Pediatric Research*. 2013; 73(3): 371–7.

20 Hertzman C, Boyce T. How experience gets under the skin to create gradients in developmental health. *Annual Review of Public Health*. 2010; 31: 329–47 3p following 47; Adler NE, Ostrove JM. Socioeconomic status and health: What we know and what we don't. In: Adler et al. *Socioeconomic Status and Health*. pp. 3–15.

21 Pinker. *The Blank Slate*.

22 Hertzman and Boyce. How experience gets under the skin.

23 Meaney MJ. Maternal care, gene expression, and the transmission of individual differences in stress reactivity across generations. *Annual Review of Neuroscience*. 2001; 24: 1161–92.

24 UCL Institute of Health Equity. *Good Quality Parenting Programmes and the Home to School Transition*. Public Health England, 2014.

25 Melhuish E. The Impact of Early Childhood Education and Care on Improved Wellbeing. In: British Academy, editor. *'If you could do one thing . . .' Nine Local Actions to Reduce Health Inequalities*. British Academy, 2014; Pordes-Bowers A, Strelitz J, Allen J, Donkin A. *An Equal Start: Improving Outcomes in Children's Centres*. London: UCL Institute of Health Equity, 2012.

26 Dumas C, Lefranc A. *Early Schooling and Later Outcomes: Evidence from Preschool Extension in France*. Thema working paper no. 2010–07. Pontoise: Université de Cergy, 2010.

5 EDUCATION AND EMPOWERMENT

1 Drèze J, Sen A. *An Uncertain Glory: India and Its Contradictions*. London: Allen Lane, 2013.

2 UNDP. *Human Development Report 2013 – The Rise of the South: Human Progress in a Diverse World*. New York: United Nations Development Programme, 2013.

3 Stiglitz JE. *Globalization and its Discontents*. London: Allen Lane, 2002.

4 UNDP. *Human Development Report 2013*.

5 Woolf SH, Aron L, editors. *U.S. Health in International Perspective: Shorter Lives, Poorer Health*. National Research Council; Institute of Medicine. Washington, DC: The National Academies Press, 2013.

6 Murphy SL, Xu JQ, Kochanek KD. *Deaths: Final Data for 2010*. National Vital Statistics Reports. 2013; 61(4).

7 Olshansky SJ, Antonucci T, Berkman L, Binstock RH, Boersch-Supan A, Cacioppo JT, et al. Differences in life expectancy due to race and educational differences are widening, and many may not catch up. *Health Affairs (Millwood)*. 2012; 31(8): 1803–13.

8 Eurostat. Life expectancy by age, sex and educational attainment (ISCED 1997) 2012 [updated 2012/07/27]. Available from: http://appsso.eurostat.ec.europa.eu/nui/show.do?dataset=demo_mlexpecedu&lang=en.

9 UCL Institute of Health Equity. *Health Inequalities in the EU – Final Report of a Consortium*. Consortium lead: Sir Michael Marmot European Commission Directorate-General for Health and Consumers, 2013.

10 Demographic and Health Surveys 2011. Available from: www.measuredhs.com/countries.

11 Drèze and Sen. *An Uncertain Glory*.

12 Hoff K, Pandey P. *Belief Systems and Durable Inequalities: an Experimental Investigation of Indian Caste*. Washington: World Bank, 2004.

13 Barber SL, Gertler PJ. The impact of Mexico's conditional cash transfer programme, Oportunidades, on birthweight. *Tropical Medicine & International Health (TM & IH)*. 2008; 13(11): 1405–14.

14 Soares FV, Ribas RP, Osorio RG. Evaluating the Impact of Brazil's Bolsa Familia: Cash Transfer Programs in Comparative Perspective. *Latin American Research Review*. 2010; 45(2): 173–90.

15 Baird S, Ferreira FHG, Ozler B, Woolcock M. *Relative Effectiveness of Conditional and Unconditional Cash Transfers for Schooling Outcomes in Developing Countries: A Systematic Review*. Campbell Systematic Reviews, 2013; 9(8).

16 Banerjee A, Duflo E. *Poor Economics: A Radical Rethinking of the Way to Fight Global Poverty*. USA: Public Affairs, 2011.

17 Ibid.

6 WORKING TO LIVE

1 Sulabh International Social Service Organisation. Lalta Nanda 2014 [27/05/2014]. Available from: http://www.sulabhinternational.org/content/lalta-nanda.

2 Growing Inclusive Markets, UNDP. Case Study: India. Sulabh International: A Movement to Liberate Scavengers by Implementing a

Low-Cost, Safe Sanitation System [27/05/2014]. Available from: http://www.sulabhinternational.org/admin/config/media/file-system/Summary%20of%20the%20Case%20Study-Sulabh%20International-A%20Movement%20to%20Liberate%20Scavengers%20by%20Implementing%20a%20Low-Cost%2C%20Safe%20Sanitation%20System-by%20UNDP.pdf.

3 Franco G. Ramazzini and workers' health. *Lancet.* 1999; 354(9181): 858–61.

4 Ibid.

5 Eurofound. *Fifth European Working Conditions Survey.* Luxembourg: Publications Office of the European Union, 2012.

6 Ibid.

7 Butler S. Bangladesh garment workers still vulnerable a year after Rana Plaza. *The Guardian.* 24 April 2014.

8 International Labour Organisation. *ILO Introductory Report: Global Trends and Challenges on Occupational Safety and Health.* 2011.

9 Marmot MG, Rose G, Shipley M, Hamilton PJS. Employment grade and coronary heart disease in British civil servants. *Journal of Epidemiology and Community Health.* 1978; 32: 244–9.

10 Marmot MG, Davey Smith G, Stansfeld SA, Patel C, North F, Head J, et al. Health inequalities among British Civil Servants: the Whitehall II study. *Lancet.* 1991; 337(8754): 1387–93.

11 Bosma H, Peter R, Siegrist J, Marmot MG. Two alternative job stress models and the risk of coronary heart disease. *American Journal of Public Health.* 1998; 88: 68–74; Chandola T, Britton A, Brunner E, Hemingway H, Malik M, Kumari M, et al. Work stress and coronary heart disease: what are the mechanisms? *European Heart Journal.* 2008; 29: 640–8; Chandola T, Brunner E, Marmot M. Chronic stress at work and the metabolic syndrome: prospective study. *British Medical Journal.* 2006; 332: 521–5.

12 Head J, Ferrie JE, Brunner E, Marmot M, Rydstedt L, Stansfeld S, et al. *The Potential Impact on Health and Sickness Absence of Management Standards for Work-Related Stress.* Research report to Health and Safety Executive. Health and Safety Executive, 2007.

13 Kivimaki M, Ferrie JE, Brunner EJ, Head J, Shipley MJ, Vahtera J, et al. Justice at work and reduced risk of coronary heart disease among employees: the Whitehall II study. *ArchInternMed.* 2005; 165(19): 2245–51; Kivimaki M, Ferrie JE, Head J, Shipley M, Vahtera J, Marmot MG. Organisational justice and change in justice as predictors of employee health: the Whitehall II study. *Journal of Epidemiology and Community Health.* 2004; 58(11): 931–7; Head et al. *The Potential Impact.*

14 Steptoe A, Kivimaki M. Stress and cardiovascular disease: an update on current knowledge. *Annual Review of Public Health.* 2013; 34: 337–54.

15 Siegrist J, Rosskam E, Leka S. Report of task group 2: Employment and working conditions including occupation, unemployment and migrant workers 2012 [updated 2012/08/13]. Available from: https://www.institute-ofhealthequity.org/members/workplans-and-draft-reports.

16 Head et al. *The Potential Impact*; Bambra CL, Whitehead MM, Sowden AJ, Akers J, Petticrew MP. Shifting schedules: the health effects of reorganizing shift work. *American Journal of Preventive Medicine*. 2008; 34(5): 427–34; Vyas MV, Garg AX, Iansavichus AV, Costella J, Donner A, Laugsand LE, et al. Shift work and vascular events: systematic review and meta-analysis. *British Medical Journal*. 2012; 345: e4800.

17 Steptoe and Kivimaki. Stress and cardiovascular disease.

18 Beveridge W. *Social Insurance and Allied Services*. London: HMSO, 1942.

19 New Policy Institute, MacInnes T, Aldridge H, Bushe S, Kenway P, Tinson A. *Monitoring Poverty and Social Exclusion 2013*. Joseph Rowntree Foundation; 2013.

20 OECD. *Growing Unequal? Income Distribution and Poverty in OECD Countries*. OECD, 2008.

21 International Labour Organisation. *Global Employment Trends 2014: Risk of a Jobless Recovery?* Geneva: ILO, 2014.

22 Marmot M. *Status Syndrome: How Your Social Standing Directly Affects Your Health and Life Expectancy*. London: Bloomsbury, 2004; Bartley M. Health and Labour Force Participation: 'Stress', Selection and the Reproduction Costs of Labour Power. *Journal of Social Policy*. 1991; 20(03): 327–64.

23 Hansard. HC 6Ser vol 191 col 413 (16 May 1991). 1991.

24 Moser K, Godblatt P, Fox J. *Unemployment and Mortality. Longitudinal Study*. London: HMSO, 1990. pp. 81–97.

25 The HAPIEE study, UCL, 1999–2005.

26 Stuckler D, Basu S, Suhrcke M, Coutts A, McKee M. The public health effect of economic crises and alternative policy responses in Europe: an empirical analysis. *Lancet*. 2009; 374(9686): 315–23.

27 Siegrist J, Rosskam E, Leka S. Report of task group 2: Employment and working conditions including occupation, unemployment and migrant workers 2012 [updated 2012/08/13]. Available from: https://www.institute-ofhealthequity.org/members/workplans-and-draft-reports.

28 Ibid.

29 Lewis M. *The Big Short: Inside the Doomsday Machine*. London: Allen Lane, 2011.

30 Reinhart C, Rogoff K. Growth in a time of debt. *American Economic Review*. 2010; 100(2): 473–8.

31 Herndon T, Ash M, Pollin R. *Does High Public Debt Consistently Stifle Economic Growth? A Critique of Reinhart and Rogoff.* Political Economy Research Institute – Working Paper Series. 2013; April(322).

32 International Monetary Fund. *World Economic Outlook October 2012: Coping with High Debt and Sluggish Growth.* Washington DC: IMF, 2012.

33 UCL Institute of Health Equity. *Reducing the Number of Young People Not in Employment, Education or Training (NEET).* Public Health England, 2014.

34 Wolfe T. *The Bonfire of the Vanities.* London: Vintage Books, 1987.

7 DO NOT GO GENTLE

1 Gawande A. *Being Mortal.* London: Profile Books, 2014.

2 United Nations Population Fund, HelpAge International. *Ageing in the Twenty-First Century: A Celebration and A Challenge.* New York: UNFPA, 2012, p. 33.

3 Kinsella K, He W, U.S. Census Bureau. *An Aging World: 2008. International Population Reports.* Washington, DC: U.S. Government Printing Office, 2009.

4 United Nations Population Division. World Population Prospects: The 2012 Revision. File MORT/6–1: Percentage of total deaths (both sexes combined), by broad age group, major area, region and country, 1950–2100. 2013 [04/06/2014]. Available from: http://esa.un.org/unpd/wpp/Excel-Data/mortality.htm.

5 Demakakos P, Cooper R, Hamer M, de Oliveira C, Hardy R, Breeze E. The Bidirectional Association between Depressive Symptoms and Gait Speed: Evidence from the English Longitudinal Study of Ageing (ELSA). PLoS One. 2013; 8(7): e68632; Studenski S, Perera S, Patel K, Rosano C, Faulkner K, Inzitari M, et al. Gait speed and survival in older adults. *JAMA: the Journal of the American Medical Association.* 2011; 305(1): 50–8.

6 Steptoe A, Demakakos P, de Oliveira C. The Psychological Well-Being, Health and Functioning of Older People in England. In: Banks J, Nazroo J, Steptoe A, editors. *The Dynamics of Ageing, Evidence from the English Longitudinal Study of Ageing 2002–2010 (Wave 5).* London: Institute for Fiscal Studies, 2012.

7 Carstensen L, Fried L. The Meaning of Old Age. In: Beard J, Biggs S, Bloom D, Fried L, Hogan P, Kalache A, et al., editors. *Global Population Ageing: Peril or Promise?* Geneva: World Economic Forum, 2012.

8 United Nations Population Fund, HelpAge International. *Ageing in the Twenty-First Century.*

9   Morris JN, Wilkinson P, Dangour AD, Deeming C, Fletcher A. Defining a minimum income for healthy living (MIHL): older age, England. *International Journal of Epidemiology*. 2007; 36(6): 1300–7.

10 National Research Council. *Aging and the Macroeconomy. Long-Term Implications of an Older Population*. Washington, DC: The National Academies Press, 2012.

11 Siegrist J, Wahrendorf M. Quality of work, health, and retirement. *Lancet*. 2009; 374(9705): 1872–3.

12 B&Q. Age Diversity. We stopped counting years ago.

13 Commission on the Social Determinants of Health. *Closing the Gap in a Generation: Health Equity through Action on the Social Determinants of Health. Final Report of the Commission on Social Determinants of Health*. Geneva: World Health Organization, 2008.

14 United Nations Population Fund, HelpAge International. *Ageing in the Twenty-First Century: A Celebration and a Challenge*. New York: UNFPA, 2012.

15 Shakespeare W. *As You Like It*, Act II, Scene vii. London: Penguin Books, 2005 [1623].

16 Shakespeare W. Sonnet 18.

17 Knoops KT, de Groot LC, Kromhout D, Perrin AE, Moreiras-Varela O, Menotti A, et al. Mediterranean diet, lifestyle factors, and 10-year mortality in elderly European men and women: the HALE project. *Journal of the American Medical Association*. 2004; 292(12): 1433–9.

18 Banks J, Lessof C, Nazroo J, Rogers N, Stafford M, Steptoe A. *Financial Circumstances, Health and Well-being of the Older Population in England. The 2008 English Longitudinal Study of Ageing (Wave 4)*. London: Institute for Fiscal Studies, 2010.

19 Fratiglioni L, Paillard-Borg S, Winblad B. An active and socially integrated lifestyle in late life might protect against dementia. *The Lancet Neurology*. 2004; 3(6): 343–53.

20 Verghese J, Lipton RB, Katz MJ, Hall CB, Derby CA, Kuslansky G, et al. Leisure activities and the risk of dementia in the elderly. *New England Journal of Medicine*. 2003; 348(25): 2508–16.

21 Abbott RD, White LR, Ross GW, Masaki KH, Curb JD, Petrovitch H. Walking and dementia in physically capable elderly men. *JAMA: the Journal of the American Medical Association*. 2004; 292(12): 1447–53.

22 Weuve J, Kang JH, Manson JE, Breteler MM, Ware JH, Grodstein F. Physical activity, including walking, and cognitive function in older women. *JAMA: the Journal of the American Medical Association*. 2004; 292(12): 1454–61.

23 Small BJ, Dixon RA, McArdle JJ, Grimm KJ. Do changes in lifestyle engagement moderate cognitive decline in normal aging? Evidence from the Victoria Longitudinal Study. *Neuropsychology*. 2012; 26(2): 144–55.

24 Holt-Lunstad J, Smith TB, Layton JB. Social relationships and mortality risk: a meta-analytic review. *PlosMed.* 2010; 7(7): e1000316.

25 Banks J, Breeze E, Lessof C, Nazroo J. *Retirement, Health and Relationships of the Older Population in England: The 2004 English Longitudinal Study of Ageing (Wave 2).* 2006.

26 Fried L. Making aging positive: The Atlantic, 2014 [updated 06/2014, 22/12/2014]. Available from: http://www.theatlantic.com/health/print/2014/06/valuing-the-elderly-improving-public-health/371245/.

27 Banks et al. *Retirement, Health and Relationships.*

8 BUILDING RESILIENT COMMUNITIES

1 CBC News. B.C. teen's suicide blamed on 'dysfunctional' child welfare system 2014 [25/06/2014]. Available from: http://www.cbc.ca/news/canada/british-columbia/b-c-teen-s-suicide-blamed-on-dysfunctional-child-welfare-system-1.2526230.

2 Chandler MJ, Lalonde CE. Cultural Continuity as a Moderator of Suicide Risk among Canada's First Nations. In: Kirmayer L, Valaskakis G, editors. *Healing Traditions: the Mental Health of Aboriginal Peoples in Canada.* Vancouver: University of Columbia Press, 2009.

3 Ibid.

4 Hummingbird L. The public health crisis of native American youth suicide. *NASN School Nurse.* 2011; 26(2): 110–4.

5 Spirits C. Aboriginal suicide rates 2014 [26/06/2014]. Available from: http://www.creativespirits.info/aboriginalculture/people/aboriginal-suicide-rates.

6 Beautrais A, Fergusson D. Indigenous suicide in New Zealand. *Archives of Suicide Research.* 2006; 10(2): 159–68.

7 Walters JH, Moore A, Berzofsky M, Langton L. *Household Burglary, 1994–2011.* NCJ 241754: US Department of Justice, 2013.

8 ONS, Home Office. *Crime in England and Wales 2010/11: Findings from the British Crime Survey and Police Recorded Crime.* (2nd edition) 2011.

9 Jones JM. Gallup Politics: Americans Still Perceive Crime as on the Rise 2010 [30/06/2014]. Available from: http://www.gallup.com/poll/144827/americans-perceive-crime-rise.aspx.

10 Stafford M, Chandola T, Marmot M. Association between fear of crime and mental health and physical functioning. *American Journal of Public Health.* 2007; 97(11): 2076–81.

11 Stafford M, De Silva M, Stansfeld SA, Marmot MG. Neighbourhood social capital and mental health: testing the link in a general population sample. *Health and Place.* 2008; 14:394–405.

12 Florence C, Shepherd J, Brennan I, Simon T. Effectiveness of anonymised information sharing and use in health service, police, and local government partnership for preventing violence related injury: experimental study and time series analysis. *BMJ.* 2011; 342: d3313.

13 Matthews K, Shepherd J, Sivarajasingham V. Violence-related injury and the price of beer in England and Wales. *Applied Economics.* 2006; 38: 661–70.

14 Bureau of Alcohol Tobacco Firearms and Explosives. ATF Releases Government of Mexico Firearms Trace Data 2012 [07/01/2015]. Available from: http://www.atf.gov/press/releases/2012/04/042612-atf-atf-releases-government-of-mexico-firearms-trace-data.html.

15 National Gang Center. OJJDP Comprehensive Gang Model [25/06/2014]. Available from: http://www.nationalgangcenter.gov/comprehensive-gang-model.

16 Violence Reduction Unit. CIRV helps reduce Glasgow gang violence [25/06/2014]. Available from: http://www.actiononviolence.co.uk/content/cirv-helps-reduce-glasgow-gang-violence.

17 Marmot Review Team. *Fair Society, Healthy Lives: Strategic Review of Health Inequalities in England Post 2010.* London: Marmot Review, 2010.

18 Hawkins JD, Oesterle S, Brown EC, Abbott RD, Catalano R. Youth Problem Behaviors 8 Years After Implementing the Communities That Care Prevention System: A Community-Randomized Trial. *JAMA Pediatrics.* 2014; 168(2): 122–9.

19 Catalano RF, Haggerty KP, Fleming CB, Hawkins JD. Social development interventions have extensive, long-lasting effects. In: Fortune AE, McCallion P, Briar-Lawson K, editors. *Social Work Practice Research for the 21st Century.* New York: Columbia University Press, 2010.

20 UNDP. *Human Development Report 2013 – The Rise of the South: Human Progress in a Diverse World.* New York: United Nations Development Programme, 2013.

21 Georgatos G. Quality of life for Australians 2nd only to Norway, but for Aboriginal peoples 122nd 2013 [25/06/2014]. Available from: http://thestringer.com.au.

22 Cooke M, Mitrou F, Lawrence D, Guimond E, Beavon D. *Indigenous Wellbeing in Four Countries: An Application of the UNDP's Human Development Index to Indigenous Peoples in Australia, Canada, New Zealand, and the United States.* BMC International Health & Human Rights. 2007; 7(9).

23 Australian Bureau of Statistics. Life Tables for Aboriginal and Torres Strait Islander Australians 2010–2012. 3302.0.55.003 2013 [25/06/2014]. Available from: http://www.ausstats.abs.gov.au.

24 Australian Institute of Health and Welfare. *Life Expectancy and Mortality of Aboriginal and Torres Strait Islander People*. Canberra: AIHW, 2011.

25 Ibid.

26 Creative Spirits. Michael Anderson: Can an Aboriginal school break the vicious circle? 2014 [25/06/2014]. Available from: http://www.creativespirits.info/aboriginalculture/education/can-an-aboriginal-school-break-the-vicious-circle.

27 Creative Spirits. Aboriginal law & justice 2013 [25/06/2014]. Available from: http://www.creativespirits.info/aboriginalculture/law/.

28 Marmot Review Team. *Fair Society, Healthy Lives.*

29 University of Sydney. Dr Charles Nelson Perrurle Perkins AO, Arrernte and Kalkadoon Man. 1936–2000. Extract from 'State Funeral' programme, Sydney Town Hall, 25 October 2000 [25/06/2014]. Available from: http://sydney.edu.au/koori/news/perkins_background.pdf.

30 Lane J. *Indigenous Participation in University Education*. No. 110, 27 May 2009. The Centre for Independent Studies Issue Analysis, 2009.

31 Australian Government Department of Social Services. Local Implementation Plans, Gunbalanya 2013 [25/06/2014]. Available from: http://www.dss.gov.au.

32 Anderson HR, Vallance P, Bland JM, Nohl F, Ebrahim S. Prospective study of mortality associated with chronic lung disease and smoking in Papua New Guinea. *International Journal of Epidemiology*. 1988; 17(1): 56–61.

33 Global Alliance for Clean Cookstoves. The Issues 2014 [25/06/2014]. Available from: http://www.cleancookstoves.org/our-work/the-issues/.

34 Marmot Review Team. *Fair Society, Healthy Lives.*

35 Clark LP, Millet DB, Marshall JD. National Patterns in Environmental Injustice and Inequality: Outdoor NO_2 Air Pollution in the United States. *PLoS One*. 2014; 9(4): e94431.

36 White MP, Alcock I, Wheeler BW, Depledge MH. Would you be happier living in a greener urban area? A fixed-effects analysis of panel data. *Psychological Science*. 2013; 24(6): 920–8.

37 University of Exeter. Green spaces deliver lasting mental health benefits 2014 [25/06/2014]. Available from: http://www.exeter.ac.uk/news/featurednews/title_349054_en.html.

38 Mitchell R, Popham F. Effect of exposure to natural environment on health inequalities: an observational population study. *Lancet*. 2008; 372(9650): 1655–60.

39 Bird D. Government advisors demand urgent shift in public investment to green England's cities. CABE (Commission for Architecture and the Built Environment), 2009.

40 Sloman L, Cavill N, Cope A, Muller L, Kennedy A. *Analysis and Synthesis of Evidence on the Effects of Investment in Six Cycling Towns*. Report for Department for Transport and Cycling England. 2009.

41 City of Copenhagen. The Bicycle Account 2013 [30/06/2014]. Available from: http://subsite.kk.dk/sitecore/content/Subsites/CityOfCopenhagen/SubsiteFrontpage/LivingInCopenhagen/CityAndTraffic.

42 Jones SJ, Lyons RA, John A, Palmer SR. Traffic calming policy can reduce inequalities in child pedestrian injuries: database study. *Injury Prevention*. 2005; 11(3): 152–6; Jacobsen PL, Racioppi F, Rutter H. Who owns the roads? How motorised traffic discourages walking and bicycling. *Injury Prevention*. 2009; 15(6): 369–73.

43 World Health Organization. *Global Age-Friendly Cities: a Guide*. Geneva: WHO, 2007.

44 Kjellstrom T. Our cities, our health, our future. Acting on social determinants for health equity in urban settings: WHO, KNUS, 2008 [updated 2012/08/13]. Available from: http://www.who.int/social_determinants/resources/knus_final_report_052008.pdf.

45 Gladwell M. *The Tipping Point*. USA: Abacus, 2000.

9 FAIR SOCIETIES

1 Judt T. *Ill Fares the Land*. London: Penguin Books, 2011.

2 Bajak F. Chile–Haiti Earthquake Comparison: Chile Was More Prepared. *Huffington Post*. 2011.

3 Ibid.

4 Banks J, Marmot M, Oldfield Z, Smith JP. Disease and disadvantage in the United States and England. *Journal of the American Medical Association*. 2006; 295(2037–45).

5 Woolf SH, Aron L, editors. *U.S. Health in International Perspective: Shorter Lives, Poorer Health*. National Research Council; Institute of Medicine. Washington, DC: The National Academies Press, 2013.

6 Drèze J, Sen A. *An Uncertain Glory: India and Its Contradictions*. London: Allen Lane, 2013.

7 Marmot M, Allen J, Bell R, Bloomer E, Goldblatt P. WHO European review of social determinants of health and the health divide. *Lancet*. 2012; 380(9846): 1011–29.

8 Marmot M, Bell R. Japanese Longevity Revisited. *Journal of the National Institute of Public Health*. 2007; 56(2).

9 Cook HJ, Bhattacharya S, Hardy A, editors. *History of the Social Determinants of Health: Global Histories, Contemporary Debates (New Perspectives in South Asian History)*. India: Orient Blackswan, 2009.

10 Drèze and Sen. *An Uncertain Glory*, p. 39.

11 OECD. Health at a Glance: Suicide mortality rates, 2011 (or nearest year) 2013 [28/10/2014]. Available from: http://dx.doi.org.

12 Lundberg O, Aberg Yngwe M, Kolegard Stjarne M, Bjork L, Fritzell J. The Nordic Experience: welfare states and public health (NEWS). *Health Equity Studies*. 2008; 12.

13 Woolf SH, Aron L, editors. *U.S. Health in International Perspective: Shorter Lives, Poorer Health*. National Research Council; Institute of Medicine. Washington, DC: The National Academies Press, 2013.

14 Stiglitz J. *The Price of Inequality*. New York: Penguin, 2013.

15 Piketty T. *Capital in the Twenty-First Century*. Cambridge, MA: Harvard University Press, 2014.

16 Vardi N. The 25 Highest-Earning Hedge Fund Managers and Traders. *Forbes*. 2014.

17 Ostry JD, Berg A, Tsangarides CG. *IMF Staff Discussion Note: Redistribution, Inequality, and Growth*. International Monetary Fund, 2014.

18 Sen A. *Inequality Reexamined*. Oxford: Oxford University Press, 1992.

19 Dahl E, van der Wel KA. Educational inequalities in health in European welfare states: a social expenditure approach. *Social Science and medicine*. 2013; 81: 60–9.

20 Santos LMP, Paes-Sousa R, Miazagi E, Silva TF, Mederios da Fonseca AM. *The Brazilian Experience with Conditional Cash Transfers: A Successful Way to Reduce Inequity and to Improve Health*. 2011.

21 Barber SL, Gertler PJ. The impact of Mexico's conditional cash transfer programme, Oportunidades, on birthweight. *Tropical medicine & international health: TM & IH*. 2008; 13(11): 1405–14.

22 Baird S, Ferreira FHG, Ozler B, Woolcock M. Relative Effectiveness of Conditional and Unconditional Cash Transfers for Schooling Outcomes in Developing Countries: A Systematic Review. *Campbell Systematic Reviews*. 2013; 9(8).

23 Mahapatra L. Consumer Spending: How much of their income do poor and rich American families spend on housing, education, healthcare, food and transportation? *International Business Times*. 6 January 2013.

24 Rutter J, Stocker K. *Childcare Costs Survey 2014*. Family and Childcare Trust, 2014.

25 Ferguson D. The costs of childcare: how Britain compares with Sweden. *The Guardian*. 31 May 2014.

26 Mackenbach JP.The persistence of health inequalities in modern welfare states: The explanation of a paradox. *Social Science & Medicine*. 2012; 75(4): 761–9.

27 Wilkinson RG, Pickett K. *The Spirit Level: Why More Equal Societies Almost Always Do Better*. London: Allen Lane, 2009.

28 Marmot MG, Sapolsky R. Of Baboons and Men: Social Circumstances, Biology, and the Social Gradient in Health. In: Weinstein M, Lane MA, editors. *Sociality, Hierarchy, Health: Comparative Biodemography: A Collection of Papers*. Washington DC: National Academies Press, 2014.

10 LIVING FAIRLY IN THE WORLD

1 Yang J. Did politics ruin 'the world's coolest mayor'? *Toronto Star*. 23 June 2014.

2 Reinhart C, Rogoff K. Growth in a time of debt. *American Economic Review*. 2010; 100(2): 473–8.

3 Herndon T, Ash M, Pollin R. *Does High Public Debt Consistently Stifle Economic Growth? A Critique of Reinhart and Rogoff*. Political Economy Research Institute – Working Paper Series. 2013; April(322).

4 Stuckler D, Basu S. *The Body Economic: Why Austerity Kills*. New York: Basic Books, 2013.

5 Eyraud L, Weber A. *The Challenge of Debt Reduction during Fiscal Consolidation*. IMF Working Paper Series No. WP/13/67: International Monetary Fund, 2013.

6 Wren-Lewis S. Mainly Macro [Internet] 2013. Available from: http://mainlymacro.blogspot.co.uk/2013/12/osbornes-plan-b.html.

7 Nelson F. In graphs: How George Osborne learned to stop worrying and love the debt: *The Spectator*, 2014 [updated 1/12/2014, 23/12/2014]. Available from: http://blogs.spectator.co.uk/coffeehouse/2014/12/in-graphs-george-osborne-fought-the-debt-and-the-debt-won/.

8 Lewis M. *The Big Short: Inside the Doomsday Machine*. London: Allen Lane, 2011.

9 Stuckler and Basu. *The Body Economic*.

10 Karanikolos M, Mladovsky P, Cylus J, Thomson S, Basu S, Stuckler D, et al. Financial crisis, austerity, and health in Europe. *Lancet*. 2013; 381(9874): 1323–31.

11 Ibid.

12 Ottersen OP, Dasgupta J, Blouin C, Buss P, Chongsuvivatwong V, Frenk J, et al. The political origins of health inequity: prospects for change. *Lancet*. 2014; 383(9917): 630–67.

13 Ibid.

14 Stuckler and Basu. *The Body Economic*.

15 World Social Protection Report 2014/15. *Building Economic Recovery, Inclusive Development and Social Justice*. Geneva: International Labour Office, 2014.

16 Drèze J, Sen A. *An Uncertain Glory: India and Its Contradictions*. London: Allen Lane, 2013.

17 UNDP. *Human Development Report 2013 – The Rise of the South: Human Progress in a Diverse World*. New York: United Nations Development Programme, 2013.

18 Ibid.

19 World Health Organization. *World Health Statistics 2014*. Geneva: WHO, 2014.

20 Drèze and Sen. *An Uncertain Glory*.

21 Ibid.

22 *World Development Report 2006. Equity and Development*. New York: World Bank/Oxford University, 2005.

23 Laird L. India's farmer suicides: are deaths linked to GM cotton? – in pictures: *The Guardian*, 2014 [updated 05/05/2014, 23/12/2014]. Available from: http://www.theguardian.com/global-development/gallery/2014/may/05/india-cotton-suicides-farmer-deaths-gm-seeds.

24 Nagaraj K. *Farmers' Suicides in India: Magnitudes, Trends and Spatial Patterns*. Madras Institute of Development Studies, 2008.

25 Sastry P. U.S. agricultural subsidies and farmer suicide in India: Roosevelt Institute, 2009 [updated 01/12/2009, 23/12/2014]. Available from: http://www.rooseveltcampusnetwork.org/blog/us-agricultural-subsidies-and-farmer-suicide-india.

26 Ibid.

27 United Nations Development Programme. *Human Development Report 2005. International Cooperation at a Crossroads: Aid, Trade and Security in an Unequal World*. UNDP, 2005.

28 Hyder S. Women's financial independence amongst female garments workers in Bangladesh: Summary of research. *Berkeley Law*, 2012.

29 Ayres A. Bangladesh: Behemoth garment industry weathers the storm: Council on Foreign Relations, 2014 [updated 20/06/2014, 23/12/2014]. Available from: http://blogs.cfr.org/asia/2014/06/20/bangladesh-behemoth-garment-industry-weathers-the-storm/.

30 Marmot M, Allen J, Bell R, Bloomer E, Goldblatt P. WHO European review of social determinants of health and the health divide. *Lancet*. 2012; 380(9846): 1011–29.

31 Global Factors Task Group. *Global Factors Task Group Final Report*. 2014.

32 The 0.7% target: An in-depth look: Millennium Project, 2006 [23/12/2014]. Available from: http://www.unmillenniumproject.org/press/07.htm.

33 Burkina Faso: Oxfam International, 2014 [23/12/2014]. Available from: http://oxf.am/HMZ.

34 Banerjee A, Duflo E. *Poor Economics: A Radical Rethinking of the Way to Fight Global Poverty.* USA: Public Affairs, 2011.

35 Deaton A. *The Great Escape: Health, Wealth, and the Origins of Inequality.* Princeton: Princeton University Press, 2013.

36 Ibid.

37 Ooms G, Hammonds R, Van Damme W. *International Assistance from Europe for Global Health: Searching for a Common Paradigm.* 2012.

38 World Cancer Research Fund, American Institute for Cancer Research. *Food, Nutrition, Physical Activity, and the Prevention of Cancer: A Global Perspective.* Washington, DC.: AICR, 2007.

39 El-Zanaty F, Way A. *Egypt: Demographic and Health Survey.* Cairo: Ministry of Health, 2009.

40 *The Economist.* Food companies: Food for thought 2012 [07/01/2015]. Available from: http://www.economist.com/news/special-report/21568064-food-companies-play-ambivalent-part-fight-against-flab-food-thought.

41 Ibid.

42 Monteiro CA, Moubarac JC, Cannon G, Ng SW, Popkin B. Ultra-processed products are becoming dominant in the global food system. *Obesity Reviews: an Official Journal of the International Association for the Study of Obesity.* 2013; 14 Suppl 2: 21–8.

43 Monteiro CA, Cannon G. The impact of transnational 'big food' companies on the South: a view from Brazil. *PLoS Med.* 2012; 9(7): e1001252.

44 Ottersen OP, Dasgupta J, Blouin C, Buss P, Chongsuvivatwong V, Frenk J, et al. The political origins of health inequity: prospects for change. *Lancet.* 2014; 383(9917): 630–67.

45 Friedman TL. *The World Is Flat: a Brief History of the Globalized World in the Twenty-First Century.* London: Allen Lane, 2005.

46 Kopetchny T. Centre for Global Development: Your Chance to Ask Nancy Birdsall About Globalization and Inequality 2007 [05/01/2015]. Available from: http://www.cgdev.org/blog/your-chance-ask-nancy-birdsall-about-globalization-and-inequality.

11 THE ORGANISATION OF HOPE

1 West Midlands Fire Service. *Improving Lives to Save Lives.* WMFS, 2014.

2 Commission for a Socially Sustainable Malmö. *Commission for a Socially Sustainable Malmö, Final Report 2013.* Available from: http://www.malmo.se.

3   UCL Institute for Health Equity. *Working for Health Equity: The Role of Health Professionals*. 2013.

4   Drèze J, Sen A. *An Uncertain Glory: India and Its Contradictions*. London: Allen Lane, 2013.

5   Banerjee A, Duflo E. *Poor Economics: A Radical Rethinking of the Way to Fight Global Poverty*. USA: Public Affairs, 2011.

6   OECD. Focus on Inequality and Growth: Does income inequality hurt economic growth? 2014.

7   *The Economist*. Economist Espresso 24 December 2014. 2014.

8   Keynes JM. *First Annual Report of the Arts Council 1945–1946*.

9   Stiglitz J. *The Price of Inequality*. New York: Penguin, 2013.

10 Navarro V. What we mean by Social Determinants of Health. *Global Health Promotion*. 2009 Mar; 16(1):5–16. doi: 10.1177/1757975908100746.

11 Navarro V, Muntaner C, Borrell C, Benach J, Quiroga A, Rodriguez-Sanz M, et al. Politics and health outcomes. *Lancet*. 2006; 2006/09/19(9540): 1033–7.

12 Hacker J, Pierson P. *Winner-Take-All Politics*. New York: Simon and Schuster, 2010.

13 Orwell G. *Politics and the English Language*. London: Horizon, 1946.

Acknowledgements

I have made clear, I hope, that the ideas, conclusions and recommendations in this book were developed over years of collaboration. In my previous book, *Status Syndrome*, I acknowledged the funding agencies in the UK, Europe and the US that supported my research and all the people who had contributed to my research and the ideas in that book. Those good colleagues in helping shape my ideas were important contributors to what I have done since. The big shift, however, was my involvement in reviews of the evidence with a view to influencing policy and practice. Through all this time I was supported by UCL, which provided an ideal working environment, and the Medical Research Council, as an MRC Research Professor.

In conducting these reviews I have been supported by a wonderful group of colleagues at UCL, which went from being the UCL secretariat for the WHO CSDH, to the Marmot Review team, to the UCL Institute of Health Equity. Current members are: Jessica Allen, Angela Donkin, Ruth Bell, Peter Goldblatt, Matilda Allen, Jillian Roberts, Dan Durcan, Luke Beswick, Laura Grobicki, Sara Thomas, Patricia Hallam, Felicity Porritt, Elaine Reinertsen. Past staff include: Ellen Bloomer, Mike Grady, Tammy Boyce, Di

McNeish, Ilaria Geddes, Alex Godoy, Ria Galeote. Without such colleagues nothing would have got done.

Matilda Allen provided invaluable help with the book, initially with research and references and then as a sensitive reader and commentator. Jessica Allen read the book and provided wise comments as did Felicity Porritt. I am so grateful for their input. I had a remarkable series of monthly meetings with Rabbi Tony Bayfield. They began with my critiquing his work in progress then shifted to his careful reading and comments on every word of this book. He was a great reader to have. Bill Swainson, Senior Editor at Bloomsbury, read the book twice and was extremely helpful. My agent, Peter Robinson, was key in shaping the original proposal. During my time at the British Medical Association, and at the World Medical Association, I have benefited greatly from the collegiality and insights of Vivienne Nathanson.

As will be seen below a vast number of people were involved in the reviews on social determinants of health and health equity that I led. This book is highly influenced by the evidence and conclusions of those reviews, but is not a summary. The probability that each of the colleagues who contributed so much to the reviews agrees with every one of my interpretations and emphases is vanishingly small. It is my view of that evidence, for which I take responsibility. That said, in our deliberations over evidence in each of the reviews there was a high degree of consensus. The first review, as described, was the WHO Commission on Social Determinants of Health (CSDH), set up by the then Director-General of WHO, J. W. Lee, and taken forward under his successor, Margaret Chan. I am grateful to these two inspirational leaders of global health. The CSDH, which I chaired, had a wonderful group of commissioners who contributed individually and collectively to our report, *Closing the Gap in a Generation*. The Commissioners were: Frances Baum, Monique Bégin, Giovanni Berlinguer, Mirai

Chatterjee, William H. Foege, Yan Guo, Kiyoshi Kurokawa, Ricardo Lagos Escobar, Alireza Marandi, Pascoal Mocumbi, Ndioro Ndiaye, Charity Kaluki Ngilu, Hoda Rashad, Amartya Sen, David Satcher, Anna Tibaijuka, Denny Vågerö, Gail Wilensky.

To provide evidence on which we deliberated, the CSDH convened nine knowledge networks, whose leaders were: Joan Benach, Josiane Bonnefoy, Jane Doherty, Sarah Escorel, Lucy Gilson, Mario Hernández, Clyde Hertzman, Lori Irwin, Heidi Johnston, Michael P Kelly, Tord Kjellstrom, Ronald Labonté, Susan Mercado, Antony Morgan, Carles Muntaner, Piroska Östlin, Jennie Popay, Laetitia Rispel, Vilma Santana, Ted Schrecker, Gita Sen, Arjumand Siddiqi. In addition, we received valuable input from the NEWS (Nordic Experience of the Welfare State) group led by Olle Lundberg and Johann Fritzell.

The CSDH Secretariat included my close colleagues in the Chair's office at UCL: Ruth Bell, Sharon Friel, Tanja A. J. Houweling, Sebastian Taylor. We worked closely with the secretariat at WHO: led by Jeanette Vega (2004–2007) and Nick Drager (2008), and including Erik Blas, Chris Brown, Hilary Brown, Alec Irwin, Rene Loewenson (consultant), Richard Poe, Gabrielle Ross, Ritu Sadana, Sarah Simpson, Orielle Solar, Nicole Valentine and Eugenio Raul Villar Montesinos; as well as, at various times, Elmira Adenova, Daniel Albrecht, Lexi Bambas-Nolan, Ahmad Reza Hosseinpoor, Theadora Koller, Lucy Mshana, Susanne Nakalembe, Giorelley Niezen, Bongiwe Peguillan, Amit Prasad, Kumanan Rasanathan, Kitt Rasmussen, Lina Reinders, Anand Sivasankara Kurup, Niko Speybroeck and Michel Thieren. Whew! It took a huge team to synthesise the world's knowledge and organise a Commission that had ten meetings and met governments in ten different countries during its three and a half years of work.

In the wake of the Global Commission I was invited by Prime Minister Gordon Brown to conduct a strategic review of health inequalities in England. We published that report as *Fair Society Healthy Lives, the Marmot Review.* The Commissioners were, as with the CSDH, a stellar group: Tony Atkinson, John Bell, Carol Black, Patricia Broadfoot, Julia Cumberlege, Ian Diamond, Ian Gilmore, Chris Ham, Molly Meacher, Geoff Mulgan. The Marmot Review team at UCL was led by Jessica Allen. Team members included Peter Goldblatt, Ruth Bell, Tammy Boyce, Di McNeish, Mike Grady, Jason Strelitz, Ilaria Geddes, Sharon Friel, Felicity Porritt, Elaine Reinertsen and Matilda Allen.

As with the CSDH, the Marmot Review was supported by Task Groups and Working Committees who reviewed and synthesised evidence on the review's key areas. These groups involved: Sharon Friel, Denny Vagero, Alan Dyson, Jane Tunstill, Clyde Hertzman, Ziba Vaghri, Helen Roberts, Johannes Siegrist, Abigail McKnight, Joan Benach, Carles Muntaner, David MacFarlane, Monste Vergara Duarte, Hans Weitkowitz, Gry Wester, Howard Glennerster, Ruth Lister, Jonathan Bradshaw, Olle Lundberg, Kay Withers, Jan Flaherty, Anne Power, Jonathan Davis, Paul Plant, Tord Kjellstrom, Catalina Turcu, Helen Eveleigh, Jonathon Porritt, Anna Coote, Paul Wilkinson, David Colin-Thomé, Maria Arnold, Helen Clarkson, Sue Dibb, Jane Franklin, Tara Garnett, Jemima Jewell, Duncan Kay, Shivani Reddy, Cathryn Tonne, Ben Tuxworth, James Woodcock, Peter Smith, David Epstein, Marc Suhrcke, John Appleby, Adam Coutts, Demetris Pillas, Carmen de Paz Nieves, Cristina Otano, Ron Labonté, Margaret Whitehead, Mark Exworthy, Sue Richards, Don Matheson, Tim Doran, Sue Povall, Anna Peckham, Emma Rowland, Helen Vieth, Amy Colori, Louis Coiffait, Matthew Andrews, Anna Matheson, Lindsey Meyers, Alan Maryon-Davis, John Doyle, Tim Lobstein, Angela Greatley, Mark Bellis, Sally Greengross, Martin Wiseman, Paul Lincoln, Clare Bambra, Kerry Joyce, David Piachaud, James Nazroo, Jennie Popay, Fran Bennett, Hillary Graham, Bobbie Jacobson, Paul Johnstone, Ken Judge, Mike

Kelly, Catherine Law, John Newton, John Fox, Rashmi Shukla, Nicky Best, Ian Plewis, Sue Atkinson, Tim Allen, Amanda Ariss, Antony Morgan, Paul Fryers, Veena Raleigh, Gwyn Bevan, Hugh Markowe, Justine Fitzpatrick, David Hunter, Gabriel Scally, Ruth Hussey, Tony Elson, Steve Weaver, Jacky Chambers, Nick Hicks, Paul Dornan, Liam Hughes, Carol Tannahill, Hari Sewell, Alison O'Sullivan, Chris Bentley, Caroline Briggs, Anne McDonald, John Beer, Jim Hillage, Jenny Savage, Daniel Lucy, Klim McPherson, Paul Johnson, Damien O'Flaherty, Matthew Bell.

I was invited by the Regional Director of WHO Europe, Dr Zsuzsanna Jakab, to lead The European Review of Social Determinants and the Health Divide. I had a group of senior advisors: Guillem Lopez, Zsuzsa Ferge, Ilona Kickbusch, Johan Mackenbach, Tilek Meimanaliev, Amartya Sen, Vladimir Starodubov, Tomris Turmen, Denny Vagero, Barbro Westerholm, Margaret Whitehead, Ex-officio representatives of WHO, Roberto Bertollini, Agis Tsouros, Erio Ziglio, and The European Commission, Michael Hübel, Charles Price. The UCL Secretariat was led by Peter Goldblatt and Jessica Allen and included Ruth Bell, Ellen Bloomer, Angela Donkin, Ilaria Geddes, Mike Grady, David Bann, Sadie Boniface, Michael Holmes, Akanksha Katyai, Anne Scott, Matilda Allen, Luke Beswick, Ria Galeote and Alex Godoy. The WHO secretariat was led by Agis Tsouros, with Johanna Hanefeld, Piroska Ostlin, Asa Nihlen, Chris Brown, Isabel Yordi, Theadora Koller, Sarah Simpson, Erio Ziglio and Richard Alderslade. Task group chairs/co-chairs: Alan Dyson, Naomi Eisenstadt, Johannes Siegrist, Jennie Popay, Olle Lundberg, Anna Coote, Gauden Galea, Witold Zatonski, Maria Kopp, Emily Grundy, Marc Suhrcke, Richard Cookson, Harry Burns, Erio Ziglio, Ronald Labonte, Karien Stronks, Martin Bobak, Claudia Stein.

If you have managed to get this far, I would like to make one more point. I said we wanted to create a social movement for health equity. The good colleagues above who have been part of compiling the evidence and approaches that fed into our reviews, and hence this book, are part of that social movement. The process has been immensely rewarding.

My family have lived this movement and these ideas over the decade during which the reviews were conducted, and several decades before that. Tolerant, loving, and contributing in all sorts of ways, they are the people to whom I dedicate this book, with love.

Index

A Note on the Author

Born in England and educated in Australia, Sir Michael Marmot is Professor of Epidemiology and Public Health at UCL. He takes up the Lown visiting professorship at Harvard in 2015 and Presidency of the World Medical Association. He chaired the WHO Commission on Social Determinants of Health (2005–8), and the European Review of Social Determinants and the Health Divide. His recommendations have been adopted by the World Health Assembly and by many countries. The British Government appointed him to conduct a review of social determinants and health inequalities. The Marmot Review and its recommendations are now being implemented in three-quarters of local authorities in England. He lives in North London.

@MichaelMarmot

A Note on the Type

The text of this book is set in Bembo, which was first used in 1495 by the Venetian printer Aldus Manutius for Cardinal Bembo's *De Aetna*. The original types were cut for Manutius by Francesco Griffo. Bembo was one of the types used by Claude Garamond (1480–1561) as a model for his Romain de l'Université, and so it was a forerunner of what became the standard European type for the following two centuries. Its modern form follows the original types and was designed for Monotype in 1929.